C000244780

61 MINUTES IN MUNICH

HOWARD GAYLE

61 MINUTES IN MUNICH

HOWARD GAYLE

IN COLLABORATION WITH SIMON HUGHES

deCoubertin
B O O K S

First published as a hardback by deCoubertin Books Ltd in 2016.

First Edition

deCoubertin Books, Studio I, Baltic Creative Campus, Liverpool, L1 OAH

www.decoubertin.co.uk

ISBN: 978-1- 909245-39- 6

Cover design by Neil Haines.

Typeset by Leslie Priestley.

Printed and bound by CPI Group (UK) Ltd, Croydon, CR0 4YY

CONTENTS

For to be free is
not merely to cast off one's chains,
but to live in a way
that respects and enhances the
freedom of others.

NELSON MANDELA, 1995

*In memory of my mum and my dad
and for my brothers and sister,
my extended family, and the people from
Norris Green and elsewhere in Liverpool
who made a positive impact on my life.*

HOWARD GAYLE, 2016

LIVERPOOL DOCKS, 1947

KIDNAPPED MEN, WOMEN AND CHILDREN BOARDED A BOAT AT THE mouth of the Sierra Leone River. From the natural harbour of Freetown, they were forcibly sailed forty minutes to Bunce Island, a small patch of jungle off the country's coastline. For more than a century this was the site of some grim trade.

Humans became slaves here. They were sold from their homes, packed inside the island's stone fort, shackled together, and shoved into holding pens. After a wait of weeks or months a ship arrived at the end of the island's stony pier. Those who survived the subsequent ten-week journey across the Atlantic Ocean would find themselves in an entirely new world: the rice plantations of the American colonies.

Slavery was not unique to Sierra Leone. It affected the whole of West Africa – an enormous area, stretching all along the Atlantic coastline and inland for several hundred miles. Within this hugely diverse region are many cultural groups, each shaped by its environment. The Fulani, Hausa, Igbo, Akan and many other peoples developed sophisticated cultures long before the arrival of the Europeans in the fifteenth century.

I cannot speak any of the languages of these distinctive tribes. Sierra Leone, indeed, is not a place I consider to be home. But it is the place where my family's story begins. What happened there centuries ago impacted especially upon my early life and continues to do so today.

1

Europeans began exploring West Africa even before they discovered the Americas. The enslavement of Africans by Portuguese traders began almost straight away.

The Portuguese had developed sugar in Brazil in the 1540s. As demand grew, plantations were established in the European colonies in the Caribbean. Other profitable commodities also entered the plantation system, including cotton, coffee and tobacco.

The movement of sugar, particularly, required a large workforce. Local labour in the Caribbean plantations was scarce because millions of indigenous people had perished after the colonisation of their lands. Many were killed in battle and others were worked to death; European diseases also wiped out considerable numbers. The consequence was colonists – other imperial countries like Spain, England, France and the Netherlands – looking towards Africa for a new supply of labour.

It was not long before Africans were being transported across the Atlantic Ocean to work in the Americas in the largest forced migration in human history.

My great-grandfather made a similar journey – beginning in Ghana and landing in Jamaica. Eventually, he joined the Maroons, a fugitive group who fled to the inland mountains and formed their own settlements, where they were able to live their own independent lives. Much later he returned to West Africa and made a home in Sierra Leone.

Europeans had used their own strict theories of civilisation to justify this manipulation and abuse of Africans, considering the prosperity and achievement of European civilisation to be essential. Because African societies and culture were unfamiliar, Europeans denounced the continent as barbaric and overrun with savage tribes and religious despotism. These racist beliefs would later be used as a justification for colonial intervention in Africa. The consequences in the twentieth century were tangible, shaping the future of the Gayle family in Liverpool, thousands of miles away.

Official UK government records suggest British connections to slavery began in 1627 when a group of British settlers landed on the Caribbean island of Barbados. During that trip, the captain of a British ship seized a Portuguese vessel and imprisoned the Africans on board. These were first black

African slaves in the British Empire. They were set to work on a sugar plantation.

British explorers had planned to convert an unpopulated wilderness in Barbados into pasture, by using their own workforce brought in from other parts of the world. Many who arrived were called 'indentured servants'. In effect these poor people had sold themselves to masters for a labour term of five years. Having already been transported, they received some sustenance and refuge. There was also the promise that, at the end of their term, they would be presented with ten acres of land. Yet the swift evolution towards slavery meant that promise, in many cases, was not kept.

In the first decades, Barbados grew by farming tobacco and cotton. Soon, thousands of slaves were being transferred across the Atlantic Ocean. The historian David Olusoga in his documentary *Britain's Forgotten Slave Owners* says it created the world's first genuine global economy.

For the businessmen involved, slavery made economic sense. A labourer would work for his master for five years; a slave was for life. Any children slaves produced automatically belonged to the master.

This process prolonged the depressing cycle of controlled ownership.

LIVERPOOL 8, OR TOXTETH, IS DIVIDED INTO TWO DISTINCT DISTRICTS: the one I grew up in on the south flank of Upper Parliament Street and then the other more prosperous-looking side, closer to Liverpool's city centre.

I was born on the site where Liverpool Women's Hospital is now, which lies directly on the border between the two.

While the area I lived in had a clear immigrant identity with much cheaper lodgings, the Georgian townhouses that lined the wealthier streets elsewhere masked a dark chapter in Britain's history. These were the homes of lawyers, doctors, vicars, sea captains and, most significantly, slave owners.

Until his death in 1851, John Gladstone resided on the majestic Rodney Street. Gladstone was a Scottish merchant, a Member of Parliament and the father of future British Prime Minister, William Ewart Gladstone.

John Gladstone was also a wealthy slave owner, an objector to the UK 1833 Slavery Abolition Act and therefore an exploiter of human life. And yet, a dock that remains in Liverpool, and flourishes today, is named after him.

Gladstone was not the only slave trader in Liverpool. From 1730 the merchants of Liverpool made huge profits from the slave trade. When a famous stage actor visited Liverpool at the end of the 1800s, he was booed when he told the audience that every brick of their town was 'cemented with the blood of an African'.

Liverpool, of course, was equally not the only city with links to slavery. The profits from slave ownership were entrenched in British society. Commanding dynasties amassed fortunes by exploiting enslaved labour in lands the majority of people in Britain had never even heard of.

Due to the huge sums of money needed to make money out of slavery, the profit-making of the slave owners started some of Britain's credit networks. Because of the huge sums of capital invested in slavery projects, this system required extremely violent suppression.

For two centuries, slavery was the engine of the British economy and, before it was abolished, slave owners wanted more: impacting on the class structure still evident today.

Abolition kept the rich very rich and the poor in their place. At the time of abolition, many members of the House of Lords were slave owners. Their position in the establishment ensured that the slave owners' interest and the nation's interest were clearly aligned. Others who were not already in parliament used money to win seats in parliament. Wealth helped them acquire political power.

The compensation from abolition – worth £17billion in today's money – seeped into every corner of the empire. Investment in industry, education, the arts and commerce followed, helping lay the foundation for our modern world.

The reality was bare and brutal: the only way to end slavery was to pay the slave owners for the loss of their property. In order to force legislation through, therefore, the anti-slave campaigners were forced to abandon their central principle: that the slaves should not be considered as property.

Abolition of slavery is considered a historic triumph of British liberalism. Yet the slave owners only walked away with the biggest bail-out in British history because government placed a price on freedom.

*

LIVERPOOL ENTERED THE SLAVE TRADE IN 1699. FROM THE 1740s, it became Britain's largest slaving port, responsible for 50 per cent of Britain's trade and nearly 5,000 voyages. Between 1790 and 1807, Liverpool was also the largest slaving port in Europe. Very few enslaved Africans were brought to Liverpool directly from Africa, however. Instead, those with African roots often arrived from the West Indies, bought by merchants to work as servants in their homes. Had my great-grandfather been born in a different time, it is possible that he would have ended up in the city rather than in Jamaica.

Liverpool's links with the slave trade are visible: everywhere you look in the city, there are reminders. Take the story of Richard Watt, for instance. As a boy, he drove a one-horse carriage in the town; later, he went to Jamaica to make his fortune. When Watt returned in 1772, he'd become a wealthy plantation owner. He bought property in Liverpool and Yorkshire and invested in shipping. In 1795, he bought Speke Hall and its estate. It remained in the family until 1921.

Then there are the docks. Liverpool's free port takes its name from the now demolished Seaforth House, which was built by John Gladstone: the plantation owner and someone who received more than £90,000 (around £83 million today) in compensation when slavery was abolished in the British Empire 1833.

Liverpool, though, retained its links with the dubious trade as cotton produced by slave labour in the American states was imported through the port and sent to the Lancashire mills. Goods made in the mills were then exported all over the world. Consequently, there was much support for the Confederate cause in Liverpool at the outbreak of the American Civil War in 1861. Many ships were built secretly on the Mersey for the Confederacy, the most famous being the steamship Alabama, built at Cammell Laird in Birkenhead. It is clear that although slavery was not permitted through the port of Liverpool, the city still grew strong from the trade of people elsewhere in the world.

Well after the abolition of slavery, African seafarers were still required to crew the ships. The palm oil trade was expanding and Liverpool's port remained as busy as ever all the way up to the 1960s. Many of those that settled in Liverpool lived in the inner-city neighbourhood riddled with social and economic

5

deprivation (such as poor housing and high unemployment) we now know as Liverpool 8: Toxteth.

My father entered Liverpool for the first time from Sierra Leone, having taken a job as a deckhand with one of the major shipping lines, Elder Dempster or Blue Funnel. Records are bleary.

My father's background was middle class by Sierra Leonean standards, but his story reflects how precarious life can be. For a long time he was comfortable. My grandparents worked as moneylenders and could afford to send him to a well-respected secondary school called St Edward's. Established in 1865 by a French Roman Catholic priest, many of the pupils there progressed to attend institutions of higher education including the universities of Oxford, Cambridge and Harvard. Students of St Edward's were easily distinguished by their uniform, which consists of a white shirt, dark shorts and a matching tie. In a country where there is no free compulsory education, attending secondary school is a rare privilege and the school uniform was and remains a badge of honour.

Some of the most famous Old Edwardians include the former prime minister of Sierra Leone, Sir Albert Margai, and President Ahmad Tejan Kabbah. In more recent times, Mohamed Kallon went to the school before embarking on a professional football career that included spells at Internazionale and Monaco.

The foundations of its success were based on a traditional British-style education of discipline, commitment and routine. The school's second headmaster, Father Mulcahy, introduced a house system at St Edward's in 1934 in order to encourage competitive sportsmanship among the pupils. Following the Eton model, St Edward's employs a system that divides the pupils into five houses. Each house has a house captain and games captain. House captains are usually selected from the sixth-form students. Games captains are chosen from the school's most talented athletes – and my father was one of them: tall, powerfully built and versatile in a sporting sense.

Life began to change for my father when his mother died. I am informed that my grandfather soon became fixated with a maid who worked in his house. Under the bewitchment of this particular lady, he was convinced that it was a good idea to remove his own family from the house and replace them with her offspring.

My dad was intelligent, fluent in French and Spanish. But with no financial support and nowhere to live, he found a job in Freetown's docks as a runner. (He was fortunate in comparison to his siblings. On a return trip to Sierra Leone later on in life, he found out that all of his brothers and sisters had died on the street.)

Setting to sea during the war years, the long months in the Atlantic were dangerous even though he was only on the trading ships.

At some point in 1947, he docked in Liverpool.

*

THIS BOOK IS A TESTIMONY TO WHO AND WHAT I HAVE BECOME in a life that has spanned from 1958 to 2016. All of the experiences that I have had in my childhood growing up in Liverpool have shaped the person I have become today, which in turn has educated me in understanding the complex issues that young people have to face.

I hope that this book goes a long way in addressing core issues around race, tolerance and mind-set and enlightens people about the things that have influenced some of the decisions that I have made as a child and also as an adult.

MUNICH

i

Dusk was setting and the brooding floodlights around the Olympic Stadium in Munich were switched on. The stage was set for a performance between two great football teams. I did not envisage that my role would become key to the narrative.

It was late April and warm, and yet Bob Paisley, Liverpool's manager, was wearing his beige trench mac, as if he was preparing for winter. 'Get the boys to go and warm up,' he croaked, speaking to Joe Fagan in his distinctive yet indecipherable County Durham accent. Those 'boys' were Avi Cohen, Jimmy Case, Ian Rush and me, Howard Gayle.

Kenny Dalglish, Liverpool's star player, was really struggling with an ankle injury. Clearly agitated, he kept patting it, as if it might somehow disappear. He tried to carry on but ultimately he could not. He signalled across to the bench that he could no longer continue.

Bob did not so much spring into action; he sat in his seat and, after a brief discussion with his assistant Fagan, he had chosen his plan.

I was the plan.

An athletics track separated the pitch from the bowl of the terracing. I stretched my hamstring, stretched my calf and tested my groin before setting off on the claret-coloured asphalt.

That's when the monkey noises started. I didn't realise what was happening at first because all of my concentration was with the warm-up; making sure my body was ready for the biggest moment in my life.

And then I looked around, away from the pitch. More monkey noises; a few grown men making Nazi salutes.

Great.

Jesus Christ, Howard, how did you get here? I thought to myself. Before I could take it all in, I spotted Ronnie Moran waving his hand furiously, having emerged from the dugout in the way that only he did, like a sentry or a patrol dog.

I sprinted in his direction before Ronnie got angry, because Ronnie could get very angry indeed. I removed my black jumper and shiny red tracksuit bottoms, tucking my gleaming white *jersey with a golden liver bird on the breast into the black shorts, tying the top strings as tightly as possible.*

I was told to play down the left-hand side, leaving David Johnson (the Doc) to forage on his own up front.

I was a month short of my 23rd birthday.

I was number 16: the last number in the match-day squad.

It was the ninth minute of the European Cup semi-final, second leg.

The linesman checked my studs.

I was going on.

CHEAPSIDE, 1976

IT WAS A ROASTING SUMMER'S DAY YET THERE WERE NO windows in the Liverpool magistrates' courtroom. The air was stuffy and the staleness of people's breath could raise the dead.

The stone-faced judge stooped forward, looking down at me from his chair high up, like a headmaster addressing a badly behaved pupil.

'The court has run out of patience with you, Mr Gayle,' he boomed. Aged eighteen, I was in the same position again – for the eighth time.

I had misjudged the seriousness of the charge. I had bitten a policeman who tried to arrest me for shoplifting in the city centre while I was out with mates.

Wrangler jackets were the height of fashion in the 1970s and the must-have item to be seen in. We had mooched around town for most of the afternoon but did not realise that plain-clothed officers had been following us.

Normally, we'd operate with more vigilance and cautiousness. The process was simple: distract staff in the shop by getting them to serve you, while others stuffed goods into bags or inside bigger coats. From the shops, middlemen would then sell the stolen goods on – many of them ending up in markets across the length and breadth of the country.

It was a lucrative business that on a good day would yield hundreds of pounds. This one was a bad day and complacency had got the better of us. I, in particular, would pay a heavy price for my role in the events that followed.

It was coming towards the end of the afternoon when we entered a camping outlet. It was my turn to do some shoplifting while the others covered for me. The target was a denim Wrangler and the plan was straightforward: two jackets into a changing room; try one on; come back out and show everyone it didn't fit; return to the changing room and put the jacket back on its hanger, while placing the spare jacket underneath the coat you arrived in; then replace just one of the jackets on the rail of the shop. That's how it was supposed to happen anyway.

As I reached the shop door, I felt a hand on my shoulder. A horrible feeling washed over me. I knew it was either going to be a policeman or a shop assistant. I hoped it would be an assistant as, normally, they wouldn't want confrontation with a gang of six lads and would just ask for the goods back.

It was a policeman, though. All hell broke loose.

One policeman grabbed me and another blocked the door. The rest of the gang were able to scatter, leaving me to try and escape alone.

A struggle ensued and a crowd gathered. I recognised some of the faces in the crowd and begged them to help me. I reckoned that, with a little help, I could free myself from the policeman and get away. But this bastard was not letting go.

The crowd swelled and, in desperation, I bit the policeman in one last attempt for freedom. The attempt was in vain.

The charge that followed was theft and assault on a policeman. It was a Friday and there was no chance of bail. So the weekend would be spent in Cheapside, Liverpool's main police bridewell'.

I am told the policeman's name was Mr Pigg. In the *Liverpool Echo*, the headline supposedly ran, 'Youth Bites Pigg'. I found the irony quite funny. It reflected my brazenness.

Crime and violence was something I had grown up around. When I was ten years old, I was suspended from primary school for head-butting another pupil and throughout my teenage years I was in and out of the police interview room regularly. Now, I had used up all my credits and I was going to receive a long-overdue punishment.

I didn't fear the sentencing. When I was given four months, I smiled at the judge, bowed my head and followed the screws down the stairs into the bowels of the bridewell to await transport to a detention centre.

I had confidence that I'd be fine. A short stretch in a young offenders' institute didn't scare me.

I was an angry young man. I was angry that my mother had died, leaving me with my father alone in the Norris Green area of Liverpool. My brothers and sister had left home. Norris Green was white and black people were scarce.

Racism was not endemic in Norris Green, but sufficiently deep-seated in certain quarters to be a threat to families like the Gayles and the few other black families that lived there, including the Bartels. Many of those living on the council estates were from families displaced by Liverpool's slum clearance programme of the 1950s. Some felt trapped by the comparative deprivation, while others used the clannish atmosphere to build a criminal power base.

I was angry with the levels of racism I was subjected to. I was angry with my father for his treatment of my mother before she died and for not realising how difficult it was being me in Norris Green.

I was angry too with the lack of opportunities, forcing me deeper into a world of petty criminality.

I remember the doors slamming shut in the court cell rooms next to the police headquarters in Cheapside, central Liverpool. A small barred window offered a vision of the world beyond the walls surrounding me. It was August and England was suffering from drought. Parts of Britain had gone 45 days without rain. As the dry weather continued, devastating heath and forest fires broke out across the country. Crops were badly hit and food prices subsequently increased dramatically. It was the hottest summer in 350 years of records. I was starting at four impenetrable concrete walls.

I did not stop to think how I'd reached this dark corner of the city I was born in. It felt like it was my destiny to follow this dubious path. Where it would end was anyone's guess. I wasn't really bothered. I had no lofty aspirations.

I had resigned myself to being this way: hustling on the streets, in and out of prison – trying to find a way to survive.

Survival was a mission enforced upon me from the day my parents were told it was necessary to move out of Liverpool 8, or Toxteth as it is known nationally. It would be seventeen years until I returned there.

I was born on Saturday 18 May 1958 in Toxteth, L8: the area that for me still represents home. Yet I grew up on the sink estates of Norris Green, to the east of Liverpool; the place that probably had the most profound impact on my life.

In the same year, America's first satellite was launched from Cape Canaveral and the microchip was developed, which formed the very early stages of the PCs we all now use at work and at home.

This was before the Beatles became the Beatles. In July, a band known as the Quarrymen paid seventeen shillings and six pence to have their first recording session, where they recorded Buddy Holly's 'That'll Be the Day' and 'In Spite of All the Danger', a McCartney/Harrison original. It was a very different world and primitive compared to the one we know today, certainly in terms of technology and – as I would learn – in terms of social acceptance too.

My earliest memory is of a lie being told. I wonder now how that affected me in the long term, especially when it was delivered by a parent, though my mum did not realise she was lying because the information supplied to her proved to be wrong.

The Gayle family included my mum Alice, my dad Purcell, Alan – my brother – who was twelve years older than me, Abdul, who was eight years my senior and Jan, my sister, four years in advance. I was the youngest.

Our house in Liverpool 8 was on 36 Carter Street, a beautiful Georgian terrace, not far away from the border with Dingle, another tough yet vibrant inner-city area.

The council had told my mum that the Gayles would have to live in Norris Green while it refurbished our house in Liverpool 8. After a few weeks, one of my mum's friends phoned her to say that the house on Carter Street had been demolished.

My mum was heartbroken and I can remember the regular visits to the housing office on Storrington Avenue where she would plead with officers to transfer us back to the south end of the city, closer to family and friends. She'd often leave in floods of tears because of the rejections, although I never knew why at the time because she kept her reasons to herself.

I grew to hate the office on Storrington Avenue. Although her brother, Uncle Willy, lived on Broadway, a twenty-minute walk from our house in Norris Green, I know my mum felt isolated in the area. It wasn't the same as the south end. My mum was a lovely woman and most of the best things that happened to me growing up was because of her. All of the good things that I am today, indeed, are because of her care.

So I remained in Norris Green. My sister Janice was there too. My two brothers Alan and Abdul did not settle and moved back to Liverpool 8 to live with my grandmother, my 'Nin' as we called her; seeing the family break up by moving in different directions made life even more difficult for Mum.

Only at weekends would I be able to return to Liverpool 8. My dad would take me for a haircut at Mr Peewee's barber shop on Granby Street – the eclectic shopping thoroughfare of the area that sold everything you could ever want – before spending the afternoons playing football in Princes Park with my two brothers.

On those Saturdays, my dad would drop me off at the barber and pick me up an hour or so later. Mr Peewee seemed to take forever with his work – he had a real pride. The clock never seemed to move. I was desperate for him to hurry up because I valued my time in Liverpool 8 and wanted to do other things while I was there – before my dad showed up. I can still hear the hum and buzz of the cutters and the sound of Radio Four in the background.

Much later, when I was in Liverpool's first team, Bob Paisley voiced concerns about the amount of time I was spending in Liverpool 8, which wrongly held a reputation as being a rough area to live. In reality it was no different to any other inner-city borough. The riots of 1981, however, changed everything.

The media played a powerful role in telling the story of what happened there. The first thing journalists did was label it 'the Toxteth Riots'. For the black community, Toxteth was always Park Road – a white area. The riots actually took place in what was widely referred to by its postcode as Liverpool 8, or the Granby ward. The media needed a tag so they called it Toxteth, which we never used in our community. It was quite clear to me that someone in London's press saw the sign 'Toxteth' without appreciating the nuances of its boundaries.

Now, when people think of Toxteth, they think of a bad day in Bosnia. Beforehand, it was a self-governing multicultural municipality where problems were sorted out internally. There was a level of respect between most of the people that lived in Liverpool 8 and to me it was a sanctuary from Norris Green, where outsiders were distrusted. Black families like ours were scarce in Norris Green. I was the only black pupil in my school year and I wasn't allowed to forget it by the majority of other kids.

All week, I'd look forward to going back to Liverpool 8, where I always felt part of the majority rather than the minority. Years later, I retraced my father's steps to Africa and I got the same feeling there. I could be myself in Liverpool 8 but in Norris Green I had to take on a tougher demeanour from day one. At home and around friends' parents, I was polite and respectful. In school, I was a brute. I had to be to get along. There was no other way; otherwise I'd have crumbled.

Liverpool 8 was the kind of place where everybody knew everybody else. In the early part of the twentieth century, it was one of the most affluent areas of Liverpool to live in. Even today, there are some majestic-looking town houses in Canning Street that used to be owned by sea captains and wealthy merchants as well as judges and bankers. On the leafy avenues off Upper Parliament Street and close to the brooding, mysterious Anglican Cathedral, there are huge Georgian and Victorian homes that are used to shoot period dramas like Peaky Blinders, which is meant to be in Birmingham.

After the Second World War, with Liverpool's docks hard hit by German bombers, a lot of the seamen moved out and worked out of other ports around the country. They left behind the houses and soon they were split up into flats. Among the bulldozers and the rubble, Liverpool 8 took on more of a working-class identity with the building of terraced accommodation stretching up towards Dingle and Aigburth.

It was during this time that my dad, Purcell, moved to Liverpool from Freetown in Sierra Leone. He was in the merchant navy and liked the city, so he stayed. My dad wasn't a talker and never really described what life was like back in Africa. It was only when we became older that he told us that he was a strong believer in the occult and black magic. It convinced him there was a curse on him and that he would suffer ill fortune if he were ever to return to Sierra Leone. He started going back in the late 1980s but on one trip in 1994 he returned from Africa and within two weeks had died of bronchial pneumonia. Maybe it was just a coincidence. Maybe it wasn't.

In the years before I was born my dad operated as a seaman out of Liverpool's port and was away for long periods. In Liverpool 8, my mum took in lodgers to help with income while he was not there. A seaman was only paid at the end of a voyage, so money was tight.

Upon moving to Norris Green, my dad got a job as a bus conductor and his route was the number 79, which ran from the Pier Head on Liverpool's waterfront to Netherley. He later worked in the Ford car plant, starting off in the paint shop, where he became a shop steward. He wasn't the sort of person to flit between jobs; he valued employment. His loyalty was almost blind, not unlike a lot of workers from his generation.

Yet my dad was also blind to a lot of life's challenges. Though I suspect he'd been through many himself before arriving in Liverpool, he wasn't the sort of person to go into detail about his problems. He had a stiff upper lip.

We never spoke about racism or the environment we lived in. Not once. Maybe inwardly he believed that the best way of dealing with it was ignoring it. It's sad that I don't really know. I wish I'd been able to speak to him: to learn from him. Outwardly, he was not an emotional man. He was very formal: smartly dressed, always in a shirt and tie. His hair was cropped short and his skin was incredibly black – much darker than mine. He was six foot four inches tall and very powerful-looking. Around friends back in Liverpool 8, he would speak in Creole.

He did not seem to appreciate that, although we lived together, my life and his life were very different and that the lives of my siblings were different as well. They managed to escape Norris Green and the problems that the area posed for a young, lonely black person pretty quickly. I did not.

When I applied for jobs, my dad did not seem to want to admit that racist attitudes were in the 1970s were prevalent and that it would stop me from finding employment. I left school without any qualifications but I wasn't the only one. Britain remained an industrial country and it seemed as though opportunities were there even if you failed at school.

On leaving education I had to find a job. I did not realise there would be so many difficulties and barriers ahead of me. I applied for so many apprenticeship schemes. I'd get phone calls from companies and they'd invite me for face-to-face interviews, which would last no more than five minutes. There were no letters explaining why I had not been successful.

After a while it got to the point where I didn't bother applying. The rejection wasn't frustrating – it was soul-destroying. I didn't feel as though I was being judged fairly. Instead, my dad concluded that I was being idle, and because of that our relationship deteriorated. It was easier for me to hustle on the streets, by which I mean dealing in stolen goods; whatever I could get my hands on. It enabled me to have a few quid in my back pocket.

Like Dad, my mum, Alice, was of West African descent. She was a gentle lady who always tried to understand the difficulties me and our Janice had to face on a daily basis.

When I close my eyes I can still hear her voice. She was well spoken and did not talk in Liverpool slang. She always wore a dress and a petticoat and had a scarf in her hair. She was mixed race, lightly skinned and very attractive. While her father came from Ghana, her mother came from a prominent white family called the Austins.

The Ethel Austin clothing retail outlet started out in Liverpool and before long there was a shop in every major town and city across the north of England. My grandmother was an Austin daughter and she had fallen in love with my Ghanaian grandfather.

Unfortunately for both of them this happened at a time when mixed relationships were not encouraged, especially in wealthy families. It led to my grandmother being shunned by the family as she chose to follow her heart instead. Sadly, it resulted in my mum and her brothers and sisters not being able to see or have any sort of relationship or contact with their grandparents or cousins.

*

LIVERPOOL IS A CITY APART, DIVIDED BY ACCENT AND ATTITUDE from the rest of the country. It has more in common with Marseilles, Naples or Dublin than it does with Birmingham, Sheffield or Leeds. Wave after wave of immigration, traditionally from West Africa, the Caribbean and Ireland, has seasoned its distinctive slang. Especially in the inner city, independence, verbal wit and physical robustness are prized characteristics of its people. Authority, on the other hand is begrudged.

Toxteth was and probably still is the grittiest of the inner suburbs. It is one of the few genuine multicultural areas of the city. But by the time I was born at the back-end of the 1950s, it maintained an ebullient image. Granby Street mimicked a bazaar with its Muslim butchers and Arab, Pakistani and Bangladeshi mini-markets selling exotic fruits, unusual vegetables and red-hot spices. West Indian mommas sat on the doorsteps of old dilapidated buildings where their husbands, wearing Panama hats, smoked hash, watching the days go by. There were faces of every creed and colour, while accents and dialects were also diverse. There were problems – like there are in any other metropolitan area of the country – but in the main Hindus, Muslims, Rastafarians and Christians got on pretty well.

The atmosphere spawned an exciting nightlife. From the seaward end of Parliament Street towards Smithdown Road on the way to Wavertree, it always seemed like there was somewhere to go. By the docks, the alehouses overflowed and ladies of the night hung around close by offering sexual favours to testosterone-filled partygoers and seamen who were passing through Liverpool en route to Asia or West Africa. In the Granby ward, I would watch customers pile into an array of drinking dens. There was the Gladray strip joint, the Somali Club, the Alahram, the Tudor Club, the Olympus, the Caribbean and the Mediterranean on my doorstep during weekends. All of them offered something towards the identity of Toxteth, but I was far too young to contemplate offering my custom.

I was very young when my parents announced that the family was moving from Toxteth and inland to Norris Green.

In Norris Green we lived upstairs in a maisonette on Stalisfield Avenue. Many of the other houses in the area were terraced with small gardens, but our prefab was even smaller, with a kitchen, a living room and three bedrooms.

Gradually we got to know a lot of other families in the area, mainly through my mum who, like most mums, would spend endless afternoons talking to other parents at the end of our front path. The Cavanaghs lived underneath us; there were the Nelsons next door and the Lowes just over the road. There were also the Todds, the Robinsons and the Whittakers.

Much later on, a few other black families were relocated into the area, but initially there was just us – standing out alone.

Upon being enrolled into St Teresa's secondary school, Alan was placed in the bottom sets. It was assumed that because he was black, he was automatically uneducated. He's a naturally intelligent person though, Alan, and within two weeks he was sent up to the top sets after they invested time in getting to know him rather than making ignorant assumptions.

Abdul converted to Islam in the 1980s. His name was Paul before. We were brought up as Christians and we went to church every weekend as children. My dad had enforced a policy in our house that if we didn't attend church on a Sunday, we couldn't go out with our mates until the following weekend. He never wavered from that rule, so most of the time we respected it. As soon as we had the opportunity not to go, we stopped.

The church, to me, spread misinformation: it was an institution that was supposed to promote love, wellbeing, happiness and togetherness, but in reality was executing a culture of the exact opposite values.

The rumours about priests touching up young boys would not go away. We also had a nun at school, Sister Gerard, who handed out punishment that was sadistic and evil. It did not matter whether you were a boy or a girl, whether you were guilty or innocent; you'd end up feeling her wrath.

If someone was heard talking during one of her religion lessons, one of her favourite tricks was to turn around and launch a blackboard duster or piece of chalk roughly in the area where she thought the noise was coming from.

It was a careless thing to do because, often, an innocent party would get hurt. I don't think it mattered to her, though. All children were guilty by association.

On another occasion during a music lesson in the main hall of the school there was a song with the lyrics '... and here we sit like birds in the wilderness...'

Bored children changed the lyric to '...and here we shit like birds in the wilderness...'

Unfortunately, one girl and one boy sang the words with a bit too much vigour and were caught by the nun. She proceeded to stop the class and drag the culprits out in front of everyone by the ear, brandishing two rulers. Rather than strike the rulers across the palms of the children's hands, she used the edge of the rulers and applied them to their knuckles.

The screams from both of them could be heard all over the school, so much so that other teachers left their classrooms to come and see what the commotion was about. This wasn't punishment, it was abuse and humiliation of the highest scale.

As a result of this brutal act, the school changed its policies on caning and designated teachers were put in place to carry out punishments. Punishments that involved knuckles were also outlawed.

*

I REMEMBER TRYING TO MAKE FRIENDS WITH SOME OF THE OTHER kids in the council estate. I'd be OK playing on the street with them, but if a gang of us tried to pile into a house, the other kids' parents would often stop me from going in. They didn't want a black kid in the house. I didn't understand it and the rejection hurt me. I'd speak to my mum and she'd tell me to hang in there: that people would learn to accept us. But I didn't bother disclosing this information to my dad. He'd have probably found a way to blame me: that I wasn't trying hard enough to fit in.

Being on the outside became normal and, as a child, I didn't realise the severity of the effect that it must have had on me. I could hear the parents saying, 'Don't be bringing that lazy nigger to the door.'

If you are told you're something often enough, you begin to believe it. Eventually, you become it. Racism can institutionalise not only the person being racist but the person on the receiving end if it happens often enough. Racism imprisons you and it's incredibly difficult to escape.

After progressing from St Teresa's infants' school on Utting Avenue, my mum enrolled me at the junior school over on Storrington Avenue.

It took me a long time to begin to integrate properly. The kids would encourage one another to make jibes at me and I'd constantly be fighting because of it. I was scrapping with boys that were older and bigger. My brothers always told me to never give in to them and if I had to pick up a brick or a glass bottle to protect myself, then I should. 'Just make sure you get your hit in first,' they said. Abdul told me that if I had to make an example of one of them then that was what I was going to have to do.

That attitude has followed me throughout life. Quite easily, I could have killed somebody because I was acting on a basis of self-defence. If someone attacked me, I'd make sure that they knew they'd been in a fight and, sometimes, I didn't know when to stop because I was constantly being challenged.

I look back at one fight at eleven or twelve years old as one of the defining moments of my schooldays.

During a sports day at the Scargreen playing fields, just around the corner from the Gayle house on Stalisfield Avenue, a boy came to me for no reason at all and called me a nigger, laughing at my hair. The insults were indiscriminate.

There was no messing around, so I started punching him in the head. Eventually, after kicking him to the floor, I pinned him down, grabbed his hands either side of his body, and head-butted him as hard as I could. It knocked him out. That prompted another boy to come over. 'What have you done, you fucking nigger?' He got hurt as well.

News of the fight spread quickly and parents of the other boys were already at school by the time I returned there. I knew it was serious. The headmaster grabbed me by my hair and hauled me into his office. No questions were asked about what happened or what had provoked the fight. All the fingers were pointed at me. My parents weren't asked to be there and I was cast as the instigator without listening to any of the facts. The result was a suspension from school. Before I was escorted from the gates, they used corporal punishment to enforce their message and the strap was applied to my hands twelve times, an unprecedented penalty. Most kids got three straps.

The pain didn't bother me a great deal. Neither did the suspension. I was more concerned about my dad's reaction. I'd take the cane, strap or slipper all day long rather than explain to my dad how I'd been chucked out of school. Getting into trouble and missing education or bringing the police to our door was the worst thing you could do.

Frustratingly, though, the only way to survive in Norris Green was to confront the aggression towards me. It meant that I was damned if I went along with the racism and damned if I confronted it. If I fought racism, I'd at least maintain a level of integrity among some of the kids, and if I let it slide, I figured that it might allow everyone to come on top of me.

I was not without friends in Norris Green, though many of those friendships were founded on my behaviour of acting tough or being outspoken. I gave others the impression that I didn't care how big someone was; over time, I gained a reputation for my fearlessness. In Norris Green, being like that won you a few mates. Inwardly, I have always been a private person and I enjoy my own space and company. In Norris Green, though, I had to be different to find friends.

If it wasn't for my mum, I wouldn't have had anybody to confide in about my problems. She was a good mum and a good wife to my dad. She was a proud woman. But my dad didn't appreciate her in the way other husbands might.

My dad had several affairs with other mystery women. He was reasonably discreet about it, but not discreet enough.

One Sunday, I came back from church and my dad was hitting my mum. I ran over and screamed at him. As a son, I'd always try to protect her. But my dad was built like a rugby player. He had hands like paint brushes and swatted me aside before jumping in the car and disappearing.

My mum reacted by pulling me to one side and begging me not to tell my brothers, who might have reacted by fighting with my dad had they found out. My brothers were older and bigger than me and as adults were not as much afraid of my dad as I was. They didn't like it in Norris Green and there were times when I didn't see them for two or three weeks. Any signs of physical violence were often clear by the time they arrived.

NORRIS GREEN, 1974

I WAS FIFTEEN YEARS OLD AND JUST ABOUT TO START MY O-LEVEL year when my mum died suddenly. It broke my world. It's a blur now. I can't remember much about the period. My mind has a mechanism that blocks memories out, especially ones I do not want to think about. In some ways it has helped me but perhaps it has prevented me from dealing with issues that have a long-term consequence. In the bad times the shutters come up. I realise now it's not a particularly healthy approach, especially if you want to improve as a person and learn from your experiences.

Initially I reacted to my mum's death with defiance. I sat in the exam hall taking a science exam with my arms behind my head having answered every question with the words: 'If you don't know – what are you asking me for?'

I now realise it was a cry for help because I couldn't understand the loss of my mum. She was the barrier between my dad and me. She shielded me. He was an old African and a disciplinarian. Like a lot of dads with a similar background, if he saw another kid from the area misbehaving, he wouldn't hesitate in giving them a slap. The area was self-governed and our family was self-governed. My dad had been brought up that way in Africa.

Now I look at myself and I don't think I've turned out a bad person and I don't think my brothers or sister have either. So the discipline must have had some sort of positive effect on me. In the right environment, discipline can be good. In the wrong one – like when you're a black boy in Norris Green – it begins to lose its meaning.

My dad never told any of us that he loved us. My mum was the opposite and, because I was the baby of the family, she gave me extra attention. When she died, the emotional release in my home life was gone. I felt like I was on my own in the house and on my own in Norris Green. The feeling of emptiness was extreme.

I was too young to get my head around it all.

On the night before her funeral my cousin Barry took me out for a walk and tried to help me. For a short space of time, I could make sense out of what had happened, but when I got to the church the following day I couldn't deal with it. I couldn't deal with the fact that death was forever and that things were going to change.

I left school with no qualifications, no mother and in Norris Green. I reacted by rebelling. Boys on the street recognised that I had the ability to take care of myself. I was broad-shouldered like my dad but nowhere near as tall, and my height was another insecurity because I was quite small for my age as a teenager.

Racism remained, but there was an acceptance that I could more than hold my own in a scrap and that earned me enough respect to get along.

Before my mum's death, I had gotten into trouble at school for fighting. It became the routine: being called a nigger, striking back, being hauled into the headmaster's office, being sent home and trying to hide the punishment from my dad.

Although I wasn't involved in serious criminality, I'd experienced brushes with the law. There was little else to do for young lads in Norris Green aside from playing football and getting into mischief.

I started hanging around with a group of lads known as the Strand Gang, who are now infamous for their role in the murder in 2007 of an innocent child, Rhys Jones, an eleven-year-old who was gunned down after being caught in the crossfire of a turf war with the Crocky Crew, who are from bordering Croxteth.

When I was a teenager, guns and drugs did not feature in any aspect of life. I used to go to watch Liverpool matches with a lot of the lads from Croxteth but that doesn't happen now. If a lad from Croxteth shows his face in Norris Green, the knives and guns are out, and vice versa if someone from Norris Green goes over to Croxteth. We used to fight at places like Sparrow Hall, Muirhead Avenue or Breck Road, but it was more sticks, stones and fists. It wasn't serious. It happened because of boredom.

To escape the routine we bunked on the bus and travelled around Liverpool looking for things to do. One afternoon we made it to Formby, a rich town far out to the northern suburban boundaries where many footballers now live.

There was a football lying in a garden so one of the lads 'borrowed' it. We started playing football on a bowling green at a nearby park. To us it was the equivalent of playing a match at Wembley.

Our escapade soon escalated. The park keeper's hut was broken into and a window got smashed. Next thing, two police vans slammed up and fifteen of us were taken to the nearest station and locked up. They lined us all up in a long corridor and the first lad denied responsibility. The policeman pulled out a leather glove and started slapping him really hard. Eventually, the lad admitted smashing two of the windows, thinking that would be the end of it. The police started the same process with me until I was forced into admitting that I'd smashed one, even though on this occasion I was only guilty of playing footy on the bowling green. If it was a choice between causing mischief or playing football, I'd always choose football. I was relieved when they gave us bail because I knew if my dad had to come up from Norris Green to pay money to get me out of the cell, it wasn't going to happen. He'd have left me there as a punishment.

Two months went by without me telling anybody at home what had happened. Then the police arrived at the door while I was out messing around with friends. I saw the police car at the end of the street and figured it would probably be a better idea if I stayed away until it was gone.

I waited until darkness fell then tried to creep up the stairs to bed without turning on the lights, alerting Dad to my presence. Guess who was waiting for me on the landing? I felt a smack and my feet didn't even touch the floor by the time I reached the bottom of the stairs. He followed me down before completing his punishment with a flurry of blows.

The incident in Formby took six months to go to court and in the end I was found guilty of criminal damage. I was given a £60 fine and two years' probation.

My dad's response to that was not physical for a second time but nevertheless harsh, insisting that I stayed in the house until I was sixteen years old. I thought he'd relent after two or three months, but most nights, he'd be waiting for me at home when I got home from school at quarter past four. If I wasn't back, he'd want to know why.

The only way past him came on the days he was on late shift-work at the Ford car plant. There was more leeway with my mum. If he got home and I wasn't there, mum would stick up for me and reason that she'd sent me to the shops. Eventually, he started to loosen his grip on me and, finally, I was free to roam the streets again.

*

WITHIN A YEAR OF MY MUM'S DEATH, I TREATED AUTHORITY AS THE absolute enemy. The unyielding discipline of my father had contributed towards it. My experiences with the police had contributed towards it. The lack of support I received from school over racist incidents contributed as well.

But if asked to pin it down to one moment that shifted my view towards authority, I can, because it's a moment that has lived with me ever since. It will never go away. It was something that was done to me and something that was wrong. It is something I will never escape from – something I have never spoken about, not even to my family until the months leading up towards the publication of this book.

I was fifteen years old and close to taking my exams at school. My mum was ill with cancer, the disease from which she subsequently died.

I took solace in football. The teacher who took charge of the fifth-year football team is dead now. His name was Mr. Mike Crossley. I liked him. He inspired trust. He organised after-school sports clubs and camping trips up to the Lake District where he originated from.

Quickly, his attitude towards me became very close. I was one of two black pupils and I thought he was trying to reassure me, give me that bit of protection I'd always craved at school.

When we finished a football training session one evening, my impression changed. He sidled up to me and, without any hesitation, started asking me questions of a sexual nature: did I have a girlfriend? Had I experienced sex before? They were asked in a friendly way – as if I was one of the lads and this was the kind of things fully grown adults speak about. Most young boys told fibs and I was no different. I wanted to seem older than I was so I responded with bravado. I claimed that I was well experienced with girls, even though I wasn't.

He was grooming me and I didn't know it. I thought it was just man-talk:

banter. Over the weeks that followed, the questions became more explicit. How regularly did I masturbate? Did I have pubic hair? I was unsettled by the questions but, being young and naïve, I was also confused. I tried to convince myself his intentions were genuine: based on friendship.

I think it was after badminton practice. He offered to drop me off home afterwards in his car. My dad was really strict on me getting home from school promptly and not being on the street so I thought it was a good idea. If my dad saw me getting out of a teacher's car, he'd find it reassuring.

So after practice, I waited for the teacher to get ready. I was invited into the teachers' changing rooms and he was the only one there.

He carried around a brown satchel with him pretty much everywhere he went. He reached for the satchel and pulled out a porn magazine. 'Have a look at that,' he said. So I did.

I'd never seen a porn magazine before. As I flicked through the pages sitting there on the bench, his questions became more and more intimate. 'Are you getting a hard-on?' Then he started to touch me.

I was terrified. He told me to touch him. He exposed himself. I told him to stop. He did not.

I ran home as fast as I could, jumping over fences. When I got there, he was waiting near my house. Maybe he planned to tell me not to say anything to anyone. But I waited for him to leave and then took the punishment that followed for being much later than expected from my dad.

Initially, I was in denial. I convinced myself that everything was normal – this is what happens. Then I started to ask myself why – why did it happen? Then the fear took over – is it going to happen again? I was embarrassed – ashamed – and scared. I couldn't disclose what had happened to anyone. I could not tell my mum because she was ill. I could not tell my dad. If I'd have told my brothers, I knew what they would have done. They'd have killed the teacher and their lives would have been ruined.

I feared ridicule too. What if I accused this man and he convinced people I was lying? He was in authority. I was not. I was a black kid. Why would anyone listen to me?

Homophobia was rife in society and I worried how friends at school might react. Would they think I was gay because I didn't fight him off? 'Puff' was an insult used regularly on the playground. I didn't expect them to understand. A term called 'queer-bashing' had emerged and it was a happening on the streets.

I had no idea of how it would affect me. I buried my head into the ground and tried to ignore it. Beneath the surface, the trauma was genuine: screaming and raw. It made me angry. How dare this person take advantage of me?

My attendance record at school slumped. I stopped playing football for the school team. When another senior teacher tried to punish my friend Cathy Bullen by grabbing her by the hair in class, I tried to stop him by jumping at him and telling him to leave her alone. I was mischievous but had never taken on a teacher before, not even verbally.

I'd never missed school before. But I stopped going. I gave up on education completely. I became distant from everyone, cutting myself off.

I didn't trust a soul.

*

FROM THE EARLIEST DAYS AS A CHILD, I CAN REMEMBER SUFFERING from racism without being able to understand why I was targeted; why people saw me differently.

This led to my rejection of authority. In the 1960s, children were taught to respect authority. It formed the framework of society. Racism was a part of society and yet, older people – authority figures you were supposed to trust – were racist towards me, making me feel rejected. How could I respect them?

Being a victim of sexual abuse from an authority figure – someone I'd respected and trusted – has made it even more difficult for me to trust people in authority positions.

This secret has been a burden that I've had to carry throughout my life.

I have mentioned elsewhere in this book how children find it difficult to talk about their problems.

Rather than telling someone about what had happened to me in an attempt to try and find a solution, I found that the only way I could deal with this was through rebellion.

*

THE SERIOUS PROBLEMS WITH THE POLICE STARTED WHEN I OBTAINED
a chequebook and a credit card by breaking into a car. I used them in Liverpool
city centre on expensive clothes. One of my friends got caught and, although
I escaped, he grassed: another one of those instances that hardly inspired me to
trust those who I thought were close to me.

I received a £20 fine and another probationary period. In the 1970s,
the probation service was so lax in Liverpool that after three or four weeks
of attendance, you did not bother. The authorities did not chase you.
The chances were, you'd just get in trouble again and the circle of petty
criminality continued.

It was an easy world to slip into. There were lots of big company factories
near Norris Green: Sayers, Schweppes and Coca-Cola had bases on Long Lane,
a road that reaches out towards Kirkby.

At sundown, we'd climb on to the factory roofs and see crate-loads of sausage
rolls, lemonade or pop being ready to be loaded on to wagons below. When the
workers had gone home, we'd break in and take with us as much as we could get
hold of. The Jacobs cracker factory produced industrial-sized boxes of biscuits
and cakes and we'd pig out on them on the way back to Norris Green and the
Strand shopping area where most lads with nothing else to do spent their evenings
together. It was petty theft. Later, though, we moved on to cars.

One night, we stole two Granadas: a Ghia and a Consul – the ones that were
made famous by The Sweeney cop show. We drove into town in the daytime and
saw some toy police lights in a 50p shop. So we pocketed them along with a pair
of walkie-talkies. For the next ten hours, we played chase around the streets of
Norris Green and did not stop until 6 a.m. without being apprehended.

It was easy to steal a car. Most motors had basic keys and by the mid-1970s,
although car manufacturers tried to improve security with slightly more advanced
locking systems, we were masters at using the serrated edge of a knife in the
ignition. I can still hear the words, ''Ave you got it?' from one of the lads while I
juggled about with the knife.

I learned to drive through stealing cars. By the age of seventeen, I was
probably robbing at least one a night and, if it was a good one, I'd stash it
somewhere and keep it for a while. I always wore a balaclava because black boys

in Norris Green stood out from the crowd and were easily identifiable in a police line-up.

We'd operate in Allerton, another prosperous area to the south of Liverpool's city centre, where there was a wider selection of top-quality cars to pinch. There was a white, limited-edition RS Capri with a turbo engine.

As usual, we returned to Norris Green because, by then, stealing cars was a competition. Everybody present agreed that this one was a great find. The police chased us but they were using RS Mexicos and had no chance.

Some of our escapades could not be considered as success stories. I was walking home one night from at a disco on Broadway in Norris Green with a friend and we spotted a Ford Capri.

Within seconds of sparking the car's engine into life, the police were on to us. They followed us for twenty to twenty-five minutes, which is long for a chase. It was only a 1300-engine Capri and we weren't able to escape. The police radioed in a fleet and they started blocking the roads off. I was in the passenger seat. We were flying round the streets but as we turned around one corner with three cars in pursuit, my mate edged a lamppost on my side. The car tipped over and my head shattered the windscreen.

I wasn't wearing a seatbelt and I was unconscious. One of the police officers, to whom I am eternally grateful, managed to pull me out of the car and rest me on the side of the road. Faintly, I could hear voices shouting, 'He's dead ... he's dead.'

I woke up the following afternoon in a hospital bed. My brothers were there but my dad was not. He chose not to visit for three weeks. It was his way of saying: 'Howard – you dickhead.'

My dad wasn't the type of person to offer sympathy to someone who'd injured themselves through doing wrong. It was a relief that he did not visit because he'd probably have been tempted to make sure I left the hospital in a body bag.

After the case went to court, I received a £120 fine – which was a lot of money. But I was expecting prison. I'd got off lightly. Again.

*

THE LATEST BRUSH WITH THE LAW WAS THE FINAL STRAW FOR my dad.

I decided to move back to Liverpool 8 and be close to my brothers, who helped me with the rent for a bed-sit on Hutchison Street. Although I'd pined for Liverpool 8 for so long, I continued to hang around with the lads back in Norris Green. I'd become institutionalised to the place. All of us were around eighteen years old and, as a gang, we were forging a reputation for ourselves.

Lessons were not being learned on my part and it was only a matter time before my actions caught up with me, as they did that Friday afternoon in Liverpool city centre when caught red-handed with a denim Wrangler jacket under my coat.

I was one of the first people in the country to get four months – usually for such an offence, you'd be committed to either three or six in prison.

The penny didn't drop. I thought it was going to be a piece of cake. Such had been my aloof behaviour, a few weeks went by before any members of my family realised I was banged up.

All of a sudden, it dawned on me that life in the immediate future was going to be very tough. I started to panic, realising that – just like when I grew up in Norris Green – I was going to have to prove myself once again in prison. Potentially, that would mean making sure that I wasn't picked on, and the likelihood was that I was going to be involved in a lot of confrontation. The self-defeating cycle would continue.

I was transferred to Werrington House in Staffordshire. It was the typical enrolment into the prison system where they take all of your possessions, including your clothes, before hosing you down with freezing water while the rules of the place were screamed at you by an angry guard.

Life before had prepared me for this. But it's the time spent alone that changes you the most, especially when it is 1976 and the hottest summer on record is being recorded outside.

I needed to change.

MUNICH

ii

Bill Shankly, Liverpool's manager, said there were only two football teams in the city of Liverpool: Liverpool FC and Liverpool FC reserves. In seventeen seasons, Liverpool FC's reserves won the old Central League an amazing fourteen times. In terms of overwhelming success, he was absolutely right. His wish for reserve-team players to possess the capacity to fill a first-team player's boots was a reality, although the first team kept on winning too so there was little change in the selection policy.

The 1980/81 Central League title was already secured by the time Blackpool's reserves visited Anfield on 18 April 1981. The personnel inside reserve teams like Blackpool's changed a lot. The incorporation of youth-team players and first-team dropouts contributed towards inconsistent results.

Liverpool's reserve team, though, remained largely the same throughout the season. We played in the same 4–4–2 formation as the first team and used the same tactics, making it easier to step up or move down if necessity called for it.

It was April and spring had sprung. The sun was shining. The pitch was rutted, as it always was by this point in the season: simultaneous campaigns of Liverpool's first team and the reserves taking its toll. For ten months of the year, a week did not go by without the pitch getting a match. It was the same at most First Division grounds. On the patches of grass, light dew remained at kick-off time.

The gate was good: nearly 2,000 people huddled together in the Main Stand. The Kop, the Anfield Road end and the Kemlyn Road Stand were closed as usual, creating a muffled atmosphere.

I was quick and I knew I had the measure of Blackpool's defence. The message from Roy Evans, our manager, was always the same: 'Get them turning early doors,' he'd say. By that, he meant for the centre-half or the full-back to knock a few quick balls into the channels for the forwards to run on to in the first five minutes. 'It puts them on the back foot straight away,' he'd say.

31

We had good, skilful players. Ian Rush, Sammy Lee and Ronnie Whelan would become legends at Liverpool, while Kevin Sheedy would take the same status at Everton. Robbie Savage, Alan Harper, Geoff Ainsworth, Avi Cohen, Richard Money, Colin Irwin and Colin Russell all played for Liverpool's reserves as well: all of them outstanding young players.

It gave me a buzz knowing that Liverpool were the best team in the country and that I was representing a big club: one expected to win week in, week out, whether it was the reserves or otherwise. The expectation excited me.

We expected to rout opposition like Blackpool. And we did, 5-0. Avi Cohen scored twice and I got a hat-trick.

'You did all right today, 'oward,' Roy said afterwards. At Liverpool, understatement reigned. 'Keep up the good work.' You never really got praise at Liverpool. Just a bit of encouragement.

I had no idea what was going to happen between the Saturday and the Monday. Liverpool's first team had drawn 0–0 at Leeds United. Their season was in danger of petering away to almost nothing. Winning the League Cup was not enough for Liverpool.

There was an injury crisis: Graeme Souness, David Johnson, Kenny Dalglish, Phil Thompson and Alan Kennedy were all struggling.

Bob Paisley was short of players.

NORRIS GREEN, 1964

IF I CLOSE MY EYES AND THINK AS FAR BACK AS I CAN, I AM TAKEN back to a scene of happiness: of green fields and football pitches.

My mind is taken to the south end of Liverpool: to Sefton Park, a beautiful open space slap-bang in between Liverpool 8 and the prosperous suburb of Aigburth, where the roads become wider, the houses are kept in better condition and the atmosphere is mellow.

I am five or six years old and I can see towering oak trees in the distance,

I can smell freshly cut grass and I can hear the sound of my brothers breaking the tranquillity by shouting orders at each other while playing football, celebrating goals.

They were long days that seemed to go on for ever. On Saturdays and Sundays, hundreds of grown men would arrive in their football kits. The amateur game was very competitive and the standard was very high. The games were noisy. You would hear instructions being shouted by players and spectators. Everyone present had something important to say.

Subconsciously, the sights and sounds of Sefton Park dripped into my consciousness, educating me about the game and what it meant to the people of Liverpool.

There were plenty of spare footballs lying about and the younger siblings of the players would start their own games on the side of the pitches where the real games were happening. We used jumpers for goalposts and tried to recreate what was going on around us – the real thing.

Back in Norris Green, in evening time, a new football programme called *Match of the Day* was being screened on television, revolutionising the way the game was received and viewed.

Working men would finish their morning shifts, head to Anfield or Goodison Park and after a few drinks in the pub would go home for dinner before slumping into their armchairs.

In the early days, the BBC had only one outside broadcasting unit. It meant that on 22 August 1964 Liverpool and Arsenal became the first teams to feature on a football highlights show on British television. Liverpool won 3–2.

Liverpool, indeed, were emerging as one of the leading clubs in the English First Division under Bill Shankly. I was too young to attend football matches so the television afforded me my first experience of the professional game.

The suggestion that I might feature and score a goal on Match of the Day – as I did when Liverpool drew 1–1 with Tottenham Hotspur in 1981 – would have been beyond my wildest dreams.

Watching *Match of the Day* became a Saturday night ritual: or, at least, I wanted it to be. Football became my first love. I quickly learned, however, that where love is concerned, punishment often follows.

From 1966 onwards *Match of the Day* had its slot on the BBC at 10.30 p.m. *Till Death Us Do Part* was usually the show on beforehand. My dad would shuffle about in his chair, slowly raising himself in the dimly lit room.

'Come on, mister,' he'd say in his deep, Creole accent. 'It's time to get off – up to bed.'

A strict, disciplined environment existed in our Norris Green house that involved both me and my sister Janice completing daily tasks. If these tasks were not carried out, my dad would use it as an excuse to send me to bed soon after the *Match of the Day* music came on.

My dad was ruthless in his approach to how he administered the discipline. For example, if I failed to take the milk bottles out one night during the week my dad wouldn't say anything to me until Saturday night – the moment I looked forward to most.

I adhered to my dad's rules. I'd often hang around outside the living room door, prolonging the walk up to bed, waiting for Kenneth Wolstenholme to introduce the day's big match. Just hearing the commentator would excite me because his voice represented *Match of the Day* and *Match of the Day* reminded me that life existed beyond these walls.

I appreciate now that maybe my dad simply didn't want me staying up late: to get into a disciplined routine that would prepare me for working life. His existence was based on pattern: waking up at 5 a.m. and going to bed at 10 p.m. during weekdays and 11 p.m. at weekends. There were few distractions to keep a person up beyond that time.

Both my mum and my dad worked very hard, my mum as an auxiliary nurse at Olive Mount, which was a mental health children's hospital, and my dad as a bus conductor and later as a paint-sprayer at the Ford car plant in Halewood. His efforts there earned him the respect to become one of the first black shop stewards in the country.

Their efforts allowed the Gayle family to have what were considered then as luxury items: a black-and-white television was one of them. I'd often see other families having to use the phone box on the street corner in order to contact friends and family working away. There were queues and waits, sometimes half an hour to an hour long. Fortunately, we were able to afford a phone. We also had a gas cooker and fire. Most households in Norris Green had an old AGA cooker and a log fire.

From Queens Drive, Liverpool's ring road, at the western end of Norris Green, Anfield was only a mile away. I knew when it was a match day because from midday on a Saturday until around 2.30, more cars were zipping about the streets. Between 3 p.m. and 5 p.m., it was a lot quieter and that meant Liverpool were playing, the magical team that played in distinctively coloured blood-red shirts, distinctively coloured blood-red shorts and distinctively coloured blood-red stockings: standing out from the rest.

When a goal was scored at Anfield you could hear the roar from Norris Green. The noise would grab my attention and make me wonder what it was like being stood in the crowd.

On school nights, I would sit in my bedroom and open the sash window. For the midweek games, there was no radio coverage and certainly no television coverage. Listening to the crowd from a few miles away was the only way to keep up with the scoreline. The anticipation of something happening was thrilling.

I quickly became used to judging the difference between a goal and a near miss. A miss would be short, sharp and disappointing, followed by a clap – the sign the crowd approved of the team's efforts.

A goal was totally different. The sound lasted for fifteen seconds and only then would you get to know the identity of the scorer because the crowd would bellow his name. It was a unique way of communicating what was going on at Anfield to the suburbs of Liverpool. It meant you didn't need to be at the game to know what the score was or, indeed, who had scored.

The Liverpool team of the 1960s was filled with brilliant players, legends of the game. Roger Hunt was my hero. I worshipped him. He was the perfect role model: tough, talented, spirited and fair.

I wonder how much money Roger would be worth in the modern game because, before Ian Rush came along all those years later, emerging from the same reserve team that I played in, Roger was Liverpool's all-time leading goal scorer. He was a comic-book centre-forward, someone who seemed invulnerable: a strong, powerful-looking man, with a shock of blond hair. I wanted to be him.

Roger was phenomenal. If he played now, I'm convinced his worth would be insurmountable. Every kid in Norris Green had a player who they modelled themselves on.

Bill Shankly built two sides. From the first Ian Callaghan, Peter Thompson, Ron Yeats, Willie Stevenson, Chris Lawler, Ian St John, Gordon Wallace, Peter Cormack, Gerry Byrne, and Tommy Lawrence were gods on the fields and schoolyards around Merseyside.

From the second, there was Ray Clemence, Alec Lindsay, Kevin Keegan, John Toshack, Emlyn Hughes, Steve Heighway and Brian Hall. One player I really liked was Tony Hateley, an old-type centre-forward who Shankly ultimately decided didn't quite fit Liverpool's style and was sold after only one season despite a healthy goals return.

I often wondered, however, why there were no Liverpool players with black skin like me. I assumed they mustn't have had the ability. There was nobody around to explain otherwise.

Very few people from Liverpool's black community went to Anfield or Goodison Park, indeed, because of racial innuendo or comments that were made towards opposing black players. Referees who made decisions the majority of the crowd did not agree with would get asked 'Who's the bastard in the black?' The undertone sat uncomfortably with me.

Cliff Marshall's problems at Everton in this period were well documented. Everton had signed Mike Trebilcock, a mixed-race player, from Plymouth Argyle and he scored twice in an FA Cup final victory for the club over Sheffield Wednesday in 1966. In doing so, he'd become only the second black player to score in an FA Cup final. The first had been Blackpool's Bill Perry thirteen years before.

After Everton sold Trebilcock to Portsmouth, Cliffy was the next black player to appear in the Everton set-up. Growing up, I'd seen him star for Liverpool and England representative teams at schoolboy level. I'd wondered why his career at Everton was not progressing until I found out that he was subjected to racist comments from within the club and on the home terraces of Goodison Park.

Cliffy Marshall was as good as if not better than the personnel Everton had on their books. He had skill, speed and aggression. Ultimately, he was not able to fulfil his ability because of racism.

Back then, as a young child, these were not issues that entered my head. I thought only of heroes and how I could realise the improbable dream of becoming a footballer.

I appreciate now that I am privileged to have been able to know and play with a lot of Liverpool's former players. We see each other regularly at games and events throughout the year. Sometimes, I don't think they realise just what an impact they had on kids like me, those kids with little hope in their lives.

They were the first generation of footballers to be truly idolised, mainly because they were the first generation to feature regularly on television. Television made it feel like you somehow knew them a bit more. In the 1950s, you wouldn't even know what a footballer sounded like because football's coverage only existed in newspapers. Suddenly, through Match of the Day, you could hear them on TV. They became friendlier and their personalities shone through. Roger Hunt seemed to be a quiet man – someone with an inner strength. I liked him mainly because of his goals. He was relentless.

My dad was an Evertonian but not in the truest sense. He rarely went to Goodison Park and I sensed he only really supported them because when he arrived in England from Sierra Leone, Everton had slightly more success than Liverpool and were probably easier to support, considering Liverpool's malaise in the 1950s when the club spent several years in the old Second Division before Bill Shankly's arrival as manager changed everything.

Shankly's presence at Anfield shook the club, grabbing it by its roots and heaving it upwards; creating a new world order. He was like the Pope; when he came on TV, people stopped what they were doing, clinging on his every word, even my mum – who had no interest in football.

Shankly was totally committed to dragging the club into the 21st century. His philosophy and ideology created a template that all Liverpool fans bought into and still do today.

Liverpool FC had been in the Second Division and Liverpool as a city was recovering from the economic decline of the docks and other industries. Within a few short years, Liverpool were an important club again and Merseybeat took off. Shankly made the people believe that anything was possible. He encouraged young people to be creative.

Throughout the 1960s, though, Everton were the wealthier club. They had all the money and invested it lavishly on players like Alan Ball and Howard Kendall. It makes me laugh now when Evertonians talk about Liverpool spending more than them. Traditionally, Everton were the elitists in the city and known nationally as the Merseyside Millionaires, as they attempted to deal with the threat of Liverpool under Shankly by spending lots of money to try and keep ahead of the challenge from across Stanley Park.

When I was ten years old, my dad's best friend Bill, who was like an uncle to me, and his wife, 'Auntie' Jean, started taking me and his two sons Stuart and Billy to both Anfield and Goodison Park on alternate weekends.

The Citrean family came from Halewood. My dad and Bill worked together on the buses and both ended up working at Ford. Their house was just a stone's throw away from the factory. I spent many happy days in Halewood, which was a brand new estate designed like Norris Green to home the overspill families of Liverpool. Most of the residents had jobs in nearby factories.

There were many things to do but what I enjoyed most was being able to play football on a huge field behind the Citrean house. On summer evenings at 6 p.m. there would be a mass gathering of kids and a playground swing would be used as goalpost frames. These were some of my happiest childhood memories. Had I been able to spend all of my summer holidays in Halewood, I would have done.

More than anywhere, though, Anfield felt like home. It felt right being there. My brothers felt the same way. When Uncle Bill and Auntie Jean took us all to Goodison Park, I didn't get the same connection with Everton. I get asked all the time by people from outside the city what defines a Liverpudlian from an Evertonian given that so many families have divided loyalties. All I can say is that it is about feeling. Nearly every lad in Liverpool has probably dabbled with both clubs in their most formative football-supporting years. I'm certain it has something to do with that buzz when you first walk inside the stadium. For me, Anfield felt like home: the green grass of the pitch, the smell of Bovril and the floodlights. It was a mystical place. It helped that Liverpool were doing well. Shankly was building something and the club's emergence fell at the same time as the Beatles. Liverpool FC and the music being created in the city meant that Liverpool felt like the centre of the universe. Unless, of course, you happened to be visiting Norris Green.

*

THE BOYS' PEN WAS A STEEL CAGE IN THE NORTHWEST CORNER OF the famous Kop stand. It could hold hundreds of kids, acting as a supposedly safe area away from the heaving masses in the Kop.

I was in my early teens when I started going to Anfield with lads from Norris Green. I quickly appreciated how easy it was to bunk in for free, especially when there were so many thousands of other people in the stand hiding you.

The pen was meant to be a satellite community of Shankly's vision: day care for the offspring of seasoned Kopites – a place where sons deemed too diminutive for the genuine thing would spend their Saturday afternoons cheering on the Reds and learning what it meant to be a Liverpool supporter. That was the theory anyway.

The reality was quite different. The Kop seemed like an all-welcoming society. The pen was a holding ground for frustrated juveniles wanting to progress into the mainstream of the Kop to experience its vibrant atmosphere. It also had its dangers for young boys. One of the hardest-working groups of people on a match day at Anfield were the workers at the St John Ambulance, who had to deal with cases of fans passing out or injuring limbs following crushes in the standing areas of the ground. Supporters were forced into viewing crushing as part of the match-day experience.

The boys' pen could also be a lonely place for newcomers outside the clique. Those that weren't inside the clique didn't hang around for long. Kids who stood in the pen were tough. Regulars in the Main Stand, just across from the pen, would witness and be the recipients of our wrath. The sound in the boys' pen was very different to the sound in the main body of the Kop. The boys' voices would be drowned out by the men because many of our voices hadn't even broken yet. It was like a choir being quelled by an adult chant.

Fighting and swearing were commonplace. There were gangs from all different areas of the city. I went with lads from Norris Green: Peter McNamara, Anthony Hannah, Micky Baldwin and Karl Yoward. Then there were other gangs from Dingle, Halewood, Speke, Scotland Road and Kirkby. Although the obvious enemy was whomever Liverpool were playing on any given Saturday afternoon, there were times inside the pen when lads would have a scrap to claim their own territory. Once the game started, all of our energies were directed at supporting the team, but beforehand it was an intimidating environment and I had to be streetwise to survive, especially being the only black boy in there.

Most of the lads inside the pen were frustrated by the fact they were too small to get into the Kop. The Kop was the place to be –being there proved you were a proper Liverpool supporter. The atmosphere the other side of the fence was unbelievable. It was electric. The noise – that roar when Liverpool scored – it gave you the feeling of togetherness; a feeling of togetherness that I craved, which was absent from other areas in my life.

Though thrilling, it was an arduous task attempting to make it over the fences and into the Kop. There was a little gap in the pen big enough for the smallest lads to get through but taller ones had to be more inventive. A typical escape attempt would involve one kid climbing over and deliberately getting caught by a steward manning the fence. The steward would throw the sacrificial lamb out of the ground and while that was happening, twenty lads would jump over and merge into the Kop without being spotted.

The most adventurous attempt to flee was via the Kop toilets. They were directly below the pen so you'd get some terrible smells wafting through. Hot air rises, so there would be a pong. The sanitary conditions in the Kop were horrendous: worse than a Turkish prison.

I probably missed some great moments on the pitch because I was so busy trying to get out of the pen. There were many routes – some of them more precarious than others. I think we sometimes annoyed the older fellas on the Kop but they must have been impressed by our determination.

It was a great way to learn about football matches. It was where I started supporting Liverpool. You get a lot of people younger than me saying they started watching Liverpool in the Kop when the pen was finally closed. I think that generation has missed out. The pen was a rite of passage.

There was a sense of community inside Anfield but that only developed, in my opinion, because of the success of the team in front of us.

Bill Shankly's sides had many qualities but, above everything else, it was the ability to recover from apparently impossible situations that set them apart. Regularly, it seemed as though Liverpool were two goals down and somehow end up winning. I think that factor ground opponents down, made them weary; arriving at Anfield already half-beaten, thinking they had to score four goals to be truly secure. This never happened, of course. The powers of recovery created a fear factor that nobody could really quantify.

Liverpool would always come good just when everyone else started to doubt them. Even though Liverpool were one of the best teams in the country, it conversely felt like we were the underdogs. Shankly had created a unique mentality and reputation for Liverpool.

That identity suited me because I felt the same way personally. I was determined to prove people wrong, to prove I was capable of rising above the challenges in my life and prove I was capable of excelling.

*

WEEKENDS FOLLOWED A SIMILAR PATTERN: PLAYING FOR THE school on a Saturday morning, heading over to Anfield or Goodison Park in the afternoon; wake up the next morning and rush out in my kit again for a Sunday league game. After dinner, there would invariably be a twenty-a-side match on Ellergreen Fields. It seemed like every kid in Norris Green knew when a game was happening. It reflects the obsession with football of both me and the majority of others in the area.

My first competitive match was for St Teresa's. I was nine years old and we faced Christ the King School, where Childwall Comprehensive is now. The idea of playing an away game was exciting. Childwall might as well have been at the other end of the earth. It made me feel older, privileged and – most of all – determined to win.

I jumped on the 61 bus to reach the meeting point at Alder Hey Hospital. From there, a teacher had organised transport that would take us the rest of the way. Being eager, I arrived at the rendezvous point an hour early. So did a few of the other lads. To pass the time, we decided to go to a corner shop and we bought sweets and ate them all. It wasn't a good idea because by the time the game started, we couldn't run. I had a stitch all the way through. It contributed towards a thumping 5–0 defeat.

Gradually, I became familiar with the unpredictable and harsh world of Sunday league football in Liverpool – a place where only the toughest or those with rapier wit survived; where insulting words like 'nigger' and 'coon' were a part of the vocabulary used by parents as well as players, especially when you were facing teams from Scotland Road or Warbreck – two of the toughest inner-city areas where attitudes were entrenched and a peculiar Celtic insularity survived.

Sometimes, it did not even take confrontation to provoke others into making racist comments. Mere competition was enough; opponents trying to set you off your game by releasing a steady stream of abuse under their breaths, making it feel really personal. It was all geared to gaining a reaction: either one where I became distracted to the point where my game suffered and my form dipped, or one where I got sent off for scrapping. It took a great deal of focus and determination to resist the temptations bubbling inside me, especially considering my reactions away from the football pitch. There were occasions when I couldn't help myself.

I started playing for on a Sunday for a team called West Derby United – run by a guy called Joe Mercer who, not to be confused with the legendary Manchester City manager, ran his own glazing business. We travelled to and from games in the back of his van.

The base tribalism that exists in football meant I never had any trouble with the lads in our team, although I'd be lying if I claimed they backed me up when the abuse started. Sometimes it was difficult for them because opponents would pick on me by whispering words, although I'm sure my team-mates must have known why I reacted.

Despite some testing experiences, these remain among my happiest childhood moments: being out on the football pitch in the driving rain, often being better than everyone else. I know it annoyed a lot of people that a black kid was the most talented in Norris Green and that encouraged me to prove the impression right. I knew I had ability and those trying to insult me were going to have a job knocking me off my stride.

The standard in the Liverpool leagues was really, really high. The achievements of Liverpool and Everton in the 1960s had inspired a generation of kids to play football and the levels of physical and technical ability on show meant that scouts from clubs across the country were visiting Merseyside.

Liverpool's Chris Lawler and Colin Irwin both came from Norris Green, as did Everton's Joe Royle and the Lodge brothers, Paul and Robert. Both of them went to St Teresa's; one signed for Liverpool, the other for Everton.

There were others, of course, who stood out at schoolboy level but never progressed beyond that. Joey McNamara, a centre-back, was one of them, as well as a goalkeeper called John Ferguson.

You always hear that shout of, 'He should have made it . . . why didn't he?' There were so many examples of kids who could have made it as a professional but never did. Football isn't the exact science that so-called experts say it is and I'm convinced many fall by the wayside due to a mixture of luck and timing.

Fortune, for example, led to me discovering a talent I didn't realise existed in me. I eventually went on to sign for a team from Fazakerley that played in the Bootle and Litherland League. It was a real pain on a Sunday because you had to get up really early to get across town for games. I earned a trial for the league's representative team but in the week before the trial I stupidly damaged my knee jumping between bollards in a car park. Although I eventually got selected for the representative team on reputation, the incident summed up my careless attitude to the game.

The casual behaviour inadvertently helped me on one occasion when I dropped a hot-water bottle on my right foot. It was shaped like a whisky jug and it broke my toe. The following day I was due to play in a cup semi-final for St Teresa's and I didn't want to miss it because we were playing our rivals St Matthews – a team we never used to beat, although the defeats tended to be narrow. They had a goalkeeper who wore an all-black kit and he was like Lev Yashin, the famous Russian – arguably the greatest in his position of all time. I'd love to know why this boy never made it professionally because he was the best keeper I faced as a junior footballer.

On this particular day, though, he couldn't stop me. In the first minute of the game, I received the ball on my left foot and I pinged a shot off the bar from 25 yards. It gave me confidence and that moment was like a switch. From then on, using my left foot seemed natural because I could run, pass and shoot with it. It opened a whole new world to me, because when you're one-footed, you tend just to go one way. If you can use both, it gives you unpredictability.

When I went on trial at Liverpool years later, the fact that I was two-footed must have had an impact on the decision to take me on. Although he never scouted me I know that the first-team scout, Geoff Twentyman, liked players that could 'go both ways' – meaning, an ability to kick with either foot. I ticked a lot of boxes: height, weight, stamina, finishing ability. But being two-footed meant I could play left, right or through the middle. Liverpool liked versatility. I'd always scored goals but I got just as much satisfaction from setting them up as well.

My other asset was speed. When I was young I ran everywhere. My mum would ask me to go to the shop round the corner for milk or bread and I'd complain before giving in. If I was watching television, I'd wait for the break to come then leg it to the shops and back as quick as I could so I didn't miss anything.

Those walking past on the street or the old dears peering out of their windows, nosing around, probably saw a black boy on the run and thought, 'What's he getting chased for?'

THE ROUTINE OF ATTENDING FOOTBALL MATCHES INTENSIFIED during my mid-teenage years as I searched for an emotional escape from Norris Green.

After a transitional period towards the end of the 1960s where it took time for Bill Shankly to realise that he needed to dispense with loyal players like Ian St John and Ron Yeats, Liverpool were really beginning to click into gear again by 1972. It coincided with my progression from the boys' pen into first the body of the Kop and then the Anfield Road end right next to the opposition supporters.

Being closer to the aggravation and the tension excited me. Despite aggravation and tension being twin themes in my home life, I wanted more of it.

Perhaps I'd become addicted.

I soon realised that no thrill could compare to the adrenalin that courses through your veins at the moment before trouble starts between rival sets of fans at an important football match. Although a sense of inevitability was attached to the moment because being a part of it became a common occurrence, the hit still felt awesome.

As soon as the gates of Anfield opened on a match day, I would enter the stadium and wait for the opposition supporters to turn up. Together with mates of mine, we'd stand and watch in the corner, with hoods over our heads and hands in our pockets, not getting involved, as pitched battles took place across the terraces. The police would form a cordon through the centre of the Anfield Road stand but those fighting were determined enough to get to each other and break through it. The noise was a rush. Everything would be quiet and suddenly, boom – it'd all kick off: fifty or a hundred men doing bad things, leaving the stadium with cuts, bruises, ripped coats and sometimes shorn of a shoe, such was the chaos.

Terrace culture was tribal. The main aim was to overrun a ground or a city with the aim of being able to go home and gloat about it. Yet whereas other hooligan groups mobilised themselves and were highly organised, at Liverpool the arrangement was organic. Aside from having a few spotters over at Lime Street station first thing in the morning, what followed was purely spontaneous. There was no team strategy about it. Someone would say to go one way and everyone followed.

The gang that travelled from Birmingham City made the greatest impression on me because beforehand I had no idea they'd bring so many numbers. The fighting on the terraces was ferocious that day. It reflected to me just how big a club Birmingham City was. I am convinced deep down in my inner consciousness, this contributed towards me deciding to sign for them years later. I respected the depth of their support.

Birmingham were promoted from the Second Division for the 1972/73 season and, ahead of their visit to Anfield, I figured that because they were supposedly a smaller club, they wouldn't be travelling with many supporters or, indeed, hooligans.

I was fourteen years old and as bold as brass as I walked up Anfield Road with the usual gang before entering the ground; standing away from where the trouble would usually start because we were too small to instigate it or even really join in at that age.

Nobody had prepared us for the scene inside, where thousands of Birmingham supporters were waiting, determined to cause trouble.

Fights were still breaking out in pockets of the stand when the game kicked off, and Birmingham raced into a 3–1 lead with a team that included Bob Latchford, Bob Hatton and Gordon Taylor.

Typically of Liverpool, though, a recovery was mounted and we ended up winning 4–3.

Birmingham, though, had made a lasting impression on me.

*

'MUGGING' WAS NOT A WORD ASSOCIATED WITH BRITISH SOCIETY until the 1970s. Suddenly mugging was in the news, a phenomenon imported from New York City.

In the eyes of many, 'muggers' – or street robbers – came from the black communities, just as they did in New York, from boroughs like Harlem. Mugging became a national obsession, only matched by football hooliganism.

Black footballers were emerging just as the atmosphere was changing on the terraces inside Britain's football stadiums, with more and more skinheads attending football matches. Although skinhead culture didn't really spread across Liverpool, it did pretty much everywhere else.

The skinheads were gangs who wore Dr Marten boots, rolled-up Levis and braces. Their image was one of violent thuggery, aimed at rival gangs – especially in football grounds, and at minorities on the street.

By the start of the 1975/76 season, but before my stint in prison, I was travelling long distances to Liverpool away matches with the lads from Norris Green.

On one trip to Middlesbrough, the plan was simple: to reach the Northeast without spending any money. So, we set off at midnight in a stolen car up the East Lancs Road.

Unfortunately the car ran out of petrol around Billinge in West Lancashire, so we decided to take another vehicle. This time it was an Audi. It was early on in the morning – daybreak – and, encouraged by our previous unimpeded recklessness, when we saw a milk float around Haydock Island, we jumped out to pinch a few crates of milk.

The milkman returned to his float and, upon finding that he'd been robbed so comprehensively, must have decided to phone the police because soon enough we were all thrown in a wagon.

Fortunately the police never found the abandoned cars and we only received a caution for stealing milk. Somehow we made it to Middlesbrough that incredibly long day, before taking the slightly safer route that involved hitching rides all the way home.

Away days at Leeds United were particularly dangerous, mainly because Elland Road is miles away from the main train station on the edge of the city close to the M62. Leeds were the top dogs in the early 1970s under Don Revie. Liverpool were the challengers and the rivalry was huge: old Lancashire versus Yorkshire.

The approach to Elland Road was safe enough, providing you travelled by car and made it in without anyone local noticing the registration plate. Any other route was perilous because the ground stands on a verge, meaning home supporters were able to throw stones at you. It was as if we were trying to enter a castle at the top of a mountain. First you had to pass through the drawbridge and the outer wall. We were sitting ducks.

The police were supposed to be impartial, protecting both sets of supporters by keeping them apart, but quite often chose the side of the town or city they were from.

Anfield was pretty much the only stadium in the country policed fairly. We certainly didn't benefit from any home comforts. There was even one infamous officer who seemed to relish confrontation. Again, he was fair. All troublemakers were treated the same by him. We called him 'Blackbeard' because he looked like Geoff Capes, the British strongman and Commonwealth medal-winning shot putter. He had hands like shovels and would walk through the crowd swiping people with his truncheon. He really was built like a brick outhouse. You didn't want to cross his path.

When we went to other cities, Liverpudlians would get no protection from the authorities. I realise you shouldn't expect it if you are determined to cause problems, but if the police's job is to uphold the peace then that's what they should do. They are meant to be the protectors of the law, not to choose sides. Aggression always came from both sides.

On one occasion at Elland Road, for example, an officer announced on a megaphone for all the Leeds fans to cross over the road to the side where we were situated, outnumbered. It was as if they wanted it all to kick off. When it did, the police stood around and did nothing until the tide turned against those fighting from their town.

The government under Margaret Thatcher later blamed crowd violence as a football problem. In my opinion, it really wasn't. Crowd violence in football stemmed from a social immobility. The slow demise of the docks and the car factories in Liverpool or the rapid demise of the coal mines that gave jobs to people all over Yorkshire and the Northeast spawned immense anger.

While older people, those made unemployed, became sad, many who never even had that opportunity in the first place were frustrated, irritated and unfulfilled.

It may sound simplistic but it resulted in an outpouring of rage. In my case, and with a lot of other lads my age in Norris Green, whether they were Liverpudlians or Evertonians, we'd let off steam at football matches. It was spontaneous. It was a way of releasing frustration: escaping the realities of life.

I guess you could see it as self-harming in disguise.

*

VIOLENCE WAS ONLY A PART OF TERRACE CULTURE. THERE WAS also fashion.

My uniform was standard: beige or white pants with flared bottoms known as Oxford bags or Wrangler jeans, a Budgie jacket with a tank top underneath, then Hush Puppies on my feet. I was proud of my roots and had Afro hair.

That was before Bombardier boots and Adidas training shoes came in; Sambas were my favourite. Some of the other lads preferred Gola or Puma.

When Londoners travelled to Merseyside, we used to laugh at the state of their clothes. Supporters of Arsenal, Spurs, West Ham or Chelsea were all the same – they dressed really badly, arriving at Lime Street in leather coats and sheepskins only to never return home wearing them. If ever a chase ensued, they'd never get away because of the heavy coats. It was naive.

I remember one weekend waiting on the concourse at Euston station on the way home from Arsenal and we bumped into a gang of West Ham supporters who were on their way home from somewhere like Luton Town.

They were coming up to Anfield the following Saturday and I said to one of the lads who was wearing a ridiculous leather coat, 'Ay, lad – you don't want to be coming up to our place wearing that . . . you won't go home in it.' I saw him the next week. He'd taken my advice.

Dipping into pockets was the norm. I wasn't very good at it because my hands were big. I might as well have done it with a boxing glove on. Subtlety isn't one of my strongest qualities.

The end of a match was a good time to go to work, or when something exciting happened in a game. If someone lost their balance, you'd help them up then someone else would delve into their pocket like the Artful Dodger from Oliver Twist. There was an element of teamwork about it.

When I think about that now I cringe and want to go back and give people their money back. Later you realise you're taking money off working-class people. You thought they were fair game when really it might have been a person's wages. Now I'm older and earning a modest wage too, I wouldn't want that happening to me.

I sometimes wonder what Bill Shankly would have made of my behaviour, which was progressively getting worse and worse; the violence and the stealing. Shankly was a people's manager and understood how people in this city looked at life, although I am sure he would have been unhappy at the thought of Liverpool supporters being the perpetrators of seemingly pointless violence inside the stadiums of a sport he loved so much.

Then again, I would reason once again the culture inside football grounds followed the general culture of the streets around Britain. At first there were gangs, then organised gangs, then skinheads, then Hell's Angels, mods, rockers and groups that separated all kinds of different creeds and colours. Society was becoming fragmented and because of the tribalism of football, it naturally followed the pattern as well.

*

IN MOST CASES PETTY CRIMINALITY LEADS TO SERIOUS CRIMINALITY because it gets to a stage where you push the boundaries of acceptability further and further, putting yourself in dangerous situations more and more often.

After being released from Werrington House, I was on probation. One of its conditions was that an offender should find employment or be actively looking for work. So I took a job making carbon-copy paper. It was boring and laborious. The pay was almost nothing.

I briefly slipped into skulduggery again, albeit on a lesser scale than before I went to prison. I signed on at the dole office and immersed myself into petty theft just so I had enough money in my pocket to get by. I stole because I had to. I wasn't a thief just for the sake of being a thief. If I stole something it was because I was either going to wear it, use it or sell it. Electrics and coffee beans were big sellers and with Norris Green being so close to a number of factories, I considered it fair game. The big companies were ripping everyone else off; that was my rationale.

I worked in a team of four, keeping the group as small as possible so less could go wrong. It became a daily routine. You were active all of the time. If you saw something in a shop, you'd think, 'I'll come back for that.' It felt like a job.

But I never stole off individuals. I wasn't a street mugger. We targeted organisations rather than individuals. Shopping retail outlets were prime targets. I only stole off companies who I thought wouldn't miss something if it was gone. There was a twisted morality to it. Robbing old ladies – you just didn't do it because she was somebody's mother. It was a warped code of conduct. That was the street.

I have no doubt that, had Liverpool not signed me, I would have fallen into serious crime. There's no doubt about that: drugs, firearms – the lot. I had been through the process of trying to earn an honest living. I wanted a trade or an apprenticeship. But there were no jobs for people like me. I'd more or less given up.

I was spinning out of control.

I was lost.

MUNICH

iii

Monday morning. Anfield. 'Boss wants to see you,' said Ronnie Moran, poking his head around the door of the dressing room, delivering the news in his typically brusque manner.

Ronnie was from a different generation: the toughest of tough men. He did not care for sentiment. He just wanted Liverpool to win, by hook or by crook. His entire working life had been spent at Anfield. First he was a player, and then he was a reserve-team coach. His role as first-team coach doubled up as physiotherapist, now that Bob Paisley – the previous incumbent – was manager.

Ronnie led Ian Rush and me down the corridor. The beige walls. The green floor. The smell of liniment. Players talking behind doors. Laughter.

I'd scored a hat-trick for the reserves two days earlier but immediately something was saying to me I was in for a telling-off. I'd been out over the weekend, partying with friends from Liverpool 8. Maybe Bob had found out. He didn't like me socialising in Liverpool 8. And that was why I was living in Mossley Hill, a few miles away.

But why was Rushy coming with me? Rushy was from Wales. He didn't go out very much. He was still in his shell. He wore the wrong clothes; said the wrong things. He was still trying to fit in.

'Wait outside, Rushy,' Ronnie said. 'Howard's in with the boss first.' So Rushy waited, perched on an orange plastic chair.

The boss was constantly on to me about how I acted off the pitch. 'How are you?' he asked. 'All right,' I said. I respected Bob. But to say I liked him would be a stretch. 'Well, you need to go home and get your stuff ready because we're going to take you away with us . . .'

Liverpool were travelling to Germany for the second leg of the European Cup semi-final against Bayern Munich. It represented the biggest game of a disappointing season where the league campaign had faltered, largely because of injuries to key players. Because of these injuries, I was being promoted.

I have no idea why Rushy went in separately. I ran off down the corridor, picked up my bag and left the other reserves in the dressing room to get changed before their bus journey to Melwood. 'Where you going, Howard?' shouts one of the lads – I can't remember who. 'Going to Munich, mate . . .'

And with that, I'm off back down the south end of Liverpool, scrambling about in search of my passport; knowing the squad is assembling at Speke airport a few hours later for the flight on Aer Lingus. Liverpool always flew with Aer Lingus. Wherever they went.

This was a new adventure for me, so getting the opportunity to travel away with the first team – even if it was just to watch a game – was exciting.

The atmosphere among the squad, though, was subdued. The reality was there: they might have to rely on some of the reserves. Phil Thompson, the captain, was already ruled out through injury and Colin Irwin was filling in for him. Alan Kennedy was injured too and that's why Richard Money was in the squad.

I sat on the plane with Sammy Lee, my best mate. The conversation was quiet as we took off; banking over the River Mersey and flying southeast, over London, over the English Channel, across France's border with Germany and into Bavaria. From the plane's window, I could see the Alps and snow glistening in the spring sun.

My mood began to change. I'd travelled with Liverpool before as a supporter. I was a player now. This felt different.

Maybe it was my week.

MELWOOD, 1977

IN ORDER TO EXPLAIN MY PATH TO LIVERPOOL FOOTBALL CLUB'S first team and in order to begin to understand the environment that existed there, it is crucial to set it in the context of the time.

My journey into football came during an era when black Britons were largely invisible in entertainment, sport and politics: in an era, indeed, where second-generation immigrants like myself were nevertheless beginning to define widespread attitudes within society. The black community was simultaneously marginalised yet thrust to the front of the political agenda when it suited those in charge.

Through maturity I have realised that it is better to try and understand other points of view even if they are diametrically opposed to what I believe in. It was only later in life that I realised the ignorance I grew up around was a consequence of what had gone before when you consider that Britain had grown rich and strong off the back of the slave trade.

After the Second World War, for the first time in its history the British government welcomed subjects from the old Commonwealth states with open arms. Although people like my dad would arrive in the country holding more rights than any immigrant had before, he and many others were greeted by an insular population holding entrenched views that had stood for centuries without forceful sociological contradiction.

I was eleven years old at the start of the 1970s and an adult at the end of the decade. I never envisaged for a second that it would be possible to break new ground and become the first black footballer to represent Liverpool at first-team level mainly because there were very few role models visible to suggest to black people that this society offered much hope of advancement.

The twin stories of Arthur Wharton and Walter Tull reflect this. Born in Jamestown, Gold Coast – now part of Accra, Ghana – in 1865, Wharton, indeed, should be recognised as one of football's most famous names.

Wharton's parents were both mixed race. His father was half-Grenadian and half-Scottish, and his mother was half-Scottish and a member of Fante Ghanaian royalty. Wharton moved to England in 1882 aged nineteen to train as a Methodist missionary but soon abandoned his plan in favour of becoming a full-time athlete.

Wharton was a fine cricketer and the 100-yard dash amateur world record holder. He became one of the best goalkeepers in England, playing with distinction for Darlington, Preston, Rotherham and Sheffield United. With that, he was also the world's first black professional footballer.

Yet after retiring Wharton disappeared from public life. He fell into destitution and alcoholism and died in 1930, being buried in an unmarked pauper's grave.

It was not until 2003 that the Football Association acknowledged his achievement formally, when he was inducted into the National Football Museum's Hall of Fame, then in Preston. In 2014, a statue was unveiled in his honour at the National Football Centre in St George's Park.

Like Wharton, Tull was mixed race. His career came a little later. Tull was brought up in an orphanage in Bethnal Green London, along with his brother, following the death of their parents; he joined Tottenham Hotspur in 1909. A journalist for the *Football Star* newspaper attended the Bristol City versus Spurs match in that year and noted the appalling racism that Tull was being subjected to. He wrote in his report: 'Let me tell those Bristol hooligans that Tull is so clean in mind and method as to be a model for all white men who play football ... In point of ability, if not actual achievement, Tull was the best forward on the field.'

Tull's abilities alerted the great Herbert Chapman, a manager who is not only credited with turning round the fortunes of both Huddersfield Town and Arsenal, but is also regarded as one of the game's first modernisers. He introduced new tactics and training techniques into the English game, as well as championing innovations such as floodlighting, European club competitions and numbered shirts, and has received many posthumous honours in recognition. In 1911 Chapman, then in charge at Northampton Town, decided to sign Tull and make him an integral part of his midfield, where he played 111 games.

Tull's promising career was cut short by the outbreak of the First World War, where he became Britain's first black army officer – an almost unimaginable achievement at the time. Despite military regulations forbidding 'any negro or person of colour' being commissioned as an officer, Walter was promoted to lieutenant in 1917 after attending the officer training school at Gailes, Scotland.

Tull fought and survived the Battle of the Somme in 1916. He was mentioned in dispatches for 'gallantry and coolness' while leading his company of 26 men on a raiding party into enemy territory in Italy in 1917. He then returned to France and was killed in action on 25 March 1918 during the Spring Offensive. He was 29 years old and his body was never recovered.

Like Wharton, it took the best part of a century for Tull's accomplishments to be really noticed by the wider public. In 1999 Northampton Town unveiled a memorial to Tull in a dedicated garden of remembrance at Sixfields Stadium. His epitaph is moving.

Through his actions, Tull ridiculed the barriers of ignorance that tried to deny people of colour equality with their contemporaries. His life stands testament to a determination to confront those people and those obstacles that sought to diminish him and the world in which he lived. It reveals a man, though rendered breathless in his prime, whose strong heart still beats loudly.

It was only as an adult, after I'd retired from football, that I became aware of Wharton and Tull, mainly because they were not celebrated for so long and also because information about their lives wasn't available to empower my own knowledge. It was as if they hadn't even existed.

James Clarke's story is similar, one of the Liverpool's greatest black swimmers. Clarke was born in British Guiana (now Guyana in South America) and he arrived in the city in 1900 aged fourteen after stowing away on a ship before being adopted by an Irish family living in the Scotland Road area. He proved himself a strong swimmer and boxer, captaining the water polo team at Wavertree Swimming Club. Children often swam in the Leeds-Liverpool Canal in an area called 'the Hotties' (because of the hot water released from the Tate and Lyle factory). Clarke regularly rescued children from the canal and received medals recognising his bravery. He died in 1946 and few remember him.

Growing up in early 1970s Liverpool, Clyde Best was one of few black faces on British television when it came to sport. Clyde was one of West Ham United's star players: a big powerful Bermudan centre-forward. I idolised him because he portrayed an image of strength and defiance.

Aside from Best, black players were few and far between. At West Ham there was Clyde's teammates Ade Coker and the Charles brothers, John and Clive. At Leeds United there was Paul Reaney, though he was mixed race and had much lighter skin. On a black-and-white television, some viewers would assume him to be white. Leeds had too the skilful South African winger Albert Johanneson, who in 1965 became the first black person to play in an FA Cup final, losing to Liverpool.

There was also Johnny Miller, who played for Ipswich Town under Bobby

Robson and Norwich City between 1968 and 1976, though his role was restricted. Ultimately, England had not yet capped a black footballer.

My own emergence as a footballer came at the same time as many other black players and is probably a result of circumstance more than anything else. I was not alone in having a father who moved to the United Kingdom in the post-war years.

Realising it needed to rebuild its infrastructure and industry after the drain of a six-year conflict, doors were opened to immigrants from the West Indies and, to a lesser extent, from West Africa – people like my dad.

Initially, black communities appeared in Britain's seaports before spreading inland towards other manufacturing and industrial centres: places like Birmingham, Manchester, Sheffield and Leeds. They arrived mainly in working-class areas where football was ingrained in the community, remembering too this was a time when Brazil began to dominate the international game, winning three out of four World Cups between 1958 (a month after I was born, in fact) and 1970, becoming the first multiracial team to achieve success on the grandest stage. Pelé, Garrincha and Jairzinho were from different minority backgrounds and performed with skill and bravery, becoming role models for a generation to follow and emulate.

By 1971 every football fan in the world appreciated that Pelé and Eusébio were the game's greatest players and yet history proves that England was either a) behind the times or b) harboured deep-seated suspicion of black footballers.

It was not until the 1970/71 football season that a black player – Ben Odeje – represented England and that was at schoolboy level. Everton's Cliff Marshall followed him. It was not until 1978 when Viv Anderson of Nottingham Forest became England's first black player to be capped by the senior side, although the gap of eight years can be accounted for by FIFA regulations, which stipulated that schoolboys could represent the country where they were educated while adults could only play for the country where a player's father had been born, therefore making immigrant players ineligible for England.

It was not just in football where people with immigrant backgrounds were deemed ineligible. It was not until 1970 when the first black person appeared in a British soap opera, Melanie Harper played by Cleo Sylvestre in *Crossroads*.

Four years later, the show introduced the first black family – the Jameses.

And yet, for twenty years *The Black and White Minstrel Show* was commissioned by the BBC, only finishing in 1978 when viewing figures declined. The fact it lasted for so long suggested it was OK to poke fun at Britain's black population and that, indeed, lots of people enjoyed watching it.

While *The Black and White Minstrel Show* always seemed to be on in the summer, *Till Death Us Do Part* was screened in the winter. It felt as though the television was poking fun all year round. In the latter, a white actor, Spike Milligan, dressed up as an Indian character called 'Paki Paddy'.

There was also a role in ITV's *Love Thy Neighbour* for a character whose racist abuse of the black actor Rudolph Walker (who in 2016 plays Patrick in EastEnders) was systematic and shocking by 21st-century standards.

In music, it took time for black British pop stars to establish themselves as well. My favourite group were from Liverpool, the Real Thing, whose first album was released in 1976. Hot Chocolate, led by Errol Brown, were the decade's most popular black group but their rise only came after the band started creating mainstream white pop rather than funk and R&B.

Politically, there was an anti-black sentiment. For a while in the 1960s and 1970s, Enoch Powell was the most famous politician in Britain. Some might call him the Nigel Farage of his time. While the Labour government of the 1960s had introduced laws that opened doors to Commonwealth immigrants in an attempt to rebuild the country after the Second World War – leading to public service improvement such as increased NHS doctor numbers – Powell resented the policy.

In 1968 Powell – a Conservative right-winger – made a hard-hitting speech attacking immigration. Addressing a Conservative Association meeting in Birmingham, Powell said Britain had to be mad to allow in 50,000 dependents of immigrants each year. He compared it to watching a nation busily engaged in heaping up its own funeral pyre.

With that, he called for an immediate reduction in immigration and the implementation of a Conservative policy of 'urgent' encouragement of those already in the UK to return home. During his infamous 'Rivers of Blood' speech, he was applauded throughout.

In the years that followed racism increased, with the National Front emerging as the most powerful party of its kind since the British Union of Fascists (BUF), which was led by Oswald Mosley in the 1930s, around the time Hitler seized control of Germany.

Electoral results in the 1970s revealed the NF's growing popularity. By 1974, economic recession contributed the idea that immigrants were 'coming over 'ere and taking our jobs'. The NF had done enough to make more than 100,000 British people vote for them.

From personal experience, I know that many people harbour racist views without ever politicising them. After leaving school, I found these attitudes were present in society. In 1977, the working environment I entered was no different.

*

HUSTLING ON THE STREETS DIDN'T BRING A GREAT DEAL OF INCOME. I was living alone in a Toxteth bedsit by the beginning of 1977, spending most of what I had on escaping the reality by socialising and sleeping it off the following morning.

Strangely, this process brought me a return to the football field and, unexpectedly, a future in the game.

Liverpool's pub and club scene had long been healthy. Having been incarcerated in Werrington House, I was desperate to enjoy my freedom. Liverpool 8 was the entertainment heart of the city, a place where clubs and bars would close for only a few daylight hours before opening again.

On Parliament Street there was the Beacon, the Yoruba (owned by boxer Joe Bygraves who was a Commonwealth champion) and the Nigerian Club. On Princes Road, you had Silver Sands, Dutch Eddies, the 101 Cub, the Federal Club and the 68 Club. On Princes Avenue were the Sierra Leone Club and Ebo – another set-up for Nigerians. The Polish Club stood on Catherine Street, Lyndas Club on Crown Street and the Pavilion Club on Lodge Lane.

The most secretive of all the places was the West Indian Club situated on the corner of Grove Street and Parliament Street, known as Montpelier Terrace at the time; it was set back from the road in the basement of a large old Victorian house. It was run by Edgar Escofree and George Gardiner and music was delivered by jukebox.

Three of my favourite places were the Top Rank, the Control Club and the Timepiece, all of them more or less in Liverpool's city centre. These were drinking dens where, mainly, black people supped on rum and Coke while listening to soul, reggae or funk.

It is widely accepted that Liverpool has experienced two, or perhaps three, great cultural eras of music. The first was the Merseybeat years of the early 1960s, which spawned the Beatles and a host of hit-paraders. The next was the scene that emerged around Eric's, a club on Mathew Street (near where the Beatles famously played a generation earlier, at the Cavern). Opened by Roger Eagle and Ken Testi in 1976, Eric's was the catalyst for the emergence of a new wave of bands who went on to enjoy various levels of mainstream success. These included the Real Thing – the band that inspired me the most. Later there was Echo and the Bunnymen, the Teardrop Explodes and Dead Or Alive, concluding with the near global domination of Frankie Goes To Hollywood, whose first three singles topped the UK pop chart in 1984. The same feat was previously achieved by another Liverpool band 21 years earlier – Gerry and the Pacemakers.

The movement from within the Timepiece certainly was grass roots – 'certainly' because it only attracted a particular section of Liverpool society: the black community. There were other clubs where the mood was similar, places like the Pun Soul Club and Babalou. For a while, I worked as a DJ in the cellar of the famous Blue Angel nightclub. The dad of my girlfriend Lorraine owned the place and he was a bodybuilder.

Unlike in other cities, Liverpool did not embrace the Northern Soul phenomenon of the 1970s – in fact, it was barely played in Liverpool at all, where a funkier groove was the order of the day. The black communities of both Liverpool and Manchester were not interested in digging around for rare 60s music when there was a wealth of great funk in the 70s.

The Timepiece was on Fleet Street. It later became the Liverpool Palace. Although black people were not welcome in many of the clubs around Liverpool, the Timepiece was where blacks and the more adventurous whites would mix. The Timepiece was famous around the country because of its all-night parties and people would travel from far and wide to attend. To the black community thirsty for reggae, it held a similar reputation to the Wigan Casino, the home of Northern Soul.

Regulars included the US servicemen stationed in Britain. Many of them were based in Burtonwood near Warrington. Some would send Les Spaine – the legendary resident DJ who went on to work for the Motown label – packages of the latest funk records when they returned home across the Atlantic. Another DJ was Steve Mason.

The nights were long and the music was liberating. When I hear some of the songs now, I am taken back to the Timepiece: Candi Staton's *Young Hearts Run Free*, *Love Hangover* by Diana Ross, *You To Me Are Everything* by the Real Thing, *You Should Be Dancing* by the Bee Gees, *(Shake, Shake, Shake) Shake Your Booty* by KC and the Sunshine Band, and Lou Rawls' *You'll Never Find Another Love Like Mine*.

We were probably getting down to something like *Get Up Offa That Thang* by James Brown one Friday night, when my brother Alan leaned over to me while we were moving around the dancefloor, looking for women, inside the Timepiece. 'Howard, fancy a game tomorrow?' he asked.

'What?'

'A game for our Saturday team – we're one player down. Kick-off is at Sefton Park at eleven.'

So off I went the following morning after getting picked up on Parliament Street in the pissing rain. I scored a goal and thereafter I was a regular with the boys at the Timepiece in the famous I Zingari League, which when translated from Italian dialect literally means 'the gypsies'. The league had been active since 1895.

Alan was the manager of the team and he'd given me a bit of breathing space after leaving Werrington House. Alan knew how much I loved football, though, and that playing for a team where I wasn't in the minority for once might help my performance and consistency.

Alan was a good footballer – maybe better than me. As a child, when I was myself a baby, he'd been sent to St Thomas More approved school in Southport because of his bad behaviour, a place that accommodated up to 125 senior boys aged between their fifteenth and seventeenth birthdays at their date of admission. The training provided by the school included baking, cabinet making, carpentry, joinery and gardening: disciplines that were designed to set pupils on the straight and narrow. There, he also played football and was invited for trials at Blackpool and Skelmersdale United, the great amateur side that Steve Heighway later played for.

Unfortunately for Alan, a knee injury curtailed his progress before his career even began. By the time I joined the Timepiece, his knee had deteriorated to the point where he wasn't able to play.

Our Alan was a great organiser, though, and he created a very strong side with the Timepiece, a team made up of black players from Liverpool 8. We were the only all-black team in the Liverpool leagues, though we had a few white players registered too, lads who would turn up for the odd game when we were short in numbers.

Sefton Park was a hub of football. Because the Timepiece represented the black community in L8, we attracted large crowds. Entire families would watch us play. On a couple of occasions, in really big games, thousands would stand on the touchline, the crowd being so deep you couldn't see the pitch if you stood behind the masses of people.

We encountered some problems when we played away from Sefton Park but they were few and far between. The Timepiece gained a reputation as a very good football team but opponents knew if they caused us problems, they'd eventually have to play us in Sefton Park later in the season, a location right in the centre of Liverpool's black community. Clubs that played against us must have been wary of using racist language against us because eventually there would be consequences one way or another. They weren't taking on just one person; they were taking on an entire team or a community. We took a huge support wherever we went. There would be a train of cars and no spare seats. Young kids would come and watch us play even when they weren't related to any of the players. Parents realised their kids would be safe following the Timepiece.

With Alan on the touchline and my other brother Abdul running down the wing, I played up front for the Timepiece with Steve Skeete, who became one of my closest friends. Everybody who knew Steve called him 'Bull' because of his formidable size.

When I was playing for Liverpool's A team Bull was in the B team. Derby games were taking place at Bellefield and I heard a huge gasp from spectators on the other pitch. Bull had headed a cross from the edge of the penalty area which did not bounce on the floor again until it fell outside the area. The crossbar was still shaking. There was so much power in his game.

While Bull's brother Leo played professionally for Oldham Athletic and became captain of Mossley in the Northern Premier League, where he was worshipped as 'the Dusky Destroyer', Steve didn't make it so far, later instead becoming the player-manager of the legendary Almithak Sunday league team, which completed the 1987/88 season victorious in all three Liverpool competitions they entered, also reaching the quarter-final of the prestigious national FA Sunday Cup. Almithak was a merger between Saana FC, who represented Liverpool's Yemeni community, and Dingle Rail, a team sponsored by a nearby British Rail station who had won the FA Sunday Cup in 1981.

With the Timepiece, success was just around the corner. We reached a cup final at Prescot Cables ground where we won 3–1 and I scored two, although it would have been a hat-trick had the referee not incorrectly ruled one out for offside. The following evening, everyone gathered with their families at the Stanley House Community Centre in Liverpool 8. It was a brilliant night: mums, dads, kids, brothers, sisters, cousins, uncles and aunties all in one place. I was the youngest player in the team and, for the first time in my life, I felt a part of something – part of a movement: part of a movement that was successful.

Anyone who believed black players were flaky or did not care enough about football should have watched this team. The Timepiece proved it was a misconception. They should have stood on the touchline at Sefton Park, Jericho Lane or Buckley Hill and watched us in the wind and the rain, destroying other teams because they couldn't compete with our speed, power and intelligence. So many players had the required ability to perform in high-level football, but so few received those opportunities.

A few years before, Bull had been at Manchester City, where there were a reasonable number of black youths in the set-up. It made him feel comfortable. There was Dave Bennett, Roger Palmer and Alex Williams, all of whom enjoyed long professional careers. Dave made his name in Coventry City's famous FA Cup final victory over Tottenham Hotspur in 1987, while Alex became one of the first black men to play in goal at any level of professional football.

Bull had just as much ability as me and together, as a centre-forward partnership, we were unstoppable – even as teenagers playing in an adult league. We'd have competitions over who could score the most goals. Sometimes it was too easy. Maybe it sounds nonchalant saying that, but it was the truth. We were dynamic players.

After signing amateur forms with Liverpool, I suggested they should have a look at Bull as well, so they took him on trial. Unfortunately for Steve, his experience was short-lived. Steve admits missing training sessions, and eventually he simply stopped going. Before Liverpool, he'd had a similar experience at Manchester City.

Steve was a fantastic player and it frustrated him that he wasn't being pushed very far by the club. He wanted to be in the reserves when he was only being selected in the B team and he felt that his face didn't fit in. In the meantime, the pair of us went on trial with a club based in Sharjah from the United Arab Emirates. We were attached to Liverpool at the time but we went on the trial anyway because we hadn't signed a contract yet. Steve in particular was getting itchy feet and thought it was a good idea. So off we went to Fulham's Craven Cottage. Jimmy Melia, the former Liverpool player, was working as an advisor to the Arabian club and he recommended that they try and sign me, although they weren't quite so sure about Steve. I didn't fancy it though. There was a lot of money on offer but things were going steadily at Liverpool.

*

IT WAS THE DONE THING TO PLAY FOR TEAMS ON BOTH SATURDAY and Sunday mornings. Although the standard of a Saturday was better and Sunday was more of a laugh with your closest mates, it was the latter route that led me to Liverpool.

Bull also played for a Sunday team called the Bedford, so I decided to go and play for them too. Like the Timepiece, the Bedford was run out of a nightclub, one that often stayed open until sunrise. It was located on Bedford Street, the thoroughfare that runs parallel with Catherine Street and Hope Street, linking Liverpool's Catholic and Anglican cathedrals in the city's striking Georgian quarter, the prosperous side of Toxteth.

The team was run by Eric Dunlop and Eric was instrumental in me becoming a professional footballer because he was the first person to really place some faith in me.

Eric's guidance made me realise I should take football really seriously – more seriously than I'd taken anything previously. I wanted to do well. I wanted to win. I realised I was quite good at it and that gave me the encouragement I needed to focus.

I wouldn't miss a big Friday night or Saturday night out in order to prepare for a game at the weekend but I wouldn't turn up in the morning breathing alcohol down opponents' necks either. Many team-mates did.

The Bedford was a mixed-race team. We had senior police officers, electricians and brickies from different parts of Liverpool's south end. Most of the lads were unemployed, though; their only income came infrequently from dock working. Some travelled over to Wirral and worked in the Cammell Laird shipyard as manual labourers. Jobs never seemed to last for long.

The Bedford was more of a laugh than the Timepiece, as Sunday league tends to be. Saturdays are for people who really want to play football: you commit to a team and are prepared to miss watching the club you support for a game. On a Saturday, the organisation is more serious.

A Sunday morning? You roll out of bed after the night before. You often spend a lot of time driving around the borough picking up people who have slept in. You throw stones at the windows to wake them up. Sometimes the referees don't turn up. The pitches aren't as good and the changing rooms resemble prisons. You have to put the goals up in the wind and the rain. The kits haven't been washed. And sometimes, you get going without completing a warm-up.

The Bedford had won the national Sunday League Cup at the beginning of the 1970s and were well known as one of the best sides around Liverpool.

The team had some really strong characters. We had a giant in goal called Willy Osu. He was one of the oldest players and was in his mid-thirties when I joined the team. He made sure that nobody picked on the young boys. Willy was the type of fella that bullied the bullies. He was six foot four and built like a house; a lot of people feared him. Sadly, he got stabbed to death in Liverpool's Chinatown in 1982.

Willy's family came from Nigeria. He had two sisters and two younger brothers, George and Tony Osu. Many of the lads came from West African backgrounds: Ghana and Sierra Leone, like me; Gambia, Senegal, Liberia. Others came from Jamaica and Trinidad. We all knew each other through our fathers, who'd first met at any one of the different African clubs in Liverpool 8. As they got to know each other better, they'd meet together in private and talk in Creole and different African languages. These gatherings were a good way for my dad and his friends to discuss what was happening back home in Africa, in countries like Sierra Leone, Ghana and Nigeria.

For the Bedford, Eric Dunlop was the glue that kept us together. There is absolutely no doubt that if I'd not met Eric, I wouldn't have played professional football. Sometimes life is about who you know rather than what you know or what you are good at.

In Sunday games, I was embarrassing fully grown men twice my age. In one game, I scored directly from a corner – and it was meant as a shot rather than a cross. I was accurate with dead balls. I remember Eric standing on the touchline, shaking his head in disbelief.

Jimmy Case and John Aldridge had played in the same south-end Sunday leagues as me. They will tell you how tough it was. Some teams wanted to play football but many just wanted to kick you. You could smell the alcohol on the breath of other teams and some players – older fellas – who'd been on the ale all night just wanted to kick the opposition.

Eric, though, insisted that we play football. He prided himself on the team he created: one that kept the ball on the ground and tried to beat the opposition the right way. If it came to it, though, we knew how to handle ourselves.

Although preparation mightn't have been taken too seriously and the standard of the football wasn't quite as high as on a Saturday, the competition was nevertheless fierce. You could not afford to take anything for granted.

Showboating was a risk. If you took the piss, there was a decent chance you'd end up getting your jaw broken. It happened because Sunday league footballers have long memories. Liverpool people are proud and do not like it if it seems they are being taken advantage of.

You had to be strong-minded, quick and, most of all, streetwise. Because I was agile and I could jump, I rode the tackles. Park football was an education. It toughened me up in terms of my general mentality. I learned that the best way to beat someone was by letting my talent express itself, rather than getting all wound up.

Eric helped me a lot. He is a taxi driver now but back then he was in the building trade. He lived in Gateacre, a few miles to the south of Liverpool 8, out towards Speke. Fortunately, John Bennison lived there too and John worked as a youth coach at Liverpool before progressing and becoming assistant manager of the reserve team, where he helped future stars such as Phil Thompson and Chris Lawler emerge through the ranks.

Eric had been telling John, or 'Benno' as he was known to everyone, for months about me. 'You need to see this kid,' Eric told him. I was scoring lots of goals and terrorising defences. Eric suspected I was a rough diamond, capable of being polished with the right guidance: something I'd never really received in any area of my life growing up – until I'd met Eric, of course.

I think Benno got tired of Eric's constant phone calls and, just to shut him up, told him to bring me down to Melwood on a Thursday night for a session with the B-team triallists.

Eric mentioned the opportunity casually to me after a game on the Sunday before. 'Do you want to go?' I had some reservations because, although I believed in myself, I thought they wouldn't fancy me if they found out about my past: Norris Green, mischief, prison. But I'd finally found someone in Eric that I trusted.

I was also nearly nineteen years old and Liverpool's apprenticeship schemes started at fifteen. Phil Thompson, for example, had already broken into the first team at eighteen – so I was well behind in my football education. I'd never worked very long in any professional environment and it worried me I wouldn't be able to stick it in a football one. Maybe another rejection would tarnish my love for the game – one of the few positive things in my life.

To be really honest, the opportunity didn't excite me as much as you might think. I'd attended trials for Merseyside county in my early teens and suffered rejection. But my brothers intervened. They told me to go. 'You've got to do it, Howard.' So I went along.

Melwood is in West Derby, which is the next district south from Norris Green to the east of Liverpool's city centre. It previously belonged to St Francis Xavier, a nearby school. The area was used as a playing field for the school; Father Melling and Father Woodlock, who taught at the school, spent hours helping the young boys play football. As a way of remembering the two priests' hard work the ground was christened using the first syllables of their names.

It was not until Bill Shankly's appointment as Liverpool manager in the year after my birth – 1959 – that the facility began to develop a mystique. Until then, it had lain in a terrible state. Shankly transformed the place into sacred ground by introducing the five-a-side games that defined his 'pass and move' philosophy. He dictated that players would meet and change for training at Anfield a few miles away and then board the team bus for the short trip to Melwood. After training, they would bus back to Anfield to shower and change again before getting a bite to eat. Shankly thus ensured all his players had warmed down correctly and he would keep his players free from injury. Indeed, in the 1965/66 season, Liverpool finished as champions using just fourteen players – and two of those only played a handful of games.

Outsiders tried to figure out what happened inside Melwood that made Liverpool so successful under Shankly and then his successor, Bob Paisley: yet the secret all along had been simplicity and executing it properly.

All of this crossed my mind as I waited for the gates to be opened that Thursday night, long after the senior players had gone home. As a child, I had stood in the same place, grabbing signatures off heroes of mine like Roger Hunt. Now, I was being let in.

I found quickly, at youth level anyway, that Melwood was a bit of a free-for-all. Hundreds of kids were in attendance and despite being one of the oldest there, most of them had more experience on me: of how to act professionally and in keeping of the expectations of a club the size of Liverpool. Although I supported the club, I didn't really know how it worked or, necessarily, what I would have to do to impress. Paul Moran, Ronnie's son, and Chris Fagan, Joe's son, were also there.

Eric had told me to simply go and play my game: to work hard off the ball and show those watching on the touchline that I wasn't scared.

The only sign that my first trial had gone well was a verbal invitation to return to Melwood the following Tuesday for a competitive game against an amateur boys' club from Runcorn who brought three sides so that matches could take place simultaneously.

I didn't know anyone else at the trials. I was the only black player. The environment was a bit impersonal anyway because of the number of kids there. It was one big scrum. I figured that I'd have to try something special to stand out from the crowd, although my afro haircut probably did that anyway.

In one of the other trial games between the 'probables' (players that had been there for a while) and the 'hopefuls' (the side I was on), I received possession of the ball around thirty yards away from goal. Turning sharply, I unleashed a volley, which struck against the crossbar. Somehow, the rebound arrived directly at my feet and from there I hit another shot that flew straight in. There were only a few people on the touchline and they were clapping. Fortunately, John Bennison and Tom Saunders, the club's youth development officer, had witnessed the moment. In the same game I sustained an ankle injury. I was aware of the stereotype that said black players disappeared when the pressure was on them, so I decided to carry on until the coaches had to pull me off.

Liverpool offered me amateur forms. Being an amateur meant training twice a week and playing matches for the A and B teams at weekends in the hope of earning a professional deal. Naturally, I was delighted. The mere fact they thought I had something about me injected me with a huge amount of confidence. No institution had ever told me I was good at anything. Being offered any deal at all by Liverpool told me that they must have thought I had a chance, even if it was a small one.

No more than a week after signing amateur forms, Bob Paisley approached me after a training session, inviting me into his office at Anfield. I sensed that

I was doing well purely by the fact I wasn't being told to do anything differently by anyone. I'd scored a lot of goals in the five-a-sides and, for the first time in my life, felt comfortable in a real working environment.

'Er, Howard,' Bob said, 'I'd like to you meet Roy Evans. He's the reserve-team manager – he'd like to speak to you about something.'

Roy was no more than thirty years old at the time. He'd played nine games as a left-half in Liverpool's first team but retired from the game aged 26 after being offered a job on Liverpool's backroom staff by Bill Shankly. He'd suffered a few injuries and his progression as a player did not match his tactical eye, so the old Boot Room had figured that he should be the newest member.

Roy was small, no taller than five foot seven. He came from Bootle and seemed to know all about me. 'Howard, we'd like you to start training with the reserves,' he said. I tried to hide my smile. Then came the 'but'.

'You're only going to get paid as an amateur.'

Full-time work for part-time wages. In normal circumstances, I might have had some doubts. But this was Liverpool.

'Do all right, Howard, and we'll review your situation in a month's time.'

'Fair enough,' I said.

Inwardly I was over the moon.

MUNICH
iv

The Olympic Stadium's public address system crackles. Liverpool's team is read out in a German accent.

Only surnames are used, as if it's a headmaster addressing a pupil at school: 'One, Clemence; two, Neal; three, Money; four, Irwin; five, R. Kennedy; six, Hansen; seven, Dalglish; eight, Lee; nine, Johnson; ten, McDermott; eleven, Souness.' Then come the substitutes: 'Twelve, Case; thirteen, Ogrizovic; fourteen, Rush; fifteen, Cohen; sixteen, Gayle.' I am the sixteenth man.

Sammy Lee begins by racing into Hans Weiner straight from the kick-off: shoving him in the back, letting him know he's there – the smallest player on the pitch.

The most distinctive opponent, though, is Karl Del'Haye: with his distinctive long blond hair and moustache. He played for Borussia Monchengladbach in the European Cup semi-final of 1978 against Liverpool. At 24 years of age, Del'Haye was a member of the West German squad that won the 1980 European Championship. That achievement enabled him to become one of the most expensive Bundesliga players in history. Bayern Munich parted with 1.26 million Deutschmarks (the equivalent of £300,000) to sign him, then a club record. And here he is, again facing Liverpool, this time at the Olympic Stadium.

Del'Haye begins as if he has a point to prove. Seven minutes have been played and, near the halfway line, Richard Money approaches him. If tonight proves to be big for me, it starts even bigger for Richard. He's played in the same reserve team as me as a centre-back. Alan Kennedy is injured. Bob Paisley selects him at left-back. Money takes Del'Haye towards his own goal, ushering him like a shepherd guiding a sheep; it forces Del'Haye to lose the ball and chase after it like a desperate man.

Kenny Dalglish is Liverpool's most important player. He doesn't turn quickly and Del'Haye launches himself into a tackle that he cannot win and one that he does not. Dalglish falls; he's in agony and the Portuguese referee, Antonio Garrido, does not care, he's unsympathetic.

He waves play on and the Germans attack.

Del'Haye has done Kenny. Kenny is our best and most influential player. Kenny tries to run it off. But then he falls again. It's the left ankle. He can barely walk. He hobbles off the pitch for treatment. Ronnie Moran, the fearsome trainer in his red Umbro tracksuit, applies his magic sponge. But it is no use. Kenny's gone. He's injured. He needs to be substituted. Joe Fagan, the assistant manager, also in a red tracksuit, helps Kenny to the dugout. It's a sad sight and a major blow to Liverpool's hopes. Liverpool's supporters tell the referee that he is a wanker.

'What are they going to do here?' I wonder to myself.

Bob Paisley and Joe Fagan are sitting next to each other at the end of the substitutes' bench. Then the message comes, passed from person to person: each substitute should get warmed up.

I suspect – along with the others – that they've decided to put Ian Rush on. He'd been selected in key games ahead of me in the weeks before.

Joe Fagan is waving at me. Roy Evans – my reserve-team manager – is in the travelling party. 'Get over 'ere, 'Oward,' he shouts.

Roy helps remove my tracksuit. He is muttering words to me, words of encouragement; although I can't remember what they were because the moment is racing by so quickly. There is no time to think.

Apparently, the commentator, Barry Davies, says with some surprise, 'Well, the youngster is going to get a chance. Here's Howard Gayle. He scored a hat-trick for the reserves at the weekend.' The linesman checks the studs on my boots, as if he thinks they are sharpened. I trot on to the pitch and Davies continues from his position in the press box: 'The task was difficult enough at the start and now they've lost their most experienced striker in European and international football ... to be replaced by Howard Gayle, an untried nineteen-year-old.'

That I am in fact nearly 23 years old, reflects how much of an unknown quantity I am. The supporters in the Olympic Stadium are whistling as I enter the arena. Are they whistling because I am a Liverpool player? Are they whistling especially because I am a black Liverpool player? Are they whistling because I am the only black player among the 22 on show?

None of these questions register with me: I am focused on what I have to do. Nothing will knock me off my stride.

Dieter Hoeness releases a shot which sails over Ray Clemence's crossbar. Ray picks up the ball from the ballboy and rolls a pass out towards Richard Money. Richard brings the ball from left-back and passes the ball to me, positioned on the left wing, five yards into opposition territory beyond the halfway line. I pass it back to Alan Hansen, our senior defender. Barry Davies speaks of Hansen, or 'Jocky' to us, executing an 'exaggerated side shuffle'; he emerges from defence majestically and knocks a long pass into the left-hand channel, a space where my pace has taken me into. One touch and I'm ahead of Wolfgang Dremmler, the midfielder *who's tracked me all the way from the halfway line. I know he's struggling. He's not meant to be in this position. Where is the right-back? Dremmler's really struggling. I'm in. I can see Walter Junghans, the Bayern Munich goalkeeper; and then … whoosh!*

The lights go out.

White noise.

MELWOOD, 1978

FULL-TIME WORK FOR PART-TIME WAGES INVOLVED TRAINING AT Melwood every day with the reserve team. Aged nineteen, I was too old to go with the B team or the A team. I was in a league of my own, a single vessel plotting an unusual route through the choppy waters of professional football. This alone singled me out as different.

I realised that it probably had to be this way in the first months at Melwood. Training with Liverpool wasn't working in a warehouse. Training with Liverpool wasn't manual labour. There was a realistic possibility that Liverpool might offer me a deal as a professional. The incentive was huge.

I was on trial. I spoke to my brothers: their message was clear. 'Keep your head down, Howard,' they said. 'Let your football do the talking.'

It was a surreal existence. By day, I was training at Melwood, sometimes with old pros like John Toshack, Steve Heighway and Ian Callaghan – injured players working their way back to fitness, or those out of favour like Tosh, who Bob Paisley wanted to sell.

I didn't meet Bob Paisley for a while so I had no impression of the man. All I really knew about him was, he'd taken the Liverpool manager's job after Bill Shankly's shock resignation in 1974 without really wanting it. The board had decided that not much should change so looked to Bob as Shanks's successor. It was quite a responsibility for a 55-year-old who'd never managed before. Although Bob had played 277 games for Liverpool before ending his career in 1954, nobody had spoken about him as management material before he reluctantly took the plunge.

Although he'd won two league titles by the time I arrived at Liverpool, as well as a European Cup, Tosh didn't think very much of him. Tosh had been signed by Shankly from Cardiff City and was a very powerful-looking Welshman with strong opinions. He rejected a move to Leicester City even though Bob had told him to go, in literally not so many words. Bob wasn't particularly good with words and had a reputation within Liverpool's squad for fudging answers on subjects that he did not feel particularly comfortable talking about. I would learn all about this when I later progressed into Liverpool's first-team environment.

For the time being, I was training hard and doing well with the reserves. For two months, I did not hear anything from Roy Evans, Tom Saunders or any of the coaching staff. I was training at Melwood and going home to a flat in Windsor Towers, Toxteth, leading a double life.

After one session, we travelled back to Anfield on the bus before having a lunch of chicken and steak. I got chatting to Phil Thompson, an established first-team player from Kirkby. I liked Phil. We'd experienced similar upbringings, although his potential quality as a footballer was recognised way before mine, having originally been on trial with Liverpool as a fourteen-year-old.

Thompson asked what was happening with my contract situation. After being told they'd make a decision after a month, it was dragging on. 'This is what you do,' Thommo said secretively, leaning over towards me with a forkful of beans in his mouth while we sat in the canteen. 'You walk into Bob Paisley's office and tell him that other clubs have been in touch.'

'I can't say that, Thommo – what if he calls my bluff and tells me to go elsewhere?'

Thommo told me to trust him, he'd seen this happen before. 'Liverpool can take the piss sometimes,' he said. 'You've got to fight your corner and make sure they value you as much as you value them.'

So I wandered off down the corridor to the end room before knocking. Bob was sitting there with his feet up on the table, wearing his slippers and overcoat. There was a draught underneath the wooden door. Bob was reading the *Racing Post* and his eyes jutted up. I got the impression he'd been waiting for me. I suspected Thommo had briefed him. 'Come back in an hour's time, son,' he said, returning to his paper. 'I'll be ready to talk then . . .'

I went for a walk and returned exactly an hour later. 'Er, boss ... I've been here for two months now. I just wondered ...'

Bob stopped me. 'Howard, son. Don't worry. We're signing you on for a year. How does three hundred pounds a week sound?'

I couldn't believe it. I was grinning like a Cheshire Cat. I wanted to hug the man. I hadn't even needed to execute Thommo's cunning plan.

And then I reached the door.

'Howard, son,' Bob said. 'Is there anything else you'd like to speak about?'

For some reason, I told him that I'd had phone calls – 'Phone calls from other clubs, boss.'

A wide smile stretched across Bob's face. He started chuckling lightly, his broad shoulders bobbing up and down. 'Why, of course you have, Howard ... of course you have.'

Clearly, it was a line that Thommo had fed to others in similar situations when it was time for contract discussions. The joke didn't bother me though. I was ecstatic. I don't think I've ever experienced as much happiness in one moment.

Had it not been for Thommo's advice, though, I'd probably still be waiting for an answer from Liverpool.

✱

ENTER MELWOOD NOW AND THERE ARE FAMOUS QUOTES PLASTERED over the walls. Enter the academy in Kirkby and there is a photograph of me, displayed as one of the club's home-grown graduates, even though I wasn't really. I signed for Liverpool at nineteen and although I started with the B team initially, I was training with the first team. I wasn't an apprentice. I was not educated the

Liverpool way from an early age. This meant I had further to travel in less time than the rest: so much to learn.

As a professional in the 1970s, Melwood was very basic. No slogans appeared on walls as inspiration. Players were expected to be savvy enough to figure out what was expected. Liverpool was a humble club. Liverpool never spoke about who they were going to beat; they just beat them. Liverpool never spoke about winning the league; they just won it.

The challenge for every player was to prove himself on a daily basis. An underlying feeling existed that there was always somebody waiting to take your place. For the first team, there were lads in the reserves gasping for an opportunity. But for the lads in the reserves, players in the A team and the B team had similar aspirations.

The level of competition was geared against complacency. I was never complacent. Deep inside me, there was a feeling that something would go wrong – paranoia almost – because everything in my life had gone wrong before. Despite earning a contract, I constantly thought something would happen to set me back. I was waiting for someone to say that I wasn't good enough – or, 'Sorry, Howard; you're not quite what we were looking for.'

It had happened before. Tom Saunders, for example, was a face I recognised, although I'm not sure whether he recognised me. He was the manager of Liverpool Schoolboys when I was at St Theresa's. I attended trials and didn't get selected. When I saw him at Melwood, his presence brought back some unhappy memories. If he didn't rate me as a player just a few years before, would he rate me now?

After three or four sessions with the schoolboys, there was a big match between the better ones and the ones considered not so good. Tom judged that I should be on the latter. Even though I played well and had the measure of the right-back marking me, when it came to selection for a game against London Schoolboys at Anfield, I was left out of his plans and asked to act as a ballboy in the old Kemlyn Road stand. It was humiliating, chasing after stray passes from players chosen ahead of me.

I saw Tom at Melwood most days. His presence didn't fill me with confidence. Although I was in the reserves and he was in charge of a younger age group,

I always wondered what was coming: whether he'd say something to put the other coaches off me. I associated his face with disappointment.

Fortunately, there were other faces that made me feel more comfortable. I wasn't the only black player in the system at Liverpool. Lawrence Iro was there, along with Stevie Cole. We were linked by the colour of our skin but were made different by our previous experiences. Lawrence came from a lower-middle-class family and later became a partner in an insurance company. Stevie, meanwhile, was the same age as me but was released before making the biggest step into the first team. He eventually became a well-known bouncer at a number of Liverpool pubs and clubs. Stevie got involved in a feud over the control of doors and in 1996 was murdered in Kirkby: hacked to death in front of his wife by a mob of twenty men. Sometimes, I wonder whether I might have met the same end.

While Lawrence and Stevie played for the reserves at different points over the next few years, I was the only regular starter. The standard was incredibly high.

Bill Shankly's comment about Liverpool and Liverpool reserves being the only two good teams in Merseyside was perceived as being a dig about the poverty of Everton's team. It wasn't. It was a statement that said Liverpool had a team that would rival anybody but Liverpool also had backup for it. Shankly wanted to manifest an idea that Liverpool were an unforgiving force with a squad of players that potentially could keep the club at the top for generations.

The reserve side I played in was outstanding, winning the Central League four out of five years. Although I often played on the wing, my goal-scoring record was consistent: in the 1977/78 season, I scored six times; in 1978/79, I got seventeen; thirteen followed the year after that, then sixteen and eight during my last full campaign spent at Liverpool in 1981/82.

With Roy Evans in charge, Liverpool's reserves were unstoppable in the Central League. We beat Newcastle United's first team on a few occasions. I honestly believe we'd have finished in the top five of the English First Division given the chance. Yet we were also probably the unluckiest group of players in history.

The first team's domination of English football meant that many of us were never given a chance to progress. It is a myth that Liverpool promoted from within, because the statistics proved they did not. Between the start of the 1970s and the middle of the 1980s, only three players emerged from the youth set-up to become regulars. They were Phil Thompson, Sammy Lee and Jimmy Case – who, like me, was spotted playing locally, albeit a bit higher with South Liverpool in the Northern Premier League. He was playing park football at the same time for Garston Woodcutters. His trajectory towards Liverpool's first team and European Cup finals was just as rapid as mine, although he enjoyed a more successful and longer career, playing into his late thirties.

Bill Shankly had said that the first result he looked for outside the first team was that of the reserves. He'd long departed the club by the time I came along but I'm not sure his mantra on this side had passed on to the next manager.

I became a Liverpool reserve when the first team was winning European Cups – dominating the game at home as well as abroad. The reserve team won title after title but only a few of us were rewarded with opportunities at senior level. The attitude at Liverpool regarding team selection was that if it wasn't broken then it didn't need fixing. Yet quite often, the first team would win and any reserve-team player in for an injured regular was given the hook the following week without reason.

Liverpool didn't need to explain to someone like me why they made their decisions but I always felt if I was given ten to fifteen games on the run, I'd establish myself. I felt the same for Colin Irwin. He was an outstanding player but his path was blocked by Alan Hansen, who'd get selected even if he was 50 per cent fit. I'm not saying Alan shouldn't have been playing because he was one of the best in the world. Quite possibly, a 50 per cent fit Alan Hansen or a 50 per cent fit David Johnson was better than a 100 per cent fit Colin Irwin or a 100 per cent fit me. But Alan has trouble with his knees now – and it is likely the condition wasn't helped by the number of games he played, or the number of injections he had to take to get on the pitch. Supporters often overlook the human cost of success. Ultimately though, Liverpool won most things around that time, so who can argue with selection policy?

The management were reluctant to make changes at any cost. Change was feared at every level the club operated. Who cares about Anfield's regeneration or an expansion, when results on the pitch are good? I'm not so sure Liverpool had a visionary in charge after Shankly. Shankly didn't just build a team, he built a club and a stadium. By the time Paisley took over, the foundations were there. Sure, he got even better results on the pitch than Shankly, but it was during his reign that other clubs began to catch up off the pitch.

This approach impacted on the progress of players in one of the best reserve teams this country has ever seen. We'd be taken on end-of-season tours for nothing games and, every single time, Bob would start with the strongest eleven available. He'd make sure the game was won before substituting anyone. It was all devised to create this aura of an invincible Liverpool. It also helped to foster the winning mentality. From day one, I was told that winning was a mentality that was hard to get into. But losing was a mentality that's even harder to get out of. No matter which game Liverpool were playing in, they went out to win it. There was no time to blood a young lad; it was a case of sinking or swimming.

I became far from happy with the lack of opportunities; but I wasn't the only one. Kevin Sheedy was brought in from Hereford for a decent fee and could play in the same position as me. He was a brilliant player and went on to become an Everton legend. But because of the standard at Liverpool he never got a genuine chance at Anfield. Part of his problem was his perceived injury record. When he first came to Liverpool he bought a new Audi to celebrate but, because the steering wheel was slightly off centre, it affected his back. After matches he was in agony and nobody could figure what was wrong with him. Eventually they figured out it was the Audi. Unfortunately for Kevin, by then Liverpool had him down as a player that was injury-prone – and Liverpool did not take kindly to injured players, who'd get ignored by the staff until they returned to the fold.

Kevin and I would often discuss our frustrations on the bus en route from Anfield to Melwood. You quickly realised it was pointless trying to force the issue with staff. The same line would get spun all of the time. 'Keep going, Howard. Your chance will come.' I didn't believe they were telling the truth because nobody's chance was coming. The only way to vent frustration was to talk about it among your team-mates. In a weird way, I think it helped foster a team spirit. Everyone was united because we could relate to one another about the slim chances of progression.

*

MY FIRST GAME AT ANFIELD FOR THE RESERVES WAS AGAINST STOKE City. It was daunting. When you dream about representing the club you support and the dream is realised as quickly as it was with me, doubts set in and you question whether you deserve to be there.

The night before, I didn't get much sleep. I woke up really early before walking to Sammy Lee's house on Brownlow Hill. I'd played against Sammy as a junior and knew him well. He was the smallest player in Liverpool's reserve team but he possessed the heart of a lion.

Sammy's mum was a really lovely lady. She cooked both of us a brunch of steak and mushrooms, fried in butter. Sammy had passed his driving test before anyone else and he drove both of us to Anfield in his red Datsun, parking in the Main Stand car park.

Liverpool's players were always allowed to wear whatever they wanted before games. Most of the lads – at first-team level and in the reserves – wore jeans. Mine were patchwork.

As I walked through Anfield's Main Stand reception entrance for the first time as a reserve player, I was asked to sign a few autographs. Although only a handful of supporters were waiting, it made me feel like a Hollywood film star.

Inside the dressing room, the atmosphere was lively. It always was. Most of the reserve lads were from the Northwest of England. Me and Sammy were brought up the closest to the city centre. I've never shared a dressing room with anyone as fanatical about the club as him. Sammy has always been a model professional and that's why he's gone so far in both his playing career and coaching career. Because of his diminutive build, he had to make up for it in another way; true, he had lots of football ability, but it was his sheer enthusiasm. A lot of people say they love Liverpool but I honestly haven't met a person who is as passionate about the club as Sammy. Because he was so desperate to fulfil his ability, it sometimes made him nervous off the pitch. But as soon as he was on it, it never showed. When you look at the tradition Liverpool had with wingers or wide midfielders – Steve Heighway, Peter Thompson and Ray Kennedy and Sammy – then those afterwards – Craig Johnston, Ray Houghton and John Barnes – you realise how good he was.

It must have broken him when Liverpool terminated his contract as a coach in June 2011. I had spoken to him shortly before the end of that season and I detected that something was wrong because I'm quite perceptive when it comes to sensing people's emotions – especially those that I know well. When I put the phone down, I was tempted to ring him back and just double-check that he was OK, but I decided not to because I don't like to interfere with private matters unless people invite me into a situation.

It turned out that I was right because, soon after, Liverpool announced he was leaving. I am told that he was called up by Kenny Dalglish, they had a two-minute conversation and by the end Sammy was told that his services were no longer required. He had only returned from his summer holiday that night. The next morning he cleared his locker and picked up his belongings from Melwood before anyone else arrived for work. It must have been very upsetting for him. For someone who has served the club for so long, always with commitment and dignity, the club were out of order handling the situation in such a ruthless way. With all the changes at the top – new owners, new directors and new coaches – I can only assume his face didn't fit and that's why they got rid of him.

Sammy's loyalty is almost blind. All that matters to him is the welfare of Liverpool Football Club. Nothing else. Nobody is bigger than the club. Whoever is leading the club at any particular time, he will support them. So if someone asks Sammy his thoughts about a manager like Rafael Benítez or even Roy Hodgson – who was a desperate failure – he would always back them. Football is full of people wanting you to take sides, especially when things are going wrong. But his loyalty has always been to Liverpool. He is like this because he has been through the Liverpool system and knows the Liverpool way. You don't speak out about your colleagues, or those in charge. It's as simple as that. You always have to back the manager in charge if you represent Liverpool.

Roy Evans was cut from the same cloth. In 1998, he was pushed out the door after the ill-fated managerial job-share with Gérard Houllier. I know he still feels hurt by the way it all happened. For a long time, he found it hard going to Anfield when really he should have been sat in the directors' box having been awarded the freedom of the stadium. He's given more than half of his life to the club and, like Sammy, his intentions were always genuine and for the best of Liverpool.

Evo was my reserve-team manager but now I regard him as a friend. From day one, he knew which buttons to press with me. The rapport we had was special. He understood and had confidence in me. He trusted me to make the right decisions and that made me make the right decisions most of the time: we were Liverpool players so we should get it right.

Evo became Liverpool's first-team manager in the 1990s and he had the same approach then. He was criticised for being too nice, which was unfair. He was a nice person and a tough manager. He wasn't confrontational all of the time but if you fell out of line, he'd let you know about it.

He liked the players to express themselves. He wanted the reserves to play expansive but collective football – just the same as every other team representing Liverpool. The policy was, if you drifted into someone else's position, you were expected to do their job until you returned to your natural shape. There was nothing dictatorial about Roy's or indeed the club's style. That came from the very top – since Shankly. Extreme tactical discipline only really became an issue at first-team level in European matches, as I would learn later.

Evo could lose his temper and, occasionally, he stretched the boundaries of acceptability. We had a reserve-team Merseyside derby at Goodison Park one year and no matter how hard I tried to make my mark on the game, I couldn't. It looked like it was going to be a 0–0 draw because Everton were never going to score either.

Evo kept telling us to keep possession but I gave it away sloppily. Evo had had enough. I looked over towards him and he said, 'If you don't pull your fucking finger out of your arse, you fucking black bastard, you're coming off.' I could sense the frustration in his tone but I was surprised and angry that he made reference to the colour of my skin.

My instinct was to verbally abuse him back. Because of our close relationship, I knew he didn't mean to offend me. Evo turned his back and, quickly, the ball was in play again. Within a few minutes, I had scored the opener and set up a second, helping us to a 2–0 victory.

I was still furious with Evo at the final whistle, though, and went looking for him. The lads could see I was angry and told me to cool off in the shower. Later, I found Evo having a drink with Colin Harvey, Everton's legendary player/coach and later manager. I stormed in and Colin goes straight away, 'Bloody hell, Evo – you really know how to push that lad's buttons, don't you?' They were laughing about it. I knew straight away that it was a deliberate ploy by Roy to get me moving. It worked. I have met a lot of racist people in my life and Roy definitely isn't one of them. He just wanted to see some fire in my belly and he knew what wound me up most. His comment inspired me to prove him wrong. There was no malice in what he said. I know the difference.

Evo was very, very good at his job. I am biased but, obviously, I am going to say he was the best reserve-team manager there has ever been. It couldn't have been easy in days when there were no coaching manuals, trying to keep fifteen or sixteen teenagers interested in what they were doing when we all knew that the opportunities above us were rare. But he managed it, season in, season out.

Evo was very young to be in charge of the reserve team and, because of that, it sometimes felt like he was one of the lads. He reminded me of Eric Dunlop at the Bedford: someone who was a little bit older but someone you could relate to.

Having retired from the game aged just twenty-six, Evo still had the attitude of a footballer as well as a coach. He would take part in training every day and if there was stick to be dealt out, he would be right at the centre of it. You could tell he loved the banter – the type you would get in any Liverpool workplace, be it in industry, the docks or the warehouses.

When Evo was manager of the reserves, he'd come and have a drink with us after the match. He'd even join us on the back of the bus and play cards. Because of that close bond, he'd always support us; encouraging Bob Paisley to give us all an opportunity in the first team. You'd always here him telling Bob, 'So-and-so had a great game last weekend.'

When he became Liverpool's first-team manager in the 1990s, the transition must have been difficult. Because he liked working within a relaxed environment, he would have found it hard distancing himself from the players. At the highest level a manager can't muck in all the time. He has to be withdrawn.

I'm not sure whether managing the club you support is always a good idea. When you lose or don't succeed, it must hit you doubly hard. I can only speak from experiences as a player but, I have to admit, losing a game for Liverpool at any level hurt a lot more than losing a game for Birmingham, Sunderland or

Blackburn, the clubs I later played for. That feeling must multiply if you're a manager because the buck stops with you.

Liverpool's success at reserve level under Evo was born out of the same formula of the first team. The club had a philosophy on how the game should be played and in each squad, whether it be the first team or the youth team, each dressing room was filled with characters that could deal with the expectations that came with representing Liverpool.

The main personalities in the reserve dressing room were Robbie Savage (not the former Leicester City midfielder but a Scouser from Sparrow Hall off the East Lancs Road), Colin Irwin (Norris Green), Geoff Ainsworth (Cantril Farm), Trevor Birch (Ormskirk) and Brian Kettle (West Derby).

Brian was our captain and had great ability with both feet. He could play in both full-back positions as well as in central midfield. His passing range was outstanding. Even though he was just as fast as Joey Jones or Richard Money, the players he was competing with for a first-team place, Brian carried a bit of weight – and that made him a very powerful player too.

Brian didn't cement himself as a first-team player at Liverpool but he later became a respected manager in non-league football with Southport and Northwich Victoria. I can see why he achieved success because he thought about the game and had strong opinions on how it should be played.

Steve Ogrizovic was the reserve-team goalkeeper and he had an unusual background. Oggy was in the police force before joining Liverpool from Chesterfield. Arrests on black people were in the news all the time towards the end of the 1970s and, naturally, some of the dressing room humour was directed between me and him. It didn't really impress Oggy, who had a drier – less obvious – sense of humour.

The Christmas parties at Liverpool were legendary – very important social occasions. Newcomers were duty bound to offer a singing performance and Steve went for the nursery rhyme, 'I Know an Old Lady Who Swallowed a Fly'. Sammy Lee did a Rod Stewart number. It was a nerve-wracking experience. I can't remember my song because I was pretty drunk by the time it came to the moment. I know this kind of initiation happened in every dressing room across the country and it certainly wasn't exclusive to Liverpool, but again, it was a deliberate test: could you handle the pressure of performing in front of a crowd? Everybody who came into the club that was new had to sing a song, no matter your standing in the game – and that included Kenny Dalglish. He was on the same bill as me because he signed in the same year I became a professional.

The venue was Tommy Smith's less than salubrious bar that used to be on Dale Street in Liverpool's city centre.

*

IT SADDENS ME TODAY TO SEE HOW RESERVE-TEAM FOOTBALL IS neglected by the FA and all clubs across England.

Every footballer wants to go through the lessons of training during the week then have the exam over the weekend. To develop, you need to be playing regularly and gaining experience. In Spain today you see B teams (the equivalent of our reserves) performing in adult professional leagues. Barcelona's B team nearly won Spain's equivalent of the Championship a few seasons ago, while Sevilla and Villarreal's B teams are also highly thought of. It's no wonder that such clubs have had so much success in promoting so many players into their own first teams. I understand that in England most fans would frown seeing a Liverpool reserve or A team playing professionally, say in League One. I can understand why, because the best traditions are always there to be upheld, and why should the FA change everything just for the desires of the big clubs? The answer is simple: reduce the number of players that can be selected for a first team's match-day squad from eighteen (including seven substitutes) to something like fourteen in total. Then those that aren't playing or working their way back to fitness can play in the reserve team. The FA or the Premier League should make a national reserve league with matches played in proper football stadiums. Going to places like Old Trafford, St James' Park and Villa Park was invaluable to my development, even if there were only a few thousand people there.

Having two or three experienced pros in Liverpool's reserve team helped enormously. From the ones that applied themselves professionally, you learned a lot about standards, and from those that didn't necessarily always, you learned about the politics of being a professional footballer at the highest level.

It was common to see first-team players appear with the reserves to get match fitness if they were recovering from an injury. Some of them would muck in, their attitude impeccable, while others made it clear that they didn't want to be there. It all depended on the individual.

One person who always fought for whatever Liverpool team he represented was Ian Callaghan. Whenever he pulled that red shirt on, he treated it seriously. He was a shining example to all of us.

Later, I started to understand through my own experience why some of the senior pros found it hard dropping down to our level. It wasn't necessarily the standard of football, because it was always very competitive. The biggest issue was playing in front of sparse crowds. I was later sent out on loan to Fulham. After six or seven games performing with people roaring at you, it's very difficult to go back to what can be like playing in a graveyard. The adrenalin isn't there.

I remember Liverpool reserves were playing at home one night and John Toshack called Evo up at five o'clock telling him that he was closing in on a move away from Liverpool and wanted to play so he could prove to the club attempting to sign him that he was fully fit. When it came to the match he didn't do a great deal. He went through the motions. A lot of the lads were frustrated by that but we couldn't say anything to him because he was a senior pro. Evo pulled Tosh over afterwards and said that he didn't know whether representatives from other clubs were indeed watching but, if they were, they wouldn't have been impressed. Tosh just shrugged his shoulders.

There was a game at Preston North End and Phil Thompson played. He was out of the first-team squad and feeling sorry for himself. We were 1–0 behind at half-time and Thommo cost us the goal. This time, Robbie Savage tore into him in the dressing room, telling him in no uncertain terms that his effort wasn't to expected levels and that his performance was pulling the team down.

In fairness to Thommo, he was outstanding after the break and led us to a victory. He was back in the first team the following Saturday.

There were other examples of senior players not really caring and some of the lads refusing to pass to them. Why should we try and help them get their form back and get a place in the first team ahead of any of us when they were showing such a disrespectful attitude?

Tommy Smith was one of them: the infamous Tommy Smith.

MUNICH

V

Sound returns like you have travelled down a plughole and landed in a river with a fierce current. The noise of whistling washes over the moment and, looking up, you see the reality: no fucking penalty.

I can't believe it.

'It looks a wild challenge to me by Dremmler,' observes Barry Davies from his position in the commentary box.

A wild challenge? Wolfgang Dremmler could have ended my career but there he is, standing tall, walking away: unpunished. No red card. No booking. No penalty.

Dremmler is a trained metalworker from Germany's industrial heartlands in the north. He's playing for Bayern Munich in the Bavarian south. He'd joined the club two years earlier and, aged 26, is a German international.

I don't hang around on the floor. I jump up; spread my arms wide open. Mr Garrido, the referee, is from Portugal. His hair is as dark as the night and it is slicked back with oil. I shout at him with a bewildered expression, 'Hey, hey, hey!' He's not interested. He doesn't care. He's made his mind up. Maybe he can't hear me. Maybe my voice is lost amid the whistles. Surely he'll realise his mistake when he sees the replay.

Frustration subsides and I return to calm. The rest of the Liverpool team has been here before: in a foreign stadium, where the crowd is hostile and the officials are reluctant to give you a decision.

Ray Kennedy is captain on the night because of Phil Thompson's injury. But Graeme Souness will soon succeed Tommo and he's in the centre circle. 'Come on, come on . . .' he encourages everyone. He turns to the defence. He rotates towards the attack and looks around the others in midfield. 'Keep this going . . . FOCUS!'

I trust Graeme. He's a true leader. He makes me feel like everything is going to be OK, just fine. He takes care of the underdog. He doesn't just hang around with the popular players. He cares about everyone. Opponents hate him. They think he's arrogant. But I love him. What a man. Everything is going to be OK, just fine.

Graeme is here: a safety blanket made out of iron.

THE SECOND DIVISION, 1980

BILL SHANKLY GREW UP IN GLENBUCK, AYRSHIRE. IT WAS A REMOTE, bleak existence. Once, he described it as being as far away from civilisation as Outer Mongolia.

After a day working in the mines, which just about sustained the village, there would not be much to do. To pass the time, Shankly listened to the wireless or – if he could afford it – read the papers. 'We were cut off from the big cities, so we talked to each other and about each other,' he said. 'We had fun, jokes, laughs and exaggeration.'

He and his friends would stand together on the street and tell yarns until it went dark. Progressively, the plots would become more outrageous. Anyone who could not keep up was mocked remorselessly. Some would not return the following day for the next instalment of storytelling.

Shankly carried these experiences throughout his life. In his career as a footballer, he helped build a spirit at Preston North End based on one-upmanship. He did the same as a manager and it followed him to Liverpool. After Shankly retired, that culture remained, imposed by the coaching staff and continued by the players.

I was unfortunate to be a part of the Liverpool culture that Bill Shankly created when Shankly was no longer there.

He retired from Liverpool in 1974 but he still occasionally turned up at Melwood by the time I started training there three years later. I detected that his presence brought resentment from Bob Paisley because he was so persistent. Bob felt his magnetic presence undermined his own authority. He never showed it to the players but there was a palpable sense of strain between the two of them.

The players liked Bill being around, though. With time, it was noticeable that Bill was turning up more and more when Bob wasn't there.

To me, Bill Shankly is the godfather of Liverpool Football Club. I'd longed to meet him properly. When I was in my early teens, I climbed on top of bins to peer over the wall at Melwood. There were fifteen to twenty kids, all doing the same thing. We'd shout for Mr Shankly to come over. He'd usually oblige, sometimes in the middle of training sessions. 'What's your name, sonny,' he'd ask. 'Howard, Mr Shankly.'

'Well, Howard; here's my autograph.' I got the impression he liked being the centre of attention: in demand. It didn't matter how many kids were there, he'd sign as many autographs as necessary. He recognised the people. He was humble. He spoke to us like adults.

His retirement shocked everyone. I was a million miles away from becoming a Liverpool player, when – in 1974 – he made the sudden announcement. It felt like there had been a death in the family.

I joined Liverpool in 1977 and in my first year he'd appear at Melwood and walk around the perimeter of the pitch, wearing slacks and a red shirt. I vividly remember the colour. It was radiating. He was a beacon. You were naturally drawn to him.

After one session, he pulled me to one side. I wanted to introduce myself to him formally but before I could say anything, he started speaking in his rasping Scottish voice. He placed his arm around my shoulder and said, 'You've got so much pace, nobody will catch you, son. And you could catch pigeons! All you need to do is knock it into space and get after it . . .'

He advised me that sometimes I tried to do too much on the ball, enabling defenders the opportunity to make a tackle. The message was clear: knock it past the defender and chase. He shook my hand, wished me good luck and wandered off with his hands behind his back. He was wearing a flat cap with a tartan pattern.

I looked around, to my left and to the right. 'Bloody hell,' I thought. 'Bill Shankly just spoke . . . to me!'

I was still making my way at Melwood. I was the young black kid that no one really knew. Bill Shankly had chosen to talk to me. He made me feel one hundred feet tall.

I don't know why but I replied: 'Thanks, boss.' I'd heard Ian Callaghan and Emlyn Hughes call him boss a million times so I decided to do the same.

Bob Paisley was the manager but Shankly remained the boss among the first-team players. Whenever he engaged in conversation with me thereafter, I realised it was only proper to call him Mr Shankly, though. I'd never played under him. He'd never been my boss so it seemed disrespectful to Bob to call him that.

I wish I'd played for Liverpool when Bill Shankly was in charge. He was one of the first managers in the game to place his trust in young players and mould them into men. His first Liverpool team in the 1960s was based around young Scots: Ron Yeats, Ian St John and Willie Stevenson. In 1970, he dismantled that side and brought in Kevin Keegan, John Toshack and Ray Clemence.

Bob Paisley surrounded himself with experience. Bill Shankly trusted youth. Bill and Bob were opposites, indeed: one could communicate, the other could not. Bill was a natural orator; Bob mumbled his words and used jargon. A lot of the time, I didn't know what Bob was talking about.

I'm not sure whether Bob understood me or appreciated where I'd come from. Bill was a people's person. He was socially savvy. Bob was awkward and shied away from all confrontation.

I wonder whether my career at Liverpool would have been more successful if Mr Shankly had been in charge rather than Bob when I was there. I needed someone to understand me. Maybe I am asking for too much.

*

I GET ASKED THE SAME QUESTION REGULARLY: 'WHAT WAS THE secret of Liverpool's success?'

Many of Liverpool's players will answer similarly and talk about the simple intensity of the coaching, the training and the instructions: the degree of trust. All of that is true. Underlying everything, though, was the culture of one-upmanship.

The importance of this cannot be underestimated. It was just as significant as ability. If a player could not deal with the mental challenges posed by all the characters at Melwood, he would fail and end up moving elsewhere. Outstanding footballers would crumble. Ian Rush was a prime example of this. Rushy was really, really shy when he came to Liverpool. He wasn't quick-witted. He spoke with an unusual accent and wore the wrong clothes. He looked out of his depth. It took him a full twelve months to get used to the remorseless criticism, which passed for banter, before he even began to establish himself within the hierarchy of the dressing room. Had he taken any longer in adjusting to this ruthless mentality, I have no doubt he would have ended up leaving the club. Crystal Palace wanted to sign him. Liverpool's record books would have a different name under the title: all-time leading goal scorer.

Liverpool's team under Bob Paisley was supremely confident. But it was not at all arrogant. Before games, you'd see nervousness in seasoned international players. Phil Neal was ritually sick. Occasionally, he'd have a shot of whisky to calm himself down. Each player appreciated he had to be at his very best to win. Just one individual mistake, and the team could lose. When you're at the top of the tree, you realise that everyone else is targeting you. There was always anticipation that something could go wrong.

The culture was a winning culture. Insecurities were seen as a weakness. If you couldn't handle what happened off the pitch, the management figured they couldn't rely on you to perform on the pitch. It was fine to have nerves because nerves were a sign of positive energy. But you had to have a mentality made out of Teflon to be a Liverpool player.

The banter at the club was designed to beat any insecurity out of you. Everything at Liverpool in terms of intensity was made more challenging by design during the week so that when you played on a Saturday, it would seem easier. Training was, indeed, simple, but that does not mean it was easy. The intensity was fierce. The theory stated that if you could deal with the intensity of training against the best players in the country, day in, day out, matches would be easy.

Likewise, if you could deal with the intensity of teasing that existed at Liverpool, no other team or individual was going to be able to take the piss during games.

Because of this, the challenge for me to succeed at Liverpool was greater from the moment I joined. I was going into the most successful club in England. A tried and trusted winning mentality existed. I had to adapt to their culture. Why should they adapt to me? I was a nobody trying to make my way in the game.

No matter where you were from or what you looked like, you had to embrace the mentality. It would have been difficult for anyone. Graeme Souness later became captain and the leader of the team but when he arrived carrying a reputation a bit of a Jack-the-lad, he was immediately brought down a peg or two. He'd been the biggest cheese at Middlesbrough, but at Liverpool he was starting at Year Zero.

As the first black player, my situation was unique. I had to show a greater mental resilience to survive and succeed.

There were black footballers after me who enjoyed a more successful time at Liverpool. After I left, John Barnes became the first black player to be signed by Liverpool from another club. He quickly earned the nickname of 'Digger', after Digger Barnes in the Dallas television series. Personally, I wouldn't have accepted that because of its closeness to the 'N' word.

Yet John and I had very different upbringings. While I was brought up in white Norris Green where there were very few black families and racism was a part of life, John lived in Jamaica around other black people. His family were reasonably wealthy and well respected in Kingston: his father was an army colonel and high up in the Jamaican Football Association. John Barnes did not have to confront racism on a daily basis. For me, racism was the norm – the routine.

Until Barnsey arrived in England as a teenager, he admits to not encountering racism at all. John has admitted that he viewed it as strange behaviour and the view of the uneducated. He did not grow up with any self-worth issues. I did.

I do not intend for my story to sound like one laced with self-pity. But I cannot ignore the reality. I had challenged all hostility towards me throughout my life.

In Norris Green, I couldn't afford to accept grey areas: the type of grey areas that existed in the humour at Melwood.

I was black: the first black player to train regularly with Liverpool's first team, the only black player at Melwood. I stood out.

Phil Thompson had a big nose so people took the piss out of him for that. David Fairclough had bright red hair, so he became a target. Later, Ian Rush wasn't the most streetwise so, as you can imagine, the teasing was intense. Me? I was black.

I wasn't accustomed to this type of humour. It was difficult to tell whether some of it was humour or whether it was really intended to offend. What is unacceptable language when it is passed off as banter?

The culture at Liverpool dictated that I was expected to just allow it to go over my head and not take things so seriously. But it wasn't in my make-up to let certain words get used without responding forcefully. So I came back at them. It contributed towards me getting the reputation as someone who had an attitude problem: someone who was reluctant to fit in.

Expectations at Liverpool were contradictory. The club demanded players to be mentally tough. So I'd challenge anyone who I considered was being racially aggressive towards me – it proved I wasn't a flake or weak.

I couldn't win no matter how I reacted. I was damned if I did and damned if I didn't. As the first black player, this ultimately made it impossible for me to progress as far as I would have had my experiences in life been different.

Lots of people – team-mates included – said that I had a chip on my shoulder. It wasn't a chip; it was a resilience not to accept racism of any kind. No black person has ever told me that I had a chip on my shoulder.

Strange that, isn't it?

Attitudes towards me were mixed. The majority did not have a problem with a young black male entering an absolutely white environment. But I could sense my presence made some uncomfortable.

This presented another problem. Some comments were made by those who I liked, those who did not mean any real harm. But even if I let those comments ride, would it create the impression for those with more entrenched views that it was OK to follow suit?

All I wanted to do was fit in and be a team-mate to everybody. I wanted to help enhance the reputation and maintain the success of the club: to be a big part of it.

I first became aware of intolerant attitudes at Melwood through people who didn't realise I was close by and within earshot. Unacceptable phrases were used. It would happen in the canteen at Anfield. It would happen on the bus en route to training or games. Such language was delivered in jest. But I was not laughing.

The racism was easier to take from the terraces because you reasoned it was down to your performance; you liked to think you were doing something right. Maybe that's naïve: I was abused frequently, whether I played well or badly.

When it comes from the people that you work with, though – people that don't understand or trust you – it hurts. Because you don't tolerate it and because you snap, the management perceives that as a weakness. How could they trust you to keep your calm in a pressure situation – just like that night in Munich?

Banter is an overused term in football and in society too – a term which can be used to disguise the way things really are. I'd barely said a word to anyone in my first few months at Liverpool when the first Christmas party came around. As part of my initiation to the group, it was arranged for a strippagram to perform a dance in front of me with the rest of the squad watching. The stripper covered herself in talcum powder and when she decided to bury my head between her breasts, my face was covered in white. Roy Chubby Brown was the compere at the party. When he said, 'Try and walk through Toxteth now,' his comment was met with raucous laughter. I felt uneasy with it. But in the spirit of the night, where everyone else was having the piss taken out of them by the comedian on the stage, I was able to laugh along with the joke.

*

TOMMY SMITH PRESENTED MY BIGGEST PROBLEM AT LIVERPOOL. Tommy had been Liverpool's captain and was known as the 'Anfield Iron'. He had a fearsome reputation in football, playing nearly 650 games for Liverpool during sixteen years at the club. He'd won four league titles and two FA Cups.

The season before my arrival, he scored in the European Cup final victory over Borussia Monchengladbach, a goal I'd celebrated wildly like all Liverpool supporters. Tommy had been one of my heroes.

My brothers had played against Tommy Smith in the 1950s when they were growing up and playing football in Liverpool's junior leagues. By the time I joined Liverpool halfway through the 1977/78 season, he was 32 years old and nearly at the end of his long, successful career. When I met him for the first time, training against him, he had an awesome presence.

Tommy Smith was brought up in the Scotland Road area of Liverpool which runs towards the city centre. Known commonly as 'Scotty', it originally was part of the stagecoach route to Scotland, hence its name. It was partly widened in 1803 and streets of working-class housing laid out either side as Liverpool expanded. Many were demolished as slums in the 1930s, to be replaced with corporation flats. In Victorian times, more than 200 pubs existed in the area.

Scotland Road was the centre of working-class life for the people of the surrounding areas of Everton, Vauxhall and Islington. Home to most of Liverpool's migrant communities, Scotland Road was almost a city within a city. It had four main migrant communities – Irish, Welsh, Scottish and Italian – as well as the native Lancastrian community and pockets of German and Polish.

By the start of the twentieth century, Scotland Road became the centre of sectarian divisions, but with the demolition of slums after the end of the Second World War, families were rehoused to new council properties in areas like Kirkby, Huyton, Croxteth and, indeed, Norris Green, where I grew up. It left Scotland Road in steady decline. It could be a place of both romantic nostalgia and brutal hardship. Those families that remained were predominantly white; attitudes towards those of ethnicity were hardened.

Tommy Smith was a living legend. Liverpool's supporters loved him and I was one of them. Yet quickly, I realised that there was a difference between the legend and the person.

Tommy seemed bitter that his career was coming to an end. He seemed bitter that the captaincy had been taken away from him a couple of years before.

He was replaced by Emlyn Hughes, who was a great Liverpool captain and one of the characters inside Liverpool's dressing room whom I trusted implicitly. Tommy clearly resented Emlyn for taking his place as captain but also his place in the team. Emlyn had been a marauding midfielder before Bill Shankly converted him to centre-back, selecting him alongside Phil Thompson instead of Tommy Smith, who was moved to full-back.

Before, Tommy had been the dominant centre-back alongside Larry Lloyd. The pair of them were from the old school of defending: tough and aggressive. Emlyn and Phil redefined the position, operating with skill, silk and speed.

Tommy had to find himself a new position to play in. But with Phil Neal emerging as right-back, Tommy's place was under threat again. In 1977, the newspapers were suggesting that Tommy was on his way out: that he'd go to Swansea City, that his Liverpool career was over.

He was a difficult person to be around. He was irritable. I don't think he had many friends inside the dressing room.

I was young, I had an edge, I was different: I was black. Tommy never said that he didn't like me. But that was my impression.

During my first six months as a Liverpool player, I'd train mainly with the reserves, but I trained with the first team too. Tommy chipped away at me with comments. At first, I wondered whether he was testing me.

Tommy went to play in the North American Soccer League in the summer of 1978 and, when he returned, signed for Swansea City as expected. He didn't want to move to Swansea, though. He lived in Crosby and continued to train at Melwood, travelling down to Wales at weekends to play games.

Tommy lingered around like a bad smell. He was constantly trying to prove himself as the player he was before, even though his knees had gone. This must have frustrated him.

I was keen to make an impression. I tried really hard in training. Tommy seemed a bit intimidated by that. One-on-one, I had the better of him: pushing the ball past him and chasing, like Bill Shankly had told me to do. Tommy tried to distract me by making nasty comments related to the colour of my skin. For a while, I somehow managed to restrain myself.

I appreciated Tommy was a former Liverpool captain and a living legend.

Here was me, a nothing. But my upbringing taught me that if you let something go once, everyone jumps on the bandwagon.

What Tommy did affected me. For a period, I didn't enjoy going to Melwood and my morale was really low. I told my brothers and they told me they'd accompany me to the training ground and fight him. Obviously I didn't want that to happen, so I had to sort it out myself.

Eventually, something was going to happen between us.

On a cold November morning, I had had enough. Some of the junior professionals, including myself, were invited to play at 'Wembley', the best patch of grass at Melwood, where the staff hosted matches at the end of training sessions. They would happen every morning and it would include some of the senior players returning from injury. The younger players involved were expected to do all of the running for the older staff members.

I received the ball, controlled it, and lashed a shot towards goal. Tommy Smith was on the other team and it hit him on the leg. It clearly stung and some of the other players started laughing. I had a smile on my face as well. I saw it as karma. Tommy responded with a tirade of abuse. It was 'black this, black that'. The place went quiet. Everybody could hear it, including the staff. He was a legend. I was a nothing. Nobody said a word.

I'd had enough of him: this bitter old man. So I went over and squared up: nose to nose. I kept my hands by my side.

I looked at him dead in the eye. 'You know what, Tommy; one night you'll be taking a piss at home and I'll be there waiting for you with a baseball bat,' I said, calmly. 'And then we'll see what you've got to say.'

I wanted to start a fight with him. His dark, seedy little eyes narrowed. And then he walked away.

I look back now and remember this moment as a real low point. I'd grown up loving Tommy Smith. He was the archetypal Liverpool player: tough, hard and committed. He was a hero of Bill Shankly's team. But you only see the player, the legend: the hero. You don't know the person. From then on, he was no hero of mine. As a human being, Tommy Smith was a disappointment, a complete let-down.

Graeme Souness was the only one that came over in the immediate aftermath.

'Well done, Howard,' he said. 'Tommy deserved that.' Graeme was a true leader. He was later made captain of Liverpool. Of all the captains to have led Liverpool in my lifetime, I consider him to be the greatest. He was the toughest of the tough, but he was empathetic too. I'm certain that he'd encountered bullies during his time as a youth player at Tottenham. Being a young Scot, he must have encountered some stick. Graeme, being intelligent as he is, would never have stood for it.

Graeme was a leader of men. He knew how to pick people up. Years later, he pulled me to one side after a pre-season friendly at Portsmouth where I'd played well. He could sense I was frustrated by the lack of opportunities in competitive matches. 'You're the only one that mixes it with me in training,' he said. 'Other players jump out of tackles. You don't.'

For weeks after the flashpoint with Tommy Smith, I waited for him to come back at me, especially with a reputation as fierce as his. Instead, he never spoke to me using racist language again.

We have barely spoken since.

The episode between us set the benchmark. Little comments may have been said behind my back but never directly to my face. Other people at Liverpool knew that I wasn't afraid – that I'd take on anyone if I thought it was necessary.

I WAS DEALING WITH ISSUES AT LIVERPOOL THAT NOBODY REALLY knew how to handle, including myself. It forced me to remain private in my personal affairs away from Melwood.

My eldest son Chris was born in 1979 when I was barely twenty years old. Chris's mum is Atonia – a very attractive young woman from our community in Liverpool 8. We went out one night for a meal, found ourselves back at my place in bed and as a result she fell pregnant.

I didn't take the news well.

I didn't want to have kids until I was into my thirties. I'd always envisaged settling down and having kids when I was ready for them – when I was mature enough.

I resented Atonia for taking that ideal away from me. I resented Chris as well. I was too young, too naive and too selfish to blame myself.

For the first few years, I thought that by denying Chris was mine it would all go away. It didn't.

I'm so sorry to Chris and Atonia for putting them through that – for being so stupid. They both needed me. I should have been a man and supported them like any father.

I don't see the point in looking back and having regrets because they only eat away at you. But if I could change one of the actions in my life, I'd approach that period differently without a shadow of a doubt. I feel very fortunate that Chris and Atonia have forgiven me. I'm very close to Chris now.

This happened while I was trying to make my way as a Liverpool player. The only person at the club who knew was Sammy Lee. Sammy was someone I could trust implicitly. We told each other everything.

I tried to keep it as quiet as possible. I was aware of the attitudes at Liverpool. The management didn't want any distractions from football. Had the club found out, it concerned me how they might react. They were always conscious and aware of what players were doing off the pitch. Anything that could impede or hinder what you were doing on the pitch was a concern to them.

The rules were not set in stone but everyone knew where the line was. You only have to consider the career of Terry McDermott to appreciate this. In 1980, Terry became one of the few players to be named both as the PFA and the Football Writers' Player of the Year, having emerged as a driving force in Liverpool's midfield. He was only thirty years old when they decided to sell him back to Newcastle two years later after too many off-the-field incidents. Liverpool had become a juggernaut and nobody was bigger than the club. Jimmy Case and Ray Kennedy fell the same way for the same reasons.

When Chris was born, my head was a mess. I realised I had a unique opportunity at Liverpool. Right at the back of my mind burrowing away was the nagging thought: I'm already up against it here. What will they think?

*

RONNIE MORAN WAS ANOTHER IMPORTANT CHARACTER AT
Melwood. He was critical of everyone and relentless with it. Ronnie had no
favourites. On any given day, you could hear Ronnie's voice above everyone
else's. It was his role to keep everyone in check: not to allow the best players
to get ahead of themselves and start believing they were great. He called them
the 'big 'eads'.

Ronnie would berate everyone. It didn't matter who you were or whether
you'd scored a hat-trick on a Saturday. By Monday, he was into you again:
a proper sergeant-major type. Ronnie got on everybody's nerves. But he was a
key figure in the Boot Room and everybody respected him.

Ronnie was born in 1934. He came from a different age. What he cherished
most was hierarchy. Elders should always be respected and youngsters put in
their place. I learned to accept him for who he was: a very angry man indeed.
I was perceptive enough to realise he wasn't very friendly at all to anyone.

Taking stick was something every player had to get used to at Liverpool.
The daily bus journey from Anfield to Melwood was a deliberate routine to get
everyone together in the morning and start the banter early. The first team sat at
the back, the coaching staff, including Ronnie, at the front and the reserves would
be in the middle or standing up.

The journey only took between ten or fifteen minutes but in many ways it was
the most important section of the day because it set the agenda. It was integral to
how the club identified itself from others. The environment was ruthless.

As a black player, I had to learn how to define the jokes from the barbs,
otherwise I wouldn't have lasted as long as I did. Ninety-nine per cent of the time,
the stick wasn't vindictive; instead it was just a case of someone throwing a fishing
rod into the river and seeing which little fishy took the bite. Some of the stick
that came my way was related to my race but I didn't consider it racism because
I didn't receive any more stick than anyone else in the dressing room.

Ian Rush had it worse than me. Rushy couldn't handle it at the beginning.
Most of the banter that came his way was because of his 'sense' of fashion
and because he was usually quite slow on the uptake of jokes. Coming from
the hills in Wales into an urban area the size of Liverpool was a huge culture
shock for him. For a time, it affected his enjoyment at the club. He's documented

in his autobiography that it had a profound effect on his outlook.

The dressing room was an unforgiving place, though; the more he went into his shell, the worse the stick became. Rushy became the greatest goal scorer in Liverpool's history but there was a time when it seemed like he'd struggle to score a goal for the reserves. His ability was clear but his fragile self-confidence, in those first six months especially, impacted on his performance.

I was very different to Rushy. Sometimes during training games, there would be incidents. You'd get kicked or you'd kick someone else. You'd get stuck into one another. It happened every day. If the incident involved two white players, they'd end up laughing. But if it was me, it was easy for the other person to jump up and call me a 'black so-and-so'. I didn't care who it was, whether they were apprentices or whether they were the best player in the first team; if that happened, I'd react forcefully. 'Don't fucking call me that,' I'd say.

I tried my best to prove to the rest of the squad that I was one of the lads. But there was a threshold to my tolerance.

Ultimately, I think that contributed towards Bob Paisley not being able to trust me.

IN JANUARY 1980, BOB PAISLEY CALLED ME INTO HIS OFFICE. 'WE'VE had an approach to take you out on loan, Howard. And we think it's a good idea.'

The offer was from Fulham.

I'd spent my first three years as a Liverpool player in the reserves, scoring goals mainly as a winger or centre-forward. I considered my performances good enough for a promotion. I considered the performances of almost all my team-mates good enough for promotion, in fact. It frustrated me that the chances weren't forthcoming. The only thing that stopped my frustration spilling over was the fact Liverpool's first team were formidable, almost invincible. The proof was in the pudding: results and trophies meant that there was no particular desire to promote from within.

Fulham were struggling down at the bottom of the old Second Division. I'd never lived outside Liverpool before. Their manager, Bobby Campbell, was a Scouser though, and he had a reputation as one of the funniest men in

My first Holy Communion.
Innocent times.

To my knowledge my dad was the only black person working at the Ford car plant in Halewood.
He earned respect and status as a shop steward.

During my first few
months at Melwood
I was small, skinny
and largely alone.
Great challenges lay ahead.
(MIRRORPIX)

I loved playing in the Merseyside derby. Although I never featured in one at senior level, the reserve team games between Liverpool and Everton were contested with the same ferocity. (MIRRORPIX)

The European Cup final in Paris. Liverpool beat Real Madrid 1-0 thanks to a late goal by Alan Kennedy. As a substitute, I celebrated like a fan. (PA)

In 1977, I was playing football in Liverpool's parks. In 1981, I returned to Liverpool Airport from Paris as a European Cup winner. (MIRRORPIX)

My first goal for Newcastle United was a match winner against Derby County the day after Boxing Day. Kevin Keegan's inclusion in the team after injury helped raise the level of my performance that afternoon. (MIRRORPIX)

Of all the managers I played for, my best relationship was with Ron Saunders. I reacted well to his mixed approach of fair discipline and leeway. (MIRRORPIX)

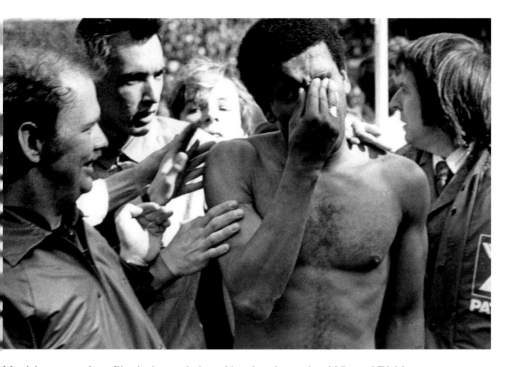

My eighteen months at Birmingham culminated in relegation to the old Second Division. The season was bittersweet because it was also marked by a call-up to the England under-21 team – a sign my progression as a footballer was being recognised. (MIRRORPIX)

I never managed to feature on a winning side against Liverpool. This game at St Andrews in 1984, where I am in hot pursuit of Alan Hansen, finished in a 0-0 draw. (PA)

The Birmingham derbies with Aston Villa were aggressive encounters.
The thrill of scoring a defining goal against the old enemy was unmatched. (MIRRORPIX)

Despite a struggle
for the club – and despite
my frosty relationship with
Lawrie McMenemy –
I enjoyed playing for
Sunderland and I enjoyed
playing at Roker Park. (PA)

tamford Bridge was not a ground I liked playing at. It was a place where many black players suffered
rom racist abuse on the terraces. (MIRRORPIX)

The 1988/89 season at Blackburn Rovers was my best goalscoring campaign as a professional footballer. Although we narrowly missed out on promotion, my relationship up front with Simon Garner was an effective one. (PA)

My first son, Chris, with his mother Atonia.

Howard Gayle in 2016.

football. Bob Paisley told me that he could have performed at the London Palladium. 'I think you'll like him, Howard.'

Bobby had played in 24 games for Liverpool under Bill Shankly when Bob Paisley was the coach. In 1961 he moved to Portsmouth and after a short spell with Aldershot remained in the south of England when injury ended his career prematurely, working on the staff at Queens Park Rangers and Arsenal.

In 1976 he took charge at Fulham when Alec Stock was sacked. These were difficult years for Fulham. Attendances were low and Craven Cottage was a bit of a dump if truth be told. The club had financial problems so Bobby called around old friends, looking for favours. He rang Bob Paisley and my name cropped up.

Bob made it clear that it wasn't Liverpool's way of moving me on. 'We want you to get experience,' he said.

Fulham had an FA Cup game at Blackburn Rovers. Bob told me to go and meet the players in the hotel before the fixture at Ewood Park and to travel back down to London with them on the bus later that night. I dreaded this prospect because I didn't know any of the players and I was the only black person. I had no idea what plans Fulham had for me in terms of accommodation.

The journey to London after a 1–1 draw was miserable and the bus was quiet. Fulham arranged for me to stay in a five-star hotel in Mayfair for the first night. It was very plush, but I felt alone. The next day, I was moved into digs in Wimbledon, which was closer to the training ground. I was an adult and I wanted my own space but there were certain rules. You had to be in at a certain time. It took me back to living with my dad in Norris Green.

Fulham ended up getting knocked out of the cup, losing 1–0 in the replay. My full professional debut soon came. It was up to Lancashire again for a game against Burnley, a town which in the 1970s and 80s had links to the National Front. Turf Moor, where I'd been before for Liverpool reserve games, was half empty. When I received the ball, there were monkey chants. I wasn't just the only black person on the pitch or in the stadium that cold afternoon – I was probably the only black person in Burnley.

Bobby Campbell selected me on the wing. It meant I was often positioned next to the stands and the banks of people abusing me. I was determined to shut them up and score a goal. In my head, I was going to run to the terraces in celebration and show them I wasn't scared.

I tried to use their energy to inspire me. I wanted to make them feel that every time I received possession, something was going to happen. There is no better feeling in football when you run past a full-back and you know you've got another couple of gears to move into; when the crowd is desperate for him to stop you but you know he is helpless – and the crowd is helpless.

And yet, at Burnley, the pitch was covered in snow and we played with an orange ball. It wasn't a particularly good debut for me. We lost 2–1. Racism was a taboo subject. Everyone inside the stadium that day would have been able to hear the monkey noises. Yet nobody asked me about it. There followed another miserable drive back to London. I sat in silence and on my own.

I spent two months at Fulham, playing in fourteen games without scoring a goal. Outwardly, it probably wouldn't have been considered a success. But inwardly, I learned a lot of things in a short period of time. Bobby Campbell proved to be a good companion and he helped me a lot, although I found him to be behind the times tactically. It made me appreciate the way things were at Liverpool more.

My responsibility at Liverpool when defending corners was to get myself into a position ten yards in front of the corner of the penalty area; ready to receive the ball if the goalkeeper threw it quickly. From there, it enabled us to launch a counter-attack. We scored a lot of goals that way.

At Fulham, the set-up was slightly different: less thoughtful and more defensive. We were 2–0 down inside the first twenty minutes to a decent Chelsea team which included Ron Harris and Clive Walker, two legendary Chelsea players.

Chelsea won a succession of corners and Bobby Campbell and his assistant, Mike Kelly, told everyone to go back and go man-to-man. Kelly was later Roy Hodgson's assistant during his brief and unsuccessful time at Liverpool. They were screaming, 'Get back and sort y'selves out!'

I shouted across to Bobby, 'We've got no one up front – what happens if we clear this corner? We're not going to be able to relieve the pressure.' Bobby went mad.

By half-time I had a dead leg anyway but Bobby substituted me. He gave me a volley of abuse for not trying hard enough. 'I want to see you tomorrow morning,' he shouted.

The next morning, I met him. 'Howard, you're going back up the road,' he said. I thought he was sending me home because I'd disobeyed his orders.

Bob Paisley had been on the phone, though.

There was an injury crisis at Anfield.

MUNICH
vi

The sound is like a plague of locusts.

When Mr Garrido from Portugal signals for half-time, the crowd inside the Olympic Stadium begin to whistle. An almighty, shrill noise.

The Liverpool team has done its job. I have done my job.

The German crowd are either unhappy with Bayern Munich, or they are unhappy with us: for sabotaging their evening. So far.

'Liverpool have contained Bayern without any real difficulty,' Barry Davies tells BBC viewers.

The dressing room is calm. Some players drink water. Others suck on oranges. A few get changed, swapping sweat-sodden jerseys for dry ones, the same for socks and shorts. Graeme Souness believed that a fresh kit encouraged a fresh mind. It gave him a psychological edge over opponents, running about in their muddy kits.

A minute passes before Bob Paisley begins to speak. He always gives us a minute at half-time: to gather our thoughts – to gather his own.

At 0–0, we knew we were in a good place. The longer it stayed the same, the more nervous the Germans would get. We only needed that one goal.

'Sit down, listen in,' he says, Simple instructions follow. Very basic reminders like: 'Sammy, keep an eye on Breitner. Never let him out of your sight – annoy him.'

To Colin Irwin: 'You're doing well: you'll need to concentrate for ninety minutes and injury time.'

Then it's my turn: 'Howard, keep going at them, son. They're frightened of you.'

I proceed to perform better in the second half than I did in the first. I know I have Bayern's defenders on toast. The only way they can get to me is by fouling.

I'm pretty certain Pál Csernai, the Bayern manager, has told Wolfgang Dremmler to follow me. He plays like a sentry.

When I steal possession from Karl-Heinz Rummenigge, having tracked him back to my own half, I race sixty yards up the pitch before Dremmler brings me down again. Dremmler escapes a booking for the second time. By now, I have accepted the referee's bias. I get up off the floor and say nothing at all.

When I turn Klaus Augenthaler, he kicks me in the thigh and finally a Bayern player receives a reprimand. I am writhing in pain. From the floor, wiping grass from my face, I can see the yellow card flashing against the blur of the floodlights.

I get up. I go again.

*

It was the very first foul I'd committed in the game – THE VERY FIRST FOUL.

Wolfgang Dremmler had tried to cut me in half. Klaus Augenthaler had scythed me down. Hans Weiner had pulled my shirt repeatedly in an attempt to stop me accelerating away.

I'd kept my cool. Said nothing. Left the referee alone to get on with his job even though he was getting it wrong.

I understood the environment. Away in Europe, decisions tend to go against you.

Ray Kennedy has knocked a pass down the line for me to chase after. Dremmler has tried to flick the ball over my head and, in response to realising his touch was quite loose, I try to flick it back. Behind Dremmler, I can see the open space and I know if I get this right I'm away from him and he won't catch me.

Dremmler falls. He's put his body in front of me and I've caught him with the side of my thigh. His reaction is pathetic: screaming like a baby, like a sniper in the crowd has caught him.

I turn around and see Mr Garrido brandishing a yellow card. For fuck's sake, he's booked me. For nothing: absolutely nothing.

My challenge wasn't malicious.

I think about the injustice of it all: that the referee has decided to book me because he'd booked so many of the Bayern players.

It was the first foul I'd committed in the game.

I'd committed it on the other side of the pitch, far away from the dugouts. I can see Bob Paisley discussing something with Joe Fagan. He's making a substitute. David Johnson is struggling with his fitness. Surely he won't last if it goes to extra time. It makes sense to bring Jimmy Case on for him and let me have a go up front. I know I've got the better of this defence.

I'm getting the hook, though.

Devastated.

MUNICH,
1981

AFTER FULHAM, I RETURNED TO MELWOOD: A VERY DIFFERENT place. Fulham were bottom of the old Second Division, heading towards the third tier of English football. Liverpool were closing in on another First Division championship, finishing the 1979/80 season two points ahead of Manchester United.

Though I never played a minute in the remainder of the campaign, I was selected on the bench for the second to last game of the season at home to Aston Villa when the title was secured with a 4-1 victory. The experience was a major thrill.

There were friendly matches and testimonials but I would have to wait a while to be involved in a competitive first team game, almost a year in fact.

Liverpool were scheduled to play a League Cup final replay against West Ham at Villa Park followed by two legs of the European Cup semi-final with Bayern Munich.

Kenny Dalglish had been struggling with his fitness. The burden of covering for Kenny was taking its toll on David Johnson. David Fairclough, Liverpool's Supersub, was injured too. Phil Thompson and Alan Kennedy: also troubled. Squad numbers were down.

'You're going down to Birmingham for the final replay,' Roy Evans told me. The game was being played at Villa Park after a 1-1 draw at Wembley.

I boarded the bus and sat next to Craig Johnston, who was in the process of signing for Liverpool from Middlesbrough. Craig was the new boy. He asked me lots of questions about Liverpool. He was clearly interested in immersing himself in the culture of the club. I liked him straight away. He had opinions and ambitions. He wasn't just coming to Liverpool to make up the numbers. He'd come to England from Australia as a teenager and, despite being turned away by Jack Charlton after his first trial, he stuck around at Middlesbrough before Charlton was replaced by John Neal. Neal took a shine to him and from there he became an important part of the Middlesbrough team. Craig told me all about himself en route to Birmingham. He possessed a really bright mind and after retiring from football suddenly at the age of 27 to care for his sick sister, he invented the Predator football boot. It did not surprise me from our first conversation that he chose to follow a different route.

We sat together again that evening in Villa Park's main stand after Bob Paisley decided to use Ian Rush in attack in what was only his second game for the club. Considering it was such an important match, it was quite a big deal for Bob to take a chance on Rushy, who was previously untested on the big occasion.

Rushy's performance was enough for him to be selected again a week later when Munich came to Anfield and played out a goalless draw in the European Cup semi-final first leg, with Paul Breitner, a World Cup winner with West Germany, claiming the Germans were now favourites to progress after parking the bus.

Again, I wasn't involved in the squad, deciding to watch the game from the Kop with my mates. I left the ground frustrated, not just as a supporter but as a player as well. Munich had players with big reputations but I thought some of their post match comments had been needless and arrogant. Breitner, who was Bayern's captain, also told the media that Liverpool had played with a lack of intelligence. It was a bold thing to say.

Liverpool had missed Kenny Dalglish's guile especially. Kenny was the link between the midfield and attack; all of Liverpool's best play went through him. He was the craft and the vision in the Liverpool team. Kenny knitted everything together. He was irreplaceable.

Unfortunately, his Achilles tendon problem was worsening. Bob Paisley revealed publicly that he was a major doubt for the return game in Munich, which was due to take place two weeks later.

Bayern had been meticulous in their planning for the first leg at Anfield.

A scout had watched Liverpool in every game since the draw was made, filing dossiers. During the scout's investigations he'd forgotten to check on one player, however, because that player only playing for Liverpool reserves.

That player was me.

*

DOWN QUEENS DRIVE, PAST ANFIELD, UP SCOTTY ROAD: INTO town, in front of St George's Hall. Liverpool had won their second European Cup and I was on the team bus.

It was 1978; I was the day before my twentieth birthday. Liverpool's opponents were FC Bruges from Belgium and the final had been played at Wembley. The week before, Roy Evans informed the reserve-team players that everyone was going to be included in the party that travelled to London. It was never explained at Liverpool but everyone understood straight away the reason why: Bob Paisley wanted the young players to experience an important match, and learn to really understand what it takes to perform at the highest level when the pressure is on.

It was my first trip away with Liverpool. Though we did not travel with the team, we met them at the Holiday Inn the night before. There were 92,500 people inside Wembley the following night and, though I'm only estimating, I reckon 80,000 were from Liverpool. The sense of occasion was enormous and Liverpool were overwhelming favourites. I couldn't see any result other than a Liverpool win. Kenny Dalglish had signed the summer before from Glasgow Celtic in a record transfer and he enjoyed an excellent first season. His goal that night sealed a 1–0 win. Though Bruges were a competent side and caused Liverpool a few problems, the margin of victory should have been greater.

We stayed over in London for a gala dinner at the hotel. The senior players in the Liverpool team all had a drink but I wanted to stay sober. Few nineteen year-olds are fortunate enough to be exposed to such moments and I wanted to take it all in. For only the second time in their history, Liverpool had won the European Cup. These are occasions you don't want to forget.

The next morning, Liverpool's players met the press and everyone had their picture taken with the European Cup. I didn't think to bring a camera with me

– I probably didn't have enough money to own one. Somewhere in the deepest *Liverpool Echo* archive, there might be a photograph of me standing alone and grinning with the cup.

At 2 p.m. we travelled from Euston station to South Liverpool station, where the new South Parkway terminal is now. The entire train was ours and the beers flowed again. From there, we jumped on an open-top bus. The scene was unbelievable. To witness that – the fervour – I'll never forget it. It was like a religious festival: a football stadium atmosphere on the streets. It was pandemonium: man-to-man Liverpool supporters.

By the time we reached the steps of St George's Hall, Sammy Lee, Colin Irwin and I were sitting down, reflecting on what was happening. Phil Thompson was a local player and a future captain. He saw us and called everyone up to the front of the bus for a prime view. One by one, we lifted the trophy and listened to the fans roar, even though the majority of them probably didn't know who any of us were. Reserve-team footballers just didn't have the exposure or the profile they do now.

Before his television career progressed, Clive Tyldesley was a presenter with Radio City and he was doing a live feed from the bus. He asked me for an interview with Sammy and, of course, both of us agreed. It was the first interview either of us had ever done.

'What do you think of this?' Clive asked.

'It's unbelievable, this – really great.' I didn't really have an insightful answer to his question. I was a bit nervous.

'Howard Gayle, would you like to win this thing yourself one day?'

'Dead right I would . . .'

*

UNDER BRIAN CLOUGH, NOTTINGHAM FOREST WON THE NEXT two European Cups, knocking Liverpool out en route to the first one following a show of endurance and tactical brilliance at Anfield, securing a 0–0 draw after a 2–0 first-leg win.

I was on the Kop that night and Liverpool's defeat made me realise how fragile a team's fortunes can be. One minute, you're the European champions, the next your defence of the competition is over.

A footballer's career lives on the same precarious levels, although that was only something I'd learn the hard way with time.

As the 1970s ended and the 1980s began, I was making decent progress as a young Liverpool player. Considering everyone else in the reserve-team dressing room had experienced an apprenticeship and I had not, I felt as though I was at the same level as them in football terms. I had quickly adjusted to the demands of professional football. Though I still found it hard to trust people and sometimes wasn't sure of how to react when meeting hostility, I started the 1980/81 season with a real sense that this might be the season I made the breakthrough.

My optimism stemmed from the fact I was selected on the bench in the second-to-last game of the season the previous May. By beating Aston Villa that day, Liverpool won the First Division title for the twelfth time in the club's history, with more than 51,000 people crammed inside Anfield.

Though I didn't get on, the buzz of being involved stayed with me throughout the summer and when I returned to pre-season, I was fitter than ever and flying in training.

Still, Liverpool being Liverpool, they like to make you wait. Just because I'd shown some promise it did not mean that night would follow day and it would earn me a permanent promotion. They did everything possible to keep me grounded. I continued to get changed in the reserve-team dressing room before training at Anfield and I continued to play for the reserves for the first few months of the new campaign. I began to suspect they'd recognised my potential but wanted to test my reactions after the positivity of reaching the first-team match-day squad by dropping me back down again. I was fine with it. I could deal with it.

My first game at first-team level had been in a testimonial for Emlyn Hughes in March 1979, replacing David Johnson as a half-time substitute at Anfield in a 1–0 defeat in front of 25,000 or so people and a party atmosphere. It took me eighteen months to make my official debut when Liverpool went to Manchester City's old Maine Road ground on 4 October 1980. Jonno was injured and David Fairclough took his place in attack, meaning I took the place on the substitutes' bench. Only one player got selected on the bench in those days and Bob Paisley usually preferred to use a striker. Goals, after all, change games. So the more options he had in that department, the better.

With 69 minutes gone and Liverpool 2–0 up and well on their way to a 3–0 victory, my moment finally came. Up went the yellow '9' board, which signalled Davie's removal before it was replaced by my number 12. I was going on.

Maine Road was one of those great traditional football grounds and I'd been there many times watching Liverpool. Just a few years earlier, I'd been thrown out for fighting on the terraces. I wondered whether any of the faces watching me from the old Kippax Stand recognised me.

The match programme didn't include my name and, though the Liverpool Echo had reported about my potential inclusion in the squad the day before, I don't think anyone really noticed the significance of the moment.

In the club's 88-year history, I had become the first black person ever to be selected for Liverpool's first team.

OCTOBER 1980 WAS A BUSY MONTH FOR LIVERPOOL, WITH EIGHT games played. For the league fixtures, substitute responsibilities switched between Ian Rush and Jimmy Case, while I was selected as one of five substitutes for the home leg of European Cup tie against Alex Ferguson's Aberdeen.

I was itching to play. I know it's a cliché, but there's something different about playing in night games, especially at Anfield under the lights when there's a full house. Ferguson had made quite a lot of noise before the fixtures, adding to the sense of anticipation. Bob Paisley, though, was not the type of manager to fall for any mind tricks and Liverpool ran out easy 5–0 winners on aggregate over the two legs.

After Aberdeen, CSKA Sofia, the Bulgarian champions, were dispatched easily in the third round, setting up a semi-final tie with Bayern Munich.

I stood in the Kop for the first leg and Bayern were the better team. Liverpool seemed to run out of ideas against a well-organised defence and a 0–0 draw was a fair reflection of the way it went. As I funnelled out of the exit gates with my hands in my pockets a few minutes before the end I didn't consider what the result meant for me. Not for a second did I think about being involved for the second leg a few weeks later in West Germany. Bob Paisley always went for the tried and trusted players on these occasions.

The odds of choosing to use an untested player with barely half an hour's first-team football behind him must have been a thousand to one. I went home and sulked like every other supporter. The odds, indeed, were stacked against Liverpool reaching the final.

*

JOE FAGAN MARCHED INTO THE LIVERPOOL DRESSING ROOM INSIDE the Olympic Stadium and said, 'There you go, lads – this is what that lot out there think of you.'

Joe pinned a translation of an interview with the Bayern captain Paul Breitner in which he criticised Liverpool's performance in the first leg as 'lacking imagination'.

Joe then pulled another sheet from his pocket. 'Look here, lads.' It was a leaflet the Germans were handing out to the home supporters inside the ground of directions to Paris where the final was taking place.

I felt like a visitor. It wasn't my place to react. I looked at Graeme Souness. His eyes were wild with rage. It was at that moment I knew that Liverpool would be the team going to Paris and not Bayern.

I knew at that point I was on the substitutes' bench for the match. Bob had told me after we'd finished our pre-match meal that I was going to be involved. I'd travelled to Munich believing that I was only there as help, in case of an emergency – if someone else pulled out with injury, because Liverpool's players were falling like flies.

Bob offered no explanation of why he chose me, nor did he explain what he expected of me, although I didn't expect him too. He wasn't a man of many words.

It was only then that it sank in that I was representing Liverpool at a European Cup semi-final. Suddenly, there was a chance – albeit a small one – I might play. It was clever management because I suppose if I'd been told a few days before, I'd have thought about it too much and become needlessly nervous. It was also clever management because the Germans, despite their reputation for meticulous preparation, did not have a clue who I was.

As a player, I was unconscious in terms of the moment's magnitude. When you are in the moment, it's difficult to enjoy it because all of your energies are focused on the ultimate aim of helping the team to win the match. I did not think about the fact that a few years earlier I'd been banging in goals for the Timepiece, being chased around boggy pitches by hulking defenders in front of thirty people on a Sunday morning; and now I was here: in Munich, pitting my wits against some of the most decorated players in Europe inside a historic football stadium where a World Cup final had been hosted, with more than 75,000 spectators watching.

When the teams lined up before the kick-off I could see Klaus Augenthaler, Paul Breitner and Karl-Heinz Rummenigge. They were legends of the game. I was a kid not long off the street. But I wasn't daunted, not one bit.

All of our preparation had been especially guarded, so maybe, looking back now, perhaps it shouldn't be viewed as a surprise that Bob had another trick up his sleeve.

There had been no training session at the Olympic Stadium. On the Wednesday morning, we went to a park and worked on set-plays, practising a routine where we'd overload the near post from corners then the kicker would aim for the back post, hoping to sneak someone in.

It was all very secretive.

THE HOSTILITY OF THE CROWD WAS NOT MY FOCUS WHEN BOB Paisley decided to bring me on for Kenny Dalglish. I was only focused on what was to follow, not what was going on around me – or even the significance of the event.

The first few minutes were like being swept away in a dream. You can hear the voices of individuals: team-mates shouting for a pass. Sometimes they get louder. But chanting is different, just a constant hum.

Liverpool supporters tell me the racist abuse from the home terraces was bad

– on another level. Afterwards, Bob spoke about it, saying he'd never heard anything like it. But it genuinely did not affect me. I was so focused, so determined to do well, so determined; I was oblivious to everything but the ball, my team-mates and the opponents in front of me.

I relished the atmosphere. The more people watching, the better, as far as I was concerned. I was an adrenalin junkie – feeding off the energy of the occasion.

As soon as I'd had the first touch of the ball, I was away. I did not realise there were monkey chants. I did not feel intimidated by the occasion. I did not feel out of my depth. I felt like I belonged in the European Cup semi-final. You might read this and consider it to be arrogance. At Liverpool, I always believed I was playing for the best club in Europe: the best team.

I had no idea of how Bayern were doing in their league campaign. Basic information like that wasn't readily available to everyone as it is now. I knew about Augenthaler, Rummenigge and Breitner because they were international-standard players. What other clubs were doing didn't interest me at all, though. I'm sure Bob Paisley did his research, especially going into a game of such importance needing to use four inexperienced players. But he never stressed the strength of other teams as if it was something to worry about. Tactically, it was a simple case of him ordering Sammy Lee to follow Breitner around the pitch. If Liverpool broke forward then Sammy could free himself of that responsibility, but as soon as Bayern regained possession, he knew that he had to track Breitner straight away.

I remember dribbling past Klaus Augenthaler and creating a chance before turning around and seeing the look on his face. He looked surprised, even scared. From then on, every time we were involved in a foot race, I knew I had two more gears on him. He knew he was in for a hard night. He had to find a way to stop me, so he threw in a foul. Then his team-mates followed.

One of the fouls should have resulted in a penalty. I received possession and legged it towards goal, beating the right-winger, Wolfgang Kraus. A few defenders had a nibble, trying to bring me down, but I was away.

Suddenly, Wolfgang Dremmler appeared from nowhere. I was darting in towards goal, then he launched into a tackle, cutting me up – almost in half – nowhere near the ball. It was the clearest penalty I've ever seen. It was an easy decision to make. As the last defender before the goalkeeper, Dremmler should have received a red card. The crowd fell silent, the whistling stopped – they knew it too.

Yet the referee – Mr Garrido da Silva from Portugal – pointed for a goal kick instead. He was quite a few yards behind play because the foot race between Dremmler and me had been rapid. Nothing, though, was impeding his view.

I watch the replay now – 35 years later – and still, it leaves me utterly bewildered. At the time, I turned around waiting to see my team-mates celebrate, only for my face to turn to horror upon realising Garrido's decision.

Only the referee can answer why he chose to award a goal kick instead of a penalty. I don't know whether he's still alive.

Friends who were watching inside the stadium and those back home believe he simply bottled it. There was a tendency for referees to favour home teams during European matches back in the 1970s and 80s. I'll admit, sometimes Liverpool probably benefited from decisions: a consequence of referees wilting in the febrile atmosphere of Anfield.

Referees certainly weren't as strong-minded – maybe as neutral-thinking – as they are now. It was a European Cup semi-final. The mood inside the Olympic Stadium was moody. There was monkey chanting. There was a swathe of opinion against me. Maybe it's unfair for me to speculate. Maybe it was simply a bad decision. Maybe he was fearful of the consequences had he gone the other way.

It's all ifs, buts and maybes, but had he got the decision right and pointed to the spot, then it's quite likely that Phil Neal would have scored to give us an early lead. Phil rarely missed. He was Mr Consistency.

It would have meant rather than just speaking of the impact I had on the game, my performance would have been marked by something palpable – something significant. 'Howard Gayle – he won us the penalty in Munich,' people would say. 'Howard Gayle really helped get us to the final.'

Maybe the moment would have been the proof Bob Paisley needed to trust me.

*

I'M SURE BOB PAISLEY WOULDN'T HAVE WANTED TO USE THREE
inexperienced players in Munich.

Aged 22, I was one of them; Colin Irwin and Richard Money were the other
two. Colin was 24 years old and had made fewer than 50 appearances for
Liverpool's first team and, though Richard was 25, he'd only started in eleven
games since signing from Fulham the previous summer.

My rise from park football to the European Cup semi-final in just under four
years was reflected by the fact nobody outside the club seemed to know my age.
Upon my introduction to the game Barry Davies, from his position in the
commentary box, said that I was just nineteen years old. It might have been a
lack of research on his part. Maybe it simply reflected how much of an unknown
I was.

And yet, I was performing very well indeed. So were Colin and Richard.
It might sound unusual to describe 24- and 25-year-olds as inexperienced
but that's the way football was back then. Reserve teams were older than they
are now, where players are often released at 21 if they haven't made their first-
team debut.

I felt like I belonged at the Olympic Stadium in a European Cup semi-final.
I could sense fear in the German team every time I received the ball. Graeme
Souness was our best player and he only passed to you if he thought you were up
to the mark. Every time Graeme gained possession, he was looking for me as an
outlet. That gave me tremendous confidence.

With Graeme in the team, I felt like I had someone backing me.
The experience was exhilarating.

Within sixty seconds in the second half, however, my mood shifted and my
optimism drained away completely.

The decision to book me for a foul on Wolfgang Dremmler was unfortunate.
Again, I think if you look at the replays, you'll agree. I barely touched him but
his screams convinced the referee to do something about it.

Mr Garrido's decision to book me was exasperating. In commentary, Barry
Davies described me as 'a really silly lad', who'd shown 'a little bit of immaturity
in this sort of atmosphere'. Considering the level of unsporting attention I'd been

subjected to by the German defenders – considering I'd not reacted to provocation once – I thought this comment from Davies to be unfair. Yes, OK, I'd fouled Dremmler, but was it worthy of a booking? I don't think it was. It was my first foul in the entire game. All you ask for from the referee as a professional footballer is consistency. It had taken several fouls by Klaus Augenthaler for him to get booked. Why was I booked for my very first – especially when it clearly wasn't malicious? I think that ultimately, the referee thought he had to book me because he'd booked so many of Bayern's players. He wilted under pressure from the crowd.

In the moments that followed, I chased after the ball, tracking back towards the defence. I'd been disciplined throughout my time on the pitch.

When there was a stoppage in play, I could see Joe Fagan and Bob Paisley in discussion. Joe then passed a message on to Ronnie Moran. Up went my number: number 16 was going off and number 12 was coming on – Jimmy Case for me.

I was absolutely gutted. I couldn't believe it. Less than sixty seconds had passed since my booking. I didn't get much of a chance to prove I could keep my cool and see the game out.

The scoreline was 0–0 and we knew that one goal for us would place enormous pressure on Bayern. I had been Liverpool's most direct route to goal.

Bob Paisley also knew, however, that I was on a booking and the tie was twenty minutes from extra time. And that was his reasoning later on when speaking to the media.

Generally, though, the Liverpool staff did not explain their reasons for the conclusions they arrived at, certainly not to players. I was left feeling like I'd done something wrong. Graeme Souness patted me on the bottom as I jogged towards the touchline. I barely touched Ronnie Moran's hand that he reached out to me when I passed Jimmy as he trundled on. I was fuming.

Jimmy had won two European Cups with Liverpool and he was a fantastic player. It was a surprise he wasn't used in the first place. Barry Davies described the decision as 'experience being used instead of impetuous youth'. Listening to Davies, you'd think I'd let the team down. Obviously, I disagree with that totally.

In cold analysis, Bob's decision surprised me because of its timing. He may have been concerned about the potential of facing extra time with ten men if

I was sent off but, in substituting me, the probability of that happening continued.

There was twenty minutes to go and he was aware that Graeme Souness and David Johnson were really struggling with injuries. It nearly backfired on Bob because a few minutes after my exit, Jonno started holding his hamstring. It forced Bob to make another tactical change because Jonno could barely walk. I guess it's up to you to decide whether it proved to be fortunate or inspired, because Jonno's inability to move forced Bob to push Ray Kennedy up front.

Liverpool ended up with ten and half men because Jonno's mobility was reduced considerably, hence why he was shunted into a wide position. Perhaps Bob understood what was needed and for that he deserves credit. Ray had arrived at Liverpool six years earlier as a striker before Bob converted him into a left-sided midfielder.

Ray's striking instincts returned in the crucial moment, scoring Liverpool's vital away goal with a superb volley. Although Bayern equalised through Karl-Heinz Rummenigge with a couple of minutes to go, we were through.

When Ray scored, I celebrated. When the final whistle was blown, I celebrated. I returned to being a fan in those moments.

Beneath the happiness, though, I was embarrassed. I'd become the first black player to play for Liverpool. But straight away, I was getting asked questions about becoming the first substitute to be substituted.

Munich had been sweet and then bitter. As we boarded the bus for the journey back to the airport, I was filled with doubts rather than positivity. I'd played well and caused some of the best defenders in European football problems. But Bob Paisley did not trust me enough to see the job through.

It should have been the greatest night of my life. Instead, I felt as though I was back at square one.

TOXTETH, 1981

BETWEEN 1979 AND 1981, BOB PAISLEY HAD ASKED ME TO MOVE OUT of Liverpool 8 on a couple of occasions. His reasoning made no sense, so I dragged my heels. I lived alone in a block of flats called Windsor Towers. I was happier than ever. I was being paid to train and, hopefully one day, play for Liverpool's first team: something I'd always dreamed of. I had my best friends and family members in close proximity. For the first time in my life, I was able to support myself financially through legitimate means rather than hustling on the streets.

I was always going to be in and out of the area on a daily basis anyway. What difference did it make if I slept elsewhere? I was never going to disconnect with a place that to me was home and always had been.

Bob had read in the papers about the social problems in Liverpool 8. As far as I'm aware, he never visited the place himself. To him, social problems spelled potential distraction. In the discussions we had, it became clear to me that he didn't really believe I was single-minded enough to ignore any of those supposed potential distractions.

I resisted Bob's pleas for as long as I could. Leaving Liverpool 8 wasn't something I wanted to do. It worried me that people might think I was turning my back on a community that had always supported me.

Yet playing professional football for Liverpool meant everything. Eventually, I yielded to Bob's request. My solution was to initially move in with my then girlfriend Lorraine and her mum, Pat Chin, in neighbouring Aigburth, a more salubrious district. Lorraine's father came from Liverpool's Chinese community. Pat became a surrogate mother to me; she was a mad Liverpool fan and she made sure I wanted for nothing.

Although I eventually found a place in Mossley Hill on Caithness Road, the move didn't necessarily make me happier. I felt disconnected from friends even though I was a ten-minute drive away. Meanwhile, it ate away at me that the club didn't trust me to make the right decision about my living arrangements. I think it's fair to say that I resented Bob for it and my attitude towards him hardened. I saw it as needless interfering. As far as I'm aware, he didn't insist on anyone else in the squad living somewhere they didn't really want to. I didn't see why it should be any different for me.

IN THE SUMMER OF 1981, DISTURBANCES TOOK PLACE IN MANY OF Britain's major cities. They were particularly intense in Liverpool. Four nights of spontaneous revolting followed by six weeks of aftershocks constituted what infamously became known as the Toxteth Riots. After insisting I move out from Toxteth, Bob Paisley must have felt vindicated.

The events were sparked when police arrested a black motorcyclist called Leroy Cooper on Selbourne Street in a heavy-handed way. A crowd gathered, saw what happened and tried to support Leroy by fending the police off. When police reinforcements arrived a battle ensued, with the crowd throwing rubble from the dilapidated roads.

Four days later, 150 buildings had been burned down including the famous Rialto cinema, while many shops had been looted; 258 police officers needed hospital treatment while 160 people were arrested. Within six weeks, 781 officers were injured and 214 police vehicles damaged. Rioters were injured too, of course, but naturally statistics there are blurred. Some would not attend hospital.

A variety of narratives exist around what provoked the riots. I see it simply as an event where black communities stood up against the police after years of mistreatment. The Conservative government led by Margaret Thatcher tried to shift the focus of the cause towards economic issues, which was a contributory factor but not a defining one.

When Thatcher came to power her mission statement was clear: to break the unions. The first place she went was the docks of Liverpool. All cities were affected, but particularly Liverpool. Thatcher targeted Liverpool because it was a Labour stronghold and a centre of the union movement.

Poverty, indeed, only played a small part in the 1981 riots. Liverpool 8 had long been top of the unemployment charts, not just in England but in Liverpool as well. Young people had limited aspirations. Even now, if you walk through Liverpool's city centre there are few black people and other minorities working in the business district in and around Old Hall Street.

Yet the riots were the product of a deliberate process from a government that wanted to keep its people down. Thatcher was a bully: giving the police force the authority to supress any disenchantment or objection to the way Britain was heading.

Britain often sneers at other countries where powerful dictators have emerged, without ever looking inwardly. This country is the author of dictatorship. Look at how it controlled India, parts of Africa and the Americas. It repressed any person who did not conform with the regime.

There was only limited discussion of policing. Newspapers such as the *Daily* and *Sunday Telegraph*, the *Daily Mail* and the *Daily Star* reported on issues of law and order, immigration policies, criminality, lack of parental control and the need to equip the police. The *Daily Mail*, for example, led with the headline on 9 July 1981 of 'FIRST CATCH THE RINGLEADERS' – arguing that 'teenage violence is uglier and more destructively anarchic than anything before'. It called for tough sentences on offenders and advised the police to turn to the Royal Ulster Constabulary, describing them as 'the specialists in contemporary urban terror'.

Only those directly affected really appreciated how it was the inevitable consequence of a history of police harassment, intimidation and brutality inflicted on Liverpool 8's black community.

The attitude from the police came from the top. The chief constable of Merseyside, Kenneth Oxford, gave an interview to the BBC's *The Listener* magazine where he spoke about Liverpool's supposed 'half-caste problem', using racist language. He said that many 'half-castes' in Liverpool 'were the product of liaisons between black seamen and white prostitutes' in Liverpool 8, the red-light district. He suggested that 'the Negroes will not except them as Blacks and the whites just assume they are coloureds. As a result, the half-caste community of Liverpool is well outside recognised society.'

In evidence to the Scarman Inquiry, after the riots, Oxford complained of 'natural proclivity towards violence' in Liverpool 8. He also dismissed the rioters as a 'crowd of black hooligans intent on making life unbearable and indulging in criminal activities'.

The Liverpool 8 Defence Committee issued a statement in July 1981 calling for Oxford's removal. 'The responsibility for the fair and proper policing of any community lies with the chief constable,' it read. 'Oxford's own racism combined with his belief that tough and repressive policing methods are the best way of keeping order, have resulted in excessive police harassment, especially of black people, which stretches back many years.'

Later the Scarman Report found that a loss of confidence and mistrust in the police and their methods had been the most significant contribution towards the riots, recommending that there should be concerted efforts to recruit more minorities into the police force, as well as changes in training and law enforcement. 'Institutional racism' did not exist, it claimed, pointing instead towards 'racial disadvantage' and 'racial discrimination'. It concluded that 'urgent action' was needed to prevent this disadvantage becoming 'an endemic ineradicable disease threatening the very survival of our society'.

Distrust of the police was not just common among men and boys. 'Stop and search' and unprovoked violence was an everyday occurrence, and women were not exempt from punishment, while working-class people in Liverpool of all backgrounds were treated with contempt. It was as if minorities and working-class people did not have the same rights as the rich. We felt like we were being picked on.

There had been race riots in Notting Hill in the year of my birth, 1958. Eighteen years later, the same thing happened in exactly the same borough of London. Tempers were boiling among young black men over police use of the 'sus' law, under which anybody could be stopped, searched and held, even if only suspected of planning a crime. Anticipating some trouble, 3,000 police officers turned up for the Notting Hill Carnival – ten times the amount for previous, relatively peaceful, events. Their presence provoked the violence that followed.

Throughout the 1970s, indeed, tabloid newspapers were filled with stories of police corruption. In 1975, *The Sweeney* was screened for the first time on British television: a show that almost glamorised the behaviours of a police force that seemed as focused on drinking alcohol and chasing women as it did solving crimes.

Acceptance of police corruption was a step too far and this was illustrated by an opinion poll in 1977, which showed that only 15 per cent of the British population considered the police to be honest.

The justice system of the time did not reflect the new complexion of Britain. This was visible at every level, most clearly in a police force that was disproportionately white. In 1970, one newspaper report offered that there were now 'ten coloured policemen in London'. Progress was painfully slow. By 1976, figures showed that there were seventy officers of ethnic background in a force of more than 22,000. Can it be surprising there were accusations of prejudice against blacks from police officers, which were often expressed in daily harassment on the streets?

The Brixton Riots of April 1981 preceded what happened in Liverpool 8. By 1981, black communities across Britain had experienced enough.

Liverpool 8 was no different.

*

I LOOK BACK AT 1981 AS THE DEFINING YEAR IN MY LIFE. IN LATE spring, I infamously became the first substitute to be substituted, having helped Liverpool to the European Cup final by beating Bayern Munich. Then in the summer, the Toxteth Riots happened.

Munich was bittersweet: the high of excelling against one of the best defences in European football swiftly being replaced by the low when Bob Paisley decided to take me off. I realised then that I was facing an uphill battle to persuade him that his reservations about my supposedly fiery temperament were misplaced.

We never discussed it, but the riots taking place so soon after Munich may have fortified his view of black people like me: people who react ferociously when they are faced with situations they don't like.

Without really appreciating it at the time, the riots probably took the focus away from what I was achieving on the football field to where I was spending my time off it. Before Munich, Bob had told me of his concerns about the amount of time I was spending in Liverpool 8. I remember him referencing 'the environment' I lived in.

As I've already mentioned, I agreed to move a few miles away to Aigburth and Mossley Hill in an attempt to placate him, but I wasn't earning enough to move my entire family – even if I had, they would have remained in Liverpool 8 anyway because they were proud of their roots. It meant that even though I'd bought a house elsewhere, the old routine remained of visiting friends and family in Liverpool 8 on a daily basis, and Bob was aware of this.

At the start of the 1980s, people believed what they read in the newspapers and many of the narratives in the newspapers did not reflect particularly well on Liverpool 8. Footballers were no different. Because of its 1989 reporting on the Hillsborough disaster where it blamed Liverpool supporters for the deaths of 96 supporters, *The Sun* newspaper passes for toilet paper on Merseyside now and rightly so. But wind back to the beginning of that decade and its reputation was very different.

On the bus between Anfield and Melwood, *The Sun* was passed around. I found its editorial line distasteful because on the one hand it was revealing scandal such as extra-marital affairs on the front page, yet inside it was selling adverts for escort agencies. So on the one hand, they were slaughtering well-known people for having sex, but on the other, they were selling it.

The only broadsheet that came into the dressing room was the *Sporting Life*. Like in any other workplace, the tabloids reigned supreme. After the riots, once we returned to pre-season training, it was still being reported. Rather than the focus in many of the tabloids being on the police's role, it instead was on the supposed perpetrators, those who were being demonised.

As ever, some team-mates – passing it off as banter – made disparaging comments about Liverpool 8 (or Toxteth as they called it). I could deal with it calmly but, in my response, I'd try and educate them about the problems that had led to the violence. This may have added to the perception that I'd react when pushed.

The riots had started on Friday, 3 July. That night, I was on a flight to the

Algarve with Sammy Lee and our partners, Lorraine and Lynn. The following morning, Sammy came running round the corner holding a newspaper and Liverpool 8 was emblazoned across the front of it. I immediately phoned home and made sure my family were OK.

A week later the holiday was over but the riots were still taking place.

I really wanted to get involved and stand up for my community, but my eldest brother Alan persuaded me that it wasn't a good idea. I was the only black professional footballer from Liverpool 8, an area with few role models. He warned me that if I was photographed throwing bricks or fighting with the police then that would spell the end of my Liverpool career.

*

DURING THE 1980/81 SEASON ONE OF MY VERY BEST FRIENDS DIED.

I realise death is difficult for anyone to deal with. My attitude towards it has always been awkward because I never fully dealt with the passing of my mum. My dad's response was to bottle everything up. He didn't talk about it and so neither did I. I've never been able to get my head around the way death is so utterly definite. My instinct is to think that somebody will get up and start walking around in front of me. That's the way I felt with my mum. I'd stand at the front door of the house, waiting for her to walk through it. I've never really admitted that death is the final act of life. I know it's an unhealthy attitude.

John Jacobs' nickname was Arouna. He was two years younger than me. His sisters were like my sister, Janice: confident and tough. John was known around Toxteth as a kind, loyal person. After moving back to the South End from Norris Green, he helped take care of me. We had the same interests, particularly musically. We both liked jazz. We both liked socialising.

His mum, Betty, was a really strong woman. She was white and from an Irish background. She'd married a Nigerian but, sadly, her husband passed away and she was left alone to take care of John and his four sisters. Despite pressures, she realised I didn't really have any parental guidance and made it clear to me that I'd always be welcome in the Jacobs' home.

The door of their house was always open to me. All I had to do on arriving was shout, 'It's only Howard.' Betty made me feel like an adopted son. She lived with the family on Beaconsfield Street near our Alan at first before moving to Upper Parliament Street after taking a job as a caretaker at a doctor's surgery. The surgery was upstairs and the family lived downstairs.

John was a very talented painter. Sadly, he developed leukaemia and I think he used painting as therapy – a distraction. He underwent chemotherapy and, despite losing his hair, he made some sort of recovery before falling victim to it again.

When John was ill, I got into the routine of visiting him after training sessions. I'd go pretty much every day to see him. By the end, he was bedridden and we'd sit together listening to jazz.

I'll never forget the day he passed away. When I went to see him one afternoon there was a strange atmosphere. Inwardly, I put that down to John suffering a bad morning. Christine Johnston, who later became a barrister, was a family friend and she was visiting John as well.

We were chatting quietly and suddenly John's body started shaking. His heart was pounding. They call it the death rattle. Christine and I tried to revive him. We offered CPR, using his chest and his mouth.

But it was too late. The doctor didn't even have time to make it down the stairs. He was gone.

In that period, I was playing for Liverpool – the greatest team in Europe. I was playing with some of my heroes. But John's death prompted me to question everything. I even thought about quitting football.

In death, thoughts are irrational. It should have been the most exciting period of my life. But I couldn't escape the feeling that things were stacking up against me, as they had been before. As I got closer to where I wanted to be – at least professionally – I had never felt so far away. There was always a different challenge wherever I went: challenges that other people – some white people – did not have to face.

I spoke to Betty about my problems. I told her I was thinking of quitting football. 'You can't do that, Howard,' she said. 'You've given a bit of hope to the young people in this community. If you walk away now, what will be left?'

MUNICH
vii

Bob Paisley is wearing a silver suit, a pin-stripe shirt and a brown tie. His hair is thin and oily. His face glistens in the muggy heat and the floodlights of Munich's Olympic Stadium.

'Bob, congratulations,' Barry Davies says.

'Thank you, Barry,' Bob responds. Unusually, for a man of few words, he volunteers further comment.

'It was a tremendous performance tonight,' he continues. 'That's our one hundred and thirteenth cup tie in Europe and I've been involved in all of them. We've had some great ones; the Rome one in particular was magnificent. But tonight, I thought, was our best performance considering all the circumstances and the injuries. Everything was going wrong on the field.'

'It really was a triumph over adversity, wasn't it?' Davies asks.

'It was, it was . . . it was just unbelievable what was happening; the way we were adjusting and replacing. When Kenny went down in the first two or three minutes I thought it wasn't going to be our cup this year. But the way the lads responded, I thought, was tremendous. Every man-jack of them played their heart out tonight.'

'Ray Kennedy, though, Bob – you pushed him up front – into his old position.'

'Yes, I did. I was worried about going into extra time with ten men. We had two players on bookings.'

WILDERNESS, 1982

I REALISE A LOT OF PEOPLE USE THEIR CHILDHOOD EXPERIENCES TO explain their behaviour later in life. At Liverpool, I was often accused of having a chip on my shoulder. If someone said something I didn't like, I'd react. I'd fight my corner.

I guess I had trust issues. Because I was black in a predominantly white area of Liverpool, I never really knew where I stood with people. There were examples of making friends with people and even families, only to discover their prejudice.

For that reason, it made it difficult for me to settle into Liverpool FC and especially difficult to understand some of the decisions made which affected me. My substitution in the 1981 European Cup semi-final second leg in Munich was one of them.

I'd always been able to fight my corner but sometimes it felt like I was fighting against an entire ring of people. Nagging right at the back of my mind was the idea that there was a mistrust of me because of my temperament rather than my colour, but my temperament was forged out of the experiences of being black. I thought that I had to do more to gain the trust of the ones who made the biggest decisions.

During my time at Liverpool a feeling lingered that the decision-makers trusted me – just not quite as much as other players. The club recruited me first and foremost because I was a talented footballer. And yet, I believe I was only able to deliver confident performances on the pitch because I didn't allow myself to be beaten down by my experiences of racism – because I was belligerent and hardened. In order to progress at Liverpool, I'd have to loosen up and sometimes let things pass. Ultimately, the challenge proved too great. I found it impossible to know which move to make when I did not know precisely what the game was.

I sometimes wonder how I made it into Liverpool: how I even played a single moment of the game in Munich. Only a few years before, I was a Sunday league park player.

I realise this book hasn't reflected particularly well on Norris Green in the 1960s. Had it not been for my experiences there, though, I'm not sure whether I'd have made it as far as I did.

A lot of my friends from Liverpool 8 simply wouldn't go to Anfield or Goodison Park because they feared the possibility of experiencing racist attitudes. By living in Norris Green, it had seemed to me a more natural thing to do because my friends were white and many of them were Liverpool fans who went to the games. I'd hear racist language being used at Anfield – if only from a small group of people. Then they'd turn to me and say, 'We don't mean you, Howard.'

'Well, who do you mean?' I'd say. 'It refers to me whether you're pointing the finger at me or not.'

There was no such thing as a sell-out at Anfield. People from Liverpool 8 could have attended if they really wanted because it was easy to pay on the gate. Yet not many bothered and I can absolutely understand why.

My path was different. I'd confronted racists on a daily basis in Norris Green. The only way to survive there was by not submitting to the will of others. As a consequence, there was no way I was going to stop going to Anfield as a supporter.

Entering Melwood, really, was no different than Norris Green, in that I was entering a place that was dominated by white professionals who did not know me. Not only was I black, but I was also quite small and scrawny as a teenager before I grew a bit taller and stronger as an adult. My physique needed a lot of work because at the beginning I wasn't as powerful as the other players. This put me at a disadvantage so I had to work incredibly hard at making sure others wouldn't underestimate me.

Like in Norris Green, if someone challenged me, I'd front it up. I wasn't scared of anyone. If someone insulted me, I'd insult them; if someone hit me, I'd hit them ten times harder; if someone spat on me, I'd fight them instead.

All of this prepared me for front-line football in the English First Division because it was something I'd encountered on a regular basis. I learned how to govern my reactions, but occasionally they were uncontrollable.

I wonder whether this ran through Bob Paisley's mind when he was deciding what to do with twenty minutes to go in Munich? He'd obviously decided I was a risk worth taking and the surprise worked. But as soon as I was booked, his faith in me seemed to drain away. He mustn't have believed that I'd be able to keep my cool in a hostile environment.

*

THE 1980/81 SEASON WAS MY BREAKTHROUGH YEAR AS A professional footballer. In making my debut for Liverpool, I'd become the first black player to represent Liverpool's first team in the club's history. I'd become the first substitute to be substituted by being taken off in a European Cup semi-final. I also became the first black player to score for Liverpool.

The league campaign had been poor by Liverpool's high standards. As reigning champions, Liverpool had won the league in four out of the previous five seasons. In April 1981, however, with Aston Villa on their way to becoming champions under a future manager of mine in Ron Saunders, Liverpool were stranded, albeit with a couple of games in hand, way down in eighth position.

After I'd played so well in Munich, several team-mates – including Graeme Souness – reassured me that my contribution on the night was valued. Despite the humiliation of being taken off, Bob Paisley said nothing to me – nor did I expect him to because that just wasn't his way.

Bob's focus was getting the senior injured players back fit for the European Cup final in Paris the following month. After Munich, I started the league game against Tottenham Hotspur at White Hart Lane three days later, but Bob had no other options by then, with so many players being unfit. Rushy and I played the whole game together up front.

At Tottenham I wore the number 7 shirt left open due to Kenny Dalglish's injury and I scored Liverpool's goal, firing across Milija Aleksic, the Spurs keeper. It felt like I'd arrived at a level I was comfortable performing at.

From there, the season wound down to a conclusion in Paris. Sunderland came to Anfield and beat Liverpool 1–0 in a game where I was substituted for a player I knew from the reserves, Colin Russell. It would be Colin's only appearance for the club. After leaving Liverpool in 1982, he played for Huddersfield Town, Bournemouth and Doncaster Rovers among others.

I was then left out of the team for Jimmy Case on the trip to Middlesbrough, where we won 2–1, but reinstalled for the final game of the season at home to Manchester City where Ray Kennedy's goal secured a 1–0 victory on a Tuesday night.

The European Cup final came eight days later. Kenny Dalglish had moved heaven and earth to get fit, so I knew I was travelling to Paris as – at best – a substitute.

Real Madrid had an illustrious history in the European Cup, but had not won the competition in fifteen years. In that time, Liverpool had lifted the trophy twice and were competing to become the first British club to win it three times.

The sense of occasion was huge. Borussia Monchengladbach and FC Brugge were beaten in the 1977 and 1978 finals but, though respected in their countries, they were not of the international standing in terms of reputation like Real Madrid.

To add spice, Laurie Cunningham, an outstanding black winger from West Bromwich Albion, was a Real Madrid player and expected to be selected. Laurie was an established player who I admired. I'd followed his career path closely and hoped I might get to experience things like him.

It was a wonderful night for Liverpool, and a bit like the game in Munich. You see, Liverpool rarely win key games like finals convincingly. There is always a struggle and the victory, sometimes, is in the struggle. Liverpool's greatest nights have always involved a level of improbability. We never win 4–0 in big games; it's more likely to be 4–3 after being 3–1 down. It's the equivalent of getting a punch on your nose and being half knocked out but still finding a way to deliver a knockout blow to the opposition.

Munich, for example, would come to rank up there with all the greatest European nights: Saint Etienne in 1977, Olympiacos in 2004 and Istanbul in 2005. We had thousands of fans out there with us. You don't travel en masse if you think you are going to get beaten. Support has always been a part of the success.

Real Madrid were very good in Paris and had opportunities to take the lead.

Our defence though – with a bit of fortune – held firm. The last person on the pitch aside from the goalkeeper that you'd expect to score the winner was Alan Kennedy, the left-back, and it was a surprise to see him as the furthest man forward when Ray Kennedy took a throw-in. With his left foot, Alan blasted his name into club folklore forever.

I celebrated the goal by running down the touchline like a fan. I lost control of all my senses. With nine minutes to go we were 1–0 up. With four minutes to go, I could see Bob Paisley talking with Joe Fagan in the dugout. I was warming up furiously down the touchline, trying my best to show that I was ready. Kenny Dalglish could go no further. Jimmy Case was the chosen one, however: a winner of two European Cups and a more experienced player.

The celebrations that night in a luxurious chandeliered hotel out near Versailles were memorable. We also visited the famous Lido cabaret lounge on the Champs-Élysées and received a standing ovation from the other guests. It was really hard to come to terms with what was happening. Liverpool had won the European Cup and I was there.

Graeme Souness and Terry McDermott led the singing into the early hours. The champagne flowed. Supporters found out where we were and joined us. Bob Paisley sat in the corner with a cup of tea and a big smile on his face.

Me? I still felt like I had something to prove.

But the possibilities at Liverpool were exciting. I had played for the first team. I had scored for the first team. I had a European Cup winners' medal.

What would next season bring?

THE TOXTETH RIOTS HAPPENED. AND THEN I REALLY MESSED UP.

Bob Paisley called me, Ronnie Whelan and Kevin Sheedy into his office on the first day of pre-season training in July 1981. I was in a good mood. It felt like I'd made the breakthrough. I was desperate to cement my place among the regular thirteen or fourteen players vying for first-team positions.

We all went in separately. Bob told me that I would be receiving a pay rise, which would equate to the cost of living. I was on £500 a week by then; Bob's proposal would have meant an increase of around £30.

I realise that most people would be happy on £530 a week even now. After all, £2,300 a month is pretty comfortable.

Yet subsequently, I found out that Ronnie and Kevin, who originally were on less than me, were being brought in line with my wage. Both had made their debuts like me the season before, playing only once each in games against Stoke City and Birmingham City.

Considering I'd made an impact in the European Cup semi-final and played in more games than them as well as being selected in more squads, I thought Bob's offer was a little bit confusing. Because I'd done a bit more than Ronnie and Kevin, I believed that my salary should reflect my progress, which had been quicker than theirs.

I'd always been challenged by the staff to prove myself, which I think I did. I'd had a particularly good season with the reserves too.

It was also nagging away at the back of my mind that players who were brought in from other clubs were treated better by Liverpool than the players that had emerged through their own system. I'd long found it strange that players signed for fees from other clubs, like Ian Rush (Chester City), Kevin Sheedy (Hereford United) and Ronnie Whelan (Home Farm in Ireland), got changed in the home-team dressing room from pretty much day one ahead of players like myself and Brian Kettle who were always asked to change in the away dressing room, even though we'd been there longer.

The changing arrangements were supposed to reflect status. And yet, despite featuring in more squads than Kevin and Ronnie – and with them still being brought in line with me in terms of wages – I remained in the away-team dressing room while they were in the first.

It didn't seem very consistent. If the powers that be were determined to keep egos in check, surely it should have been one rule for all? Kevin, Ronnie and Rushy were all playing in the same reserve games as me and Brian, for example. At that specific time, they weren't any further ahead in their progress; in fact, I thought I was ahead of them.

I was annoyed and too determined to think any other way. I felt like I was being unfairly treated. So I did not sign the contract.

I didn't relay any of my feelings to Bob initially, though. I took the contract away with me and rode it out until he came to ask me again. 'Howard, about that contract – are you going to sign it?'

It was only then that I explained to him about my frustrations with the system. I'd come a long way in a short space of time – much further than anyone else at the club – but felt someone was manipulating the fact I was local and not bought from elsewhere.

Bob reacted calmly. 'OK, son – go away and have another think about it.' I reminded him I wasn't asking for a transfer or anything like that. 'There's no way I want to leave the club, boss.' I only wanted what I thought was fair.

What a stupid thing to do. I should have realised Liverpool's contract offer was their way of keeping everyone on the same level. Even the top players like Kenny Dalglish weren't on much more money than anyone else.

I reacted instinctively – and defensively. I did not have anyone advising me. Within the squad, I was private and did not discuss the impasse with anyone. On Liverpool's part, I thought it was brinksmanship. I did not appreciate the offer was final and not up for discussion.

Through paranoia, in believing others would try and take advantage at every turn, I did not stop to consider what might happen if I played hardball with Liverpool. My hard stance, indeed, may have fortified Bob Paisley's and the other decision-makers' views of me and their element of mistrust: maybe that I wasn't totally committed towards my football career and motivated more by money. It may have also given the club the impression that I thought I'd made it as a footballer at Liverpool; that I'd cracked it.

I wish I'd just gone along with it all. Then I would have known for certain what Liverpool thought of me. I didn't want to sign a contract that may have kept me in the reserves. The deal Liverpool were offering was relatively good.

But I realised too through past experiences how difficult it was for a black person to find work. I was thinking about what would happen after my career. What happens if I sign the contract and I don't play games? What happens if I end up in the reserves and get a serious injury that ends my career? Where am I left then?

I should have just backed myself to do well. I trusted myself but I didn't trust the system.

With the experience I have now, I'd approach the moment differently and accept Liverpool's offer straight away. The momentum gained by my efforts and performances the previous season was lost pretty quickly.

I returned to the football wilderness.

My regret is huge.

*

AN ENTIRE YEAR PASSED. MY LIVERPOOL CAREER CRASHED AND burned quicker than it had risen.

Banished back to the reserves, I knew where I had gone wrong. The odds were already stacked against me, so going against the club was the stupidest thing I could have done in terms of career progression. Going the other way wouldn't have been a case of climbing the greasy pole as so many others do. It simply would have been the correct decision at a vital time in my life, where I really needed to kick on and establish myself. It's difficult managing ambition and patience. Sometimes it was a case of saying the right things to get along. At Liverpool – and probably any other football club for that matter – you had to be prepared to take a step back and be courteous, even if it betrayed who you really are.

I scored just eight goals for the reserves in the 1981/82 season. In the previous three seasons, I'd scored seventeen, thirteen and sixteen, while also contributing a healthy number of assists.

My form tailed away. My focus wasn't as it should have been. I partied more with friends. I was going through the motions for the reserves – unable to raise myself for games in front of a couple of hundred people in places like Bury.

In November 1981, I was the sixteenth man and an unused substitute during a 3–2 victory over AZ Alkmaar in a European Cup second-round tie at Anfield. I was then on the bench twice, first against Dundalk and against Helsinki. After that never again did I get to warm up – never mind play – in a red Liverpool shirt in a competitive first-team game.

The pre-season campaign of 1982/83 made me realise I needed to start thinking about a career away from Liverpool. We travelled down to Portsmouth for a testimonial game to open our pre-season schedule and I wasn't selected in the squad of sixteen. New seasons usually give fresh hope but I was feeling stale. Graeme Souness could tell I was down.

Everyone has an opinion on Graeme because he's such a forceful personality. You either love him or you hate him. I fell into the love camp. He couldn't do enough for the young players at Liverpool. Of all the senior pros, I felt as though I had Graeme's support the most. Some viewed him as flash, and he was to an extent, but chip away and get to know him and you realise that beneath the surface, he's an incredibly intelligent and kind person.

Graeme told me not to sulk, to get my head down and, even if my chance wasn't to be at Liverpool, someone else might fancy me and want to take me to another club.

I flew to La Manga for a pre-season training camp after the Portsmouth game, where we drew with Malaga in Marbella. Unfortunately, I missed one of the kicks in the penalty shoot-out.

Bob Paisley hadn't spoken to me for a long time. I remember boarding the team bus back to the hotel listening to jazz music on a Walkman. They were becoming fashionable. Bob leaned forward and said in his own inimitable way, 'You should have had them headphones in last night . . .'

It wasn't delivered in a jokey manner. It was him telling me to remove them. So I did without saying anything to him.

Inwardly, I was thinking: *Give us a break! I didn't mean to miss the fucking penalty!* I could have hidden and not taken one. But I'd been on the sidelines for so long, I wanted to make an impact, so I put myself forward.

It was another sign my time at Liverpool was up.

INITIALLY, THE LOAN OFFER FROM NEWCASTLE UNITED CAME AS A relief. Someone wanted me.

Kevin Keegan had sustained an eye injury and Arthur Cox, Newcastle's manager, needed a short-term replacement in the run-up to Christmas 1982. I was on a three-year contract at Liverpool and had eighteen months left at this point. The thought of spending another eighteen months on the fringes at Melwood terrified me.

Arthur was well respected within the game. Newcastle had also signed Terry McDermott from Liverpool the summer before and I knew all about him – one of the biggest characters in the Liverpool dressing room. He was loved by everyone, Terry. After stretching the boundaries of acceptability as far as he could by his behaviour on nights out, though, Bob Paisley decided to get shut of him. His departure sent out a warning to the rest of the squad. We all needed to buck our ideas up.

I was driven up to Newcastle on a Friday morning by Terry Littlewood, the chauffeur for all the Liverpool players whenever they went somewhere on official business. I felt really sad as the hours passed. It felt as though my time at Liverpool was coming to an end. On a few occasions, I was close to telling Terry to turn around and go home. My heart was in Liverpool and deep down I did not want to leave. Sitting alone in the back of the car, there were a few tears.

Newcastle is a cold, bleak place in winter. When I arrived at St James' Park, it was snowing quite heavily. Arthur made it clear to me that if I did well, he'd do everything in his power to make the move permanent.

Newcastle were vying for promotion from the Second Division. They had fallen on hard times but were very ambitious. St James' Park wasn't like you see it now, where it probably stands as the most impressive inner-city football ground in Britain. It was run-down, not always filled to capacity and a difficult place to play, particularly if you were a home player – mainly due to the frustration on the terraces.

Kevin Keegan had been signed from Southampton and his arrival was viewed as the beginning of good times again. His recruitment was massive for Newcastle, when you consider not long before he'd been the European Footballer of the Year and that Newcastle were not even a First Division club.

In addition to Keegan and Terry Mac, Arthur Cox had signed David McCreery from Queens Park Rangers. He'd been a promising midfielder at Manchester United. John Anderson was the lynchpin that the defence was built around, while Chris Waddle was emerging as a young, talented winger.

The team, though, was not quite meeting expectations by the time I joined in the last week of November, sitting mid-table. I scored my first goal for the club in front of the famous Gallowgate End, a header against Derby County, the day after Boxing Day and it proved to be the match winner. Kevin Keegan made his comeback from injury in that game and he was a level above everyone else on the pitch. The following afternoon, we travelled to Grimsby and I scored again in a 2–2 draw. Grimsby was probably my best game for Newcastle. Kevin's presence gave everyone a lift and he enhanced my performance. I played well with better players.

I remember a song being chanted in the away end at Blundell Park: 'He's black, he's broon, he's playing for the Toon.' I figured that I'd had worse songs chanted about me. It was the Newcastle supporters' way of showing some affection. There were no other black players in the Newcastle team that day. Arthur Wharton, the black goalkeeper, had guested for Newcastle and District FC in friendly matches a century before.

By playing for Newcastle United in 1982, I had become only the second black player to represent the club in its history.

*

I WAS GIVEN THE KEYS TO AN APARTMENT AT THE SWALLOW Hotel, not far from St James' Park. It meant that I could walk to the stadium for home games. I loved that about Newcastle: the fact it's one of the few remaining clubs that are located right in the middle of the action.

I quickly began to appreciate that as long as the football team in Newcastle are doing well, everything else pales into insignificance. Life's problems fade away. On a Friday night in Newcastle's city centre, you could sense a football match was going to happen the following day.

Newcastle were sponsored by Newcastle Brown Ale and the players could drink in the brewery tap for free. Terry McDermott acted as my mentor during my two and a bit months there. I don't think he would mind me saying that he was a seasoned drinker and more than capable of indulging in a two-day binge before going out and playing the match of his life. I couldn't do that. I needed to be fresh and focused to be at my best. Sometimes, though, I didn't really know how to say no either. When you're a black professional in a predominantly white environment, you stand out anyway. You don't want to give people another reason to talk about you, so with something like drinking, you end up going with the flow.

I didn't want to be on the outside. There was an underlying feeling, particularly at Liverpool, that it was the other players that got you into the team. The management wanted to see whether you fitted into their social framework: whether you were one of the lads.

At Liverpool, Kenny Dalglish did not drink so much as the others. Maybe he'd have a beer on the back of the bus coming back from an away game and then head home to Southport as soon as we arrived at Anfield, while everyone else moved into town.

Kenny, though, was the club's most expensive signing and proving himself to be a top player, so he could do as he pleased. I was young, on the edge of things, and unsure of how to prove myself. Often the best way of doing that was by performances on the pitch but opportunities, for reasons already explained, weren't readily available.

Most of my socialising with other footballers came after games. At Liverpool we'd drink in Kirklands on Hardman Street. It had just opened as a wine bar and it quickly became popular with Bruce Grobbelaar, Sammy Lee and Graeme Souness particularly. On the parallel alleyway was a place called Streets. Le Bateau opened on Duke Street and we went there a lot too because the music was diverse.

The mood at Newcastle was lower-key. Every Friday night before home games, Terry and I would play snooker just to while a few hours away. Terry probably did it because he enjoyed playing snooker but, deep down, I knew it was my way of dealing with the anticipation of what was to follow. The adrenalin always started to kick in the night before for me. I struggled sleeping in hotel beds. Frequently, I'd take a Mogadon sleeping tablet and wake up the next morning a bit drowsy as a consequence.

The social scene wasn't quite as active in Newcastle as in Liverpool. Terry was banned from driving at the time and I'd never passed my test, so after games, journeys back to Liverpool (where we both continued to live while playing for Newcastle) were always on the train with a few cans of lager. If Newcastle played at home – they were always 3 p.m. kick-offs – we'd be on the train by 6 p.m. and back in Liverpool by 10 p.m. at the latest. It meant there was plenty of time to join our friends in the early stages of their nights out. Terry lived in Kirkby and would often head out around the pubs there. Meanwhile, I'd stay in town. Monday was usually a day off so we'd meet again at Lime Street late that afternoon and head up back to the Northeast.

My time at Newcastle finished after a nightmare performance against Bolton Wanderers. I had a drink with Terry the night before and maybe I had one too many – although I certainly wasn't drunk. After the game, I decided to be honest with the press. 'I was absolutely crap today,' I admitted. 'I haven't done myself any favours if I want to get a move here.' That created a headline in the local paper, something like 'Gayle Doubts Over Permanent Newcastle Switch'.

On the Monday morning, Arthur Cox gave me a bollocking. 'Never give the press a story like that,' he said. He thought I was feeling sorry for myself.

A few days later, Arthur called me into his office again. He told me that Birmingham City had made an offer for me and that Liverpool had accepted it. 'Well, I want to stay here,' I told him. Arthur explained that Newcastle could afford my wages but not the transfer fee Birmingham were offering, which came in at around £75,000. Arthur said that Liverpool were going to call me back to Melwood regardless of whether I wanted to remain at Newcastle, so it was advisable to listen to what Birmingham had to say.

I thought to myself, 'Fuck this, I'll go to Birmingham, then.' As you know, I am quite impulsive.

Norman Bodell, the driver for Birmingham, picked me up from Newcastle train station in a taxi. It was a long drive and I had a lot to think about. Birmingham were in the First Division and Ron Saunders, Birmingham's manager, was paying a reasonable amount of money for me so, naturally, he'd expect some return on that and the only way he was going to get it was by selecting me.

I asked Ron if I could spend the weekend thinking about it. The only people I really spoke to about it was my girlfriend at the time and my brothers. The options were: a) sign for Birmingham and play, or b) go back and play in Liverpool's reserves. Nobody from Liverpool called me to try and explain how they viewed me, or indeed to persuade me to stay. I weighed up the pros and cons.

My family had lived through my Liverpool career with me. It was their view that I should leave.

Early on a Sunday, there was a call from Ron. 'Have you made your mind up yet?'

'Yeah, about that, Ron. I'd like a car for my missus . . .'

'OK,' Ron said. 'That's fine.'

'I'm only joking!' I said, desperate not to come across as greedy. I hadn't learned from my experience negotiating contracts with Liverpool. All I wanted to do with Ron was test how much he wanted me. It could have backfired.

'Get down here tomorrow, Howard,' Ron told me. 'We'll get this sorted.'

BIRMINGHAM, 1983

I'VE ALWAYS BEEN SUSPICIOUS OF THE MEDIA. IT PARTLY EXPLAINS why I've taken so long to write a book. Life has taught me it is difficult finding someone who will tell your story in the way you believe it should be portrayed.

I didn't trust the media over the wider coverage of the Toxteth Riots. Later, I didn't trust the media because of *The Sun's* lies following the Hillsborough disaster. I certainly didn't trust them after my experiences at Birmingham City.

I felt as though I was stitched up over an interview I gave to the *News of the World* right at the start of my time at Birmingham where the article intimated that I'd made disparaging remarks about Bob Paisley.

Though you might read some of this book and think I've been critical of Bob here – more than thirty years ago – I'd never have dreamed about going public with my views about the way it was at Liverpool. One thing I implicitly understood was, it wasn't the Liverpool way to wash your dirty laundry in public. The article resulted in me travelling back to Merseyside, where I apologised to Bob in person.

After that episode, I rarely spoke to anyone from the press. Maybe it's unfair, because I realise all journalists are different. Ron Saunders, Birmingham's manager, used to tell us about his views of the media. 'Look!' he'd say, holding up a newspaper. 'Each report from the weekend's game will have a different take on what happened. They'll usually choose a different man of the match – yet a lot of people believe everything they read.' He made me realise it was safer to say nothing at all – to keep your head down when someone asks you for a quote.

I only played for Birmingham for eighteen months and my stay culminated in relegation from the old First Division. Yet, when I look back, some of my fondest memories are there.

I became a first-team regular, a consistent goal scorer, I found a manager who trusted me and, most of all, I went from a situation where it felt like nobody really wanted me at Liverpool to one where I felt really valued.

When Arthur Cox, Newcastle's manager, told me Birmingham had made an offer, I returned to the Swallow Hotel and reached across my bed for the newspaper, looking at the First Division table. Because I'd been playing for Newcastle in the Second Division, I hadn't paid much attention to what was happening in the top flight – aside from Liverpool's results, of course.

Birmingham were bottom of the First Division, having won just four games. Their highest position all season had been nineteenth and that had been achieved in the second game of the campaign, following a goalless draw with Liverpool at St Andrew's. Great.

Birmingham's offer and Liverpool's acceptance of it presented the realisation that there was no way home. The cold truth was: my Liverpool career was over. There was no going back. Ever. Very few players get a second chance at Liverpool. As far as I'm aware, only three players in the club's history have been re-signed and they all came after me. Ian Rush and Robbie Fowler are established as two of the club's greatest goal scorers, while Craig Bellamy also had two spells.

I'd made my bed so I had to lie in it. I wasn't filled with joy when I joined Birmingham. I remember driving down the M6 with the rain battering down and my face leaning against the car window, wondering what the future held. I'd found adjusting to life in London with Fulham and then Newcastle quite difficult. Being away again from the community where I felt comfortable in Liverpool 8 didn't really appeal to me.

Ron Saunders was Birmingham City's manager. Immediately, we struck a rapport. He sold Birmingham to me. Ron was originally from Birkenhead, which is just over the River Mersey from Liverpool, so we had something in common.

Ron had started his playing career in the early 1950s with Everton before settling at Portsmouth. His managerial career had found greater success, winning the First Division title with Aston Villa then progressing well in the European Cup. Villa were in the quarter-finals of a competition that they would go on to win under Tony Barton when Saunders resigned over a contract dispute.

Ron had such a forceful personality, he wasn't afraid of the repercussions when he walked straight into a new job across the city with Villa's arch-rivals. I admire any person who possesses the courage to go his own way. Ron Saunders was my type of football manager.

Widely, Ron was misunderstood. Publicly, he came across as dour and unapproachable, but within the confines of the club – in the dressing room and around the training ground – he was an outstanding mentor who made players want to deliver performances for him. He did not trust the press but did not use that as a negative among his players. Instead, he cultivated an 'us and them' mentality, which was healthy.

Ron was a disciplinarian. He'd let you know if you crossed the line and did not think twice about doling out punishments. But he was consistent. His management – particularly his ruthlessness – was what I needed. He wasn't punitive; he was very fair. Unlike Bob Paisley, he was a communicator.

The atmosphere at Birmingham was totally different to Liverpool. At Melwood the Boot Room members rather than the manager enforced the rules on a day-to-day basis. Ronnie Moran was the shouter and screamer, but others would have their say too if they saw something they didn't like. Joe Fagan, Roy Evans and Bob Paisley were vocal, as well as Reuben Bennett. At Birmingham, Ron was the all-seeing eye. His control was absolute and he was the person you didn't want to disappoint.

The systems might explain why Liverpool were so secure as the most successful club in England for so long. I have been at clubs where players turn on the manager and stop playing for him. At Liverpool, it was impossible to do that because you weren't just playing for a manager – you were playing for an entire staff. The staff had different opinions but, fundamentally, they all wanted the same thing. As a player, it meant you had a number of people to impress at the same time and therefore it led to an increase in standards. You could never afford to rest on your laurels. In many ways, the Boot Room was a union – the safety in numbers protected jobs. Ultimately, it made Liverpool stronger.

At Birmingham, Ron's was the only head on the block. There was no Boot Room at Birmingham. He had an assistant manager, a first-team trainer and a chief scout who recommended players. He would take advice from these figures but not in the same way as Bob Paisley took advice at Liverpool. As far as I'm aware, there were no long meetings at Birmingham: certainly no debriefings at St Andrew's like there were at Anfield on Sunday mornings between staff after every game.

Ron wasn't afraid to make big decisions. He told me in our first discussion that Birmingham was a sleeping giant. He wanted to remove the players who were on big money but, as he said, 'not earning it'. He thought the team he inherited was too soft and it was time for a change.

I felt like Ron trusted me. Ron asked whether there were any other players at Liverpool I'd recommend. 'Tough lads, Howard,' he said. 'We need tough lads.'

Mick Halsall was the first name that entered my mind. I'd played with Mick for years in Liverpool's reserves. He was some way down the pecking order in Liverpool's midfield but he was a great pro. Mick was born in Bootle, the same suburb where Jamie Carragher later came from, and Bootle lads are tough. Mick also had a calm left foot and Birmingham needed some balance in the team. 'Go for Mick, Ron – he's an ideal Birmingham player: not the quickest but strong in the tackle and a good character in the dressing room.' So Ron went and signed him.

Other Scousers came and went. Mark McCarrick had a background in non-league football and he joined from Witton Albion. Later, Billy Wright came from Everton.

I developed close relationships with players that were already at Birmingham by the time I signed, though. Those friends were: Noel Blake, Robert Hopkins, Tony Coton, Mick Harford and Kevin Dillon.

I'd grown up playing against Blakey and Hoppy for Liverpool's reserves. Hoppy was a hard-as-nails winger who made full-backs squeal. Blakey had been a formidable opponent in the centre of defence: a proper leader and very physical. His roots were in Kingston, Jamaica, and for the first time in my career, his presence in the Birmingham dressing room meant I was not the only black player. Daniel Sturridge's dad Michael was there as an apprentice as well. Suddenly, I wasn't alone.

Ron wanted to rebuild the team around quick, athletic players. That's what he'd achieved at Aston Villa and he saw me as an important part of his plans because of my pace and ability to expose the opposition using the counter-attack.

Like most English managers, Ron played 4–4–2 every single week and the idea was basic: break quickly, using the wingers to supply the centre-forwards. The ball had to be moved fast and if that meant going long from time to time then so be it. Ron used me up front and on the right and left wing. I could shoot, pass and control with either foot. He recognised my versatility as an asset and I think that was one of the main reasons why he decided to buy me for £75,000. I was conscious, though, that while versatile players are always in demand, they don't necessarily play every single week. So from day one at Birmingham I realised I had to nail a position that would give me a little bit more security.

For the first time in my football career, I felt really wanted. Liverpool is a bubble and I'd never thought once about taking myself out of that bubble. I realised that I needed to prove myself but, in the long term, Liverpool was always where I wanted to be. And yet, I'd always felt near the bottom of the pile there: miles away from achieving my goal. I never stopped to consider what it might be like at other clubs – whether, indeed, those environments would be better for me.

Inwardly, I'd always craved some reassurance. I wanted someone to tell me they had my back. Under Ron, I felt his support straight away. Being a bought player changed the way I was viewed. It cost Liverpool nothing to bring me in from park football. Birmingham had spent money to take me there. They were in trouble and needed a quick fix.

Maybe it's a superficial way of looking at it but the club had invested £75,000 in hard cash to get me so they had to justify their outlay. It made sense for them to roll out the carpet a bit more and make me feel welcome because, ultimately, they needed me to perform well.

From the first moment at Birmingham, I was viewed as a first-team player. I was never viewed in the same way at Liverpool, where I was Howard Gayle – the young black player trying to push others out of the way to reach the top. I wasn't alone in that sense because every day Ronnie Moran would remind everyone that their place wasn't certain – you'd need at least 250 games behind you to think you were established and I only played five.

At Birmingham, because I was a signed player – and because they'd seen where I'd come from: Liverpool, the most successful club in England – it afforded me a bit more respect.

*

RON HAD BEEN IN CHARGE OF BIRMINGHAM FOR A YEAR BY THE time I arrived. He didn't go into much detail – managers rarely do when there are problems – but it was clear to me that morale was on the floor and there needed to be greater unity among the players.

Ultimately, a manager can desire a spirit all he wants but without a few positive results it is impossible. There is no substitute for the unique taste of victory and what it inspires. Throughout my time at Liverpool, I wanted to win because it was Liverpool, and it felt like a duty to win because Liverpool was my club. There was a culture of success. It was expected. It was a routine.

It was only when I signed for Birmingham that I really began to appreciate the difference between winning and losing; how a place changed depending on the result at the weekend. At Liverpool winning was normal, it seemed the natural thing to do.

At Birmingham, though, the club was in survival mode. Football is a vicious circle. Results sustain momentum and momentum sustains spirit. Somehow, you have to find a way to step on that ladder of positivity, otherwise you'll slip away into a spiral of decline.

Birmingham's position in the table appeared really bleak and the only way to change it was through hard work. As fate would have it my league debut would follow the next Saturday at Anfield – of all places.

I travelled back to Lime Street station by train and twisted my ankle on a kerb getting into a taxi. I couldn't believe it. My ankle ballooned. I phoned Ron the next morning and explained the situation. It was understandable that he thought it was a consequence of being drunk but the reality was rather more mundane. For the rest of the week, I was on the treatment table: hot and cold water, ice packs and massages. He'd paid a reasonable sum of money for me. There was no way I was going to miss a trip to Anfield.

I had stepped on to the Anfield turf many, many times as a Liverpool reserve-team player: when the stadium was almost empty, echoey and you could hear the shouts between team-mates. As a first-team player, it happened only twice, losing 1–0 to Sunderland and beating Manchester City by the same scoreline. Those were very different experiences. The season was drifting towards a conclusion and, though supporters clearly cared whether we won or lost, there wasn't much significance weighing on the outcome. Anfield wasn't quite as loud as it might have been otherwise. The atmosphere wasn't quite as intense.

Nevertheless, the experience was exhilarating. It was where I wanted to be – where I wanted to play. Going back to reserve-team football after that was a massive comedown. The adrenalin was not the same.

Never did I think about playing at Anfield as an opposition player. Going there with Birmingham for my league debut acted as a cold reminder that my Liverpool career was over. It's strange how many times a footballer has left one club only to return with his new club soon after. For me, it helped bring about some form of closure on my Liverpool career quicker than I might have done. I was confronted with the realisation that my career was taking a different path. Although Liverpool had agreed to sell me, the decision to go was ultimately mine.

Walking into Anfield that afternoon, it felt like a dream. You wonder whether Bob Paisley might come over, finally put his hands on your shoulder and say, 'It's OK, son. Let's forget the past. You can come back.' You hope, somehow, it might happen.

This Birmingham team was lacking in confidence. There were some good players: Tony Coton, Noel Blake, Mark Dennis, Robert Hopkins, Mick Harford, Kevin Dillon and David Langan. The makings of a decent side was there but it was clear that we were short by two or three top performers. At the very highest level, that can be the difference between success and failure. Over the previous decade, Birmingham had become a selling club. They had sold Bob Latchford to Everton before he'd reached his peak, for a British transfer record fee. They then sold Trevor Francis to Nottingham Forest, also for a British record. I wondered how this impacted upon the mentality of the players and the fans. For the players, you appreciated that if you did well, there was a chance of a move to a bigger club. For the fans, that must have been incredibly frustrating. Ultimately, if you continue to sell your best players and don't have an idea what to do with the money, you end up slipping down the league – and that's where Birmingham found itself when I joined in 1983.

Birmingham's kit was blue shirts, white shorts and red socks. Because Liverpool played in the famous red strip, we wore white socks. Again, pulling them on reminded me that my allegiances had changed. Yet my memories of everything that happened after the kick-off are blurred. All I remember is spending most of the game chasing after former team-mates. At Liverpool, training and matches seemed easy because of the standard of player you were sharing a pitch with. Playing against Liverpool in a real-life situation where points were at stake was different. It wasn't enjoyable because Liverpool moved the ball around so quickly and they rarely gave it away. It is damaging psychologically when you don't see much of the ball. You are halfway towards a defeat. I became frustrated and it seemed inevitable from early on that we'd end up losing.

In the first ten minutes, I was struggling and playing with a strapping on my ankle. I heard a Birmingham fan shout, 'Fucking move yourself, Gayle.' It was cold and blustery and around 30,000 fans had turned up. Liverpool won 1–0 thanks to a goal by Phil Neal. It was a strange experience. I didn't play well.

I MADE MY HOME DEBUT AT ST ANDREW'S AGAINST WEST HAM United. Birmingham won for the first time in the league in more than a month and in a 3–0 victory I scored the third goal in front of more than 12,000 people. St Andrew's was more open than Anfield, with deep, sweeping, uncovered terraces. It can't have been a particularly nice place to play for visiting teams because it wasn't particularly nice for Birmingham's players. That said, the fans were really supportive. Towards the end of the game, they started singing my name – something that had never happened at Liverpool. Hearing that was like a shot of adrenalin in the arm. It made me want to run faster.

I played really well. A friend of mine, Tom Parry, had come down to watch me and he stood with the Birmingham fans. Tom was the head chef in a seafood restaurant in Liverpool's city centre and he'd met my brother, Alan, who used to work in the market stall that delivered vegetables to his kitchen. Tom was an avid Liverpool fan and we became close over the years.

Tom was a cultured football supporter. He knew about systems, players and their characters. I'd lean on him for advice and he certainly wasn't one who told you what you wanted to hear. He became a really close confidant: someone I respected. I didn't have an agent – few players did back then, but Tom was the closest person I had to one.

'One of the Birmingham guys described you as being a Rolls-Royce engine in an old banger,' he told me. I'd never received a compliment like this before. I'd never really felt appreciated. Instantly, I liked being at Birmingham. I liked the people. They were working-class, like Liverpool supporters.

The victory over West Ham did not prove to be a catalyst for a positive run of form, however. Over the next three months, Birmingham won only two more games and when a 3–1 defeat at Luton Town cemented our position at the foot of the First Division table, I had visions of away-days at places like Grimsby and Carlisle the following season in the Second Division.

I missed much of this period through injury, having torn my ankle ligaments in a tackle with Aston Villa's Steve McMahon. I tried to carry on for a few weeks but my ankle was hurting badly. I'd played against McMahon many times when he was in the reserves at Everton and I was at Liverpool. He was a boyhood Evertonian and the most ferocious player in their team. I didn't like him, and he didn't like me, I think. He was one of those opponents I simply didn't get on with because he was always on the front foot in terms of confrontation. By all accounts, he was the same way with a lot of team-mates in his own dressing room.

Despite McMahon's background as an Everton captain, Kenny Dalglish later made him his first Liverpool signing as manager from Villa and it didn't surprise me: firstly because McMahon was a very good player and secondly because he didn't appear to be the type of personality to allow allegiances to get in the way of personal achievement.

After the Luton match, and with my season finished, we had six games remaining; to have any chance of saving ourselves from relegation, we needed at least four wins and other results to go our way. Somehow, we did it. Coventry City, Everton and Sunderland were all beaten by the odd goal before a draw at Brighton and Hove Albion stunted our progress. In the final home game of the season, we beat Tottenham Hotspur 2–0 – essentially thanks to bullying them off the park. Then on the last day we went to Southampton, still needing three points to be sure of survival.

I still get goose pimples when I think of the moment Mick Harford struck the winner, sending the travelling Birmingham supporters inside the Dell crazy.

WHEN FOOTBALL TEAMS DEVELOP THE WINNING HABIT, THEY cling on to routines. The manner of Birmingham City's escape from relegation shaped the next twelve months socially.

Most days after training, from April 1983 onwards, we'd head into Birmingham's city centre to a restaurant called Gino's in the famous Bullring shopping centre. One of the lads had heard on the TV how pasta was meant to be nutritious and particularly beneficial for athletes. Nobody at the club advised us to do it because there just wasn't that level of insight in the 1980s.

After eating a spaghetti Bolognese, we'd head out for a couple of drinks. Our intentions at the beginning were healthy but naturally, as footballers from my generation tended to do, someone would suggest a pint or two and the night would open up from there.

Ron Saunders had become 'the gaffer' to me by then in the way that Bob Paisley never was, largely due to the fact I played so few games for Bob and a lot more for Ron. It is only through playing games that you develop a trust and a level of camaraderie with the people around you and the people you work for. Otherwise, you are simply an outsider looking in – hoping to join the party.

The gaffer made it clear to us that he was happy for everyone to drink as much as they wanted providing it never interfered with football matters.

He wanted us to arrive at training on time and to perform in matches. So long as we managed that, he was happy. He knew we always went out on a Wednesday night so he'd run the bollocks off us on a Thursday morning. Every other day of the week, he'd send one of his coaching staff in the changing rooms to try and figure out whether we'd been drinking. You'd only have to pop your head in because the whiff of alcohol was so obvious on someone's breath. Even if it was just from one person, he'd punish the group by running, running and more running.

It is fair to say that the gaffer would have been quite within reason to punish us for other reasons. The run towards the end of the 1982/83 season manifested a spirit that carried on across the summer and into the following campaign. Relatively, it was a short period, but in that time the bond between the players became pretty tight pretty quickly.

The pre-season campaign involved a tour of Sweden. Considering we made it on to the ITN News at Ten for non-football reasons, I suppose you could say it was a memorable trip. It certainly brought us closer together as a group.

Noel Blake and I were walking between bars through some random town – I can't remember its name – a few hours away from Stockholm. We were having a few drinks but it was all very low-key. Suddenly, a gang approached the pair of us on the street, one of them brandishing a meat cleaver. It was massive. Racist language was used and a fight ensued. Somehow, I ran around a small block to get away, not realising Blakey hadn't followed me. So I ran back round the other way behind the assailant with the blade, cracking him over the head before he could attack Blakey.

Some of the other Birmingham players were in a bar just around the corner. All hell broke loose and I got hit by one of those staves that gardeners use to plant trees. It was just a glancing blow but blood started pouring from my nose straight away. Police rounded everyone up and – considering the others were armed with weapons – it was clear who the aggressors were. It only took a few hours for the story to get back to England and the British media, naturally, weren't very sympathetic towards us. They believed it to be a classic case of young footballers causing trouble on a night out when, really, we were attacked and forced to defend ourselves.

The local papers labelled us the 'Birmingham Six'. I immediately thought the headline was disrespectful, considering the moniker had originally been used a decade before after the six supposed IRA bombers set devices off, ripping the city centre apart. Although they were later found to be wrongly convicted, the attack was still raw in the minds of many people. There were, indeed, a few hell-raisers in our group but our actions did not equate to anything near as serious.

There were so many incidents in that period, it's difficult to know where to start. Wimbledon were known in the latter part of the decade as the Crazy Gang, but the Birmingham City squad of 1983/84 preceded Wimbledon in terms of wild behaviour.

Aside from the fights with Villa supporters, there were stories published about scuffles with taxi drivers, trashed cars and someone getting run over by a bus. Some of the stories were true. Some were not. Some were exaggerated. The identities of the six were well established and known and accepted, though: Mick Harford, Mark Dennis, Noel Blake, Tony Coton, Robert Hopkins and myself, although others came into the group over the course of time, with some leaving.

Mark Dennis had the nickname 'Damien', after the character in The Omen film so I'll refer to him in this book by that name. Damien owned a pit bull terrier, and in his back garden he put a tyre on his washing line. To entertain the dog, he'd spin the tyre round as fast as he could. The dog would latch on. Damien would go out for a few hours and when he returned, the dog would still be attached to the tyre. Damien was the craziest of the Birmingham Six and in the end Ron decided to sell him.

Damien was an outstanding footballer with a brilliant left foot but his reputation went before him. He was from East London and as tough as they come. In his twelve-year career he was sent off a dozen times.

I'd not long signed for Birmingham and we were out in a nightclub called Faces. Our other favourite places became Rum Runner, Peppermint Place and Mr Moons. Damien was standing by the bar in Faces all night talking to someone. I figured that he must have known him as they appeared to be getting on well. Next thing, the fella is on the floor – Damien has sparked him.

'Why did you do that?'

'I'd had enough of him, Howard – he's been talking shite all night,' was his response. The victim was a Birmingham City supporter. Damien didn't care.

During his time at Birmingham, he was married to an East London girl and within our dressing room she had a reputation of being just as uncompromising as him. On another occasion, the squad had planned a night out and Damien was struggling to escape her clutches. So at 9.30 p.m., he left the house, promising to return shortly with a curry. Instead, he stayed out for two nights in succession – without ringing or going home once.

Alan Curbishley, the Birmingham midfielder who later became Charlton Athletic's manager, lived on the same street as Damien. Bearing in mind this was before mobile phones, Curbs was the first person she called trying to establish where Damien was. She rang everywhere. By the end of the second day, she was ringing the office of the club every ten minutes: 'Is he there yet?'

Damien, of course, had been into training and told everyone to say that he wasn't around. 'We haven't seen Mr Dennis – we're looking for him as well,' I could hear someone saying from the secretary's office down the corridor.

In the end, Damien realised it was time for him to return after his two days of fun. Somehow, he persuaded Curbs to go with him. 'Just say I've been to the hospital with you if she kicks off,' was his excuse.

After getting out the taxi at the end of the road, Curbs accompanied Damien to the door before edging back towards the gates, fearing what the reaction might be. Damien put his key in the lock and turned to Curbs, winking at him – indicating everything was going to be OK. Suddenly, Curbs heard a scream that must have woke the street up. Damien was greeted at the door with a fork being applied to his shoulder blade. The hospital had been Damien's excuse. He ended up going there.

Damien's poor disciplinary record at Birmingham was legendary and ultimately the gaffer decided that he should be sold. Most managers had the same philosophy in those days: the best way to pick a team was to keep it the same. If a player was going to be suspended a lot, it potentially compromised the manager's selection policy. Ron Saunders was no different. So Damien went to Southampton.

*

WE TRAVELLED TO LA MANGA FOR WARM-WEATHER TRAINING IN the middle of the season. Now you might think, 'Here we go: footballers on a trip abroad – what a laugh that must be.' The reality was very different.

Quickly, boredom sets in, especially in between training sessions and during the evening. In the 1980s, evening time meant a few drinks. We were at a golfing resort owned by Seve Ballesteros.

One of the Birmingham players got so drunk that he took a picture off the wall and smashed it. The residents complained about us and the hotel manager wanted us out but the gaffer apologised on our behalf.

We'd arrived on a Sunday and were due to go home on the Thursday, so there was a lot of time to pass in between the training sessions. You really have to appreciate that it's not like it is now when a football squad travels abroad and they have media commitments. The only reporter that followed us to Spain was a journalist from the *Birmingham Mail*.

In all the clubs I've played for, footballers have always filled the gaps with little mind games. So one afternoon, we sat on the beach and sunbathed in between dares. Gradually, the dares became riskier until someone said to Noel Blake, 'I dare you to sunbathe on this beach naked,' appreciating, of course, that Blakey is considerably endowed – certainly greater in that department than anyone else in the group. Blakey was one of our leaders and, naturally, he could not resist responding by bathing stark naked on the sun lounger with his hands behind his head.

During my stay at Birmingham, the sentence, 'Gaffer wants to see you lot,' became a theme. It would be followed by the response, 'It wasn't us, boss – it was someone else.' Before we were due to catch the plane home, we were escorted upstairs in the hotel, where Ron was waiting.

'Who got their cock out down at the beach?' he asked.

'Wasn't us,' we all said at more or less the same time. He explained that he'd overheard a British lady speaking to the concierge at the hotel reception about a group of men larking about before one of them stripped off.

'She's talking about going to the police,' Ron said.

'Wasn't us, gaffer,' we said. 'Wasn't us.'

The gaffer knew that the culprit was black and that meant he also knew it was either Blakey or me.

'You two are going have to stay here and sort it out with the police,' he said, pointing at Blakey and me. 'Otherwise I'll fine you two weeks' wages.

Obviously, I didn't have much trust in the police in England and even though I knew it wasn't me, I didn't fancy taking my chances with the police in Spain because the Garda Civil had a fierce reputation.

OK, gaffer, I was thinking, *I'll take the two-week fine and come home with you!*

Yet Blakey – being the leader he was – stepped forward and admitted his guilt. The gaffer loved Blakey because he knew he could rely on him on the pitch.

At that point, the gaffer announced he was imposing a two-week fine on Blakey and a one-week fine on everyone else for covering for him, including me of course.

Deep down, I think he respected the fact we'd stuck together. There were no snitches. Birmingham City, indeed, were not soft any more.

*

OVER THE COURSE OF THE NEXT FEW MONTHS WE'D ENCOUNTER A lot of Aston Villa supporters on our nights out and they were not shy in coming forward, giving us abuse. When groups of lads have had a drink and feel challenged, no matter what their profession, they end up reacting and we were no different. Birmingham City's players were involved in quite a few street scraps with Villa supporters and I was at the forefront of those confrontations.

One Sunday evening we were in a nightclub called Kaleidoscope, having been on the ale all afternoon. It was a proper 1980s place with sticky floors, soft furnishing, disco balls and bad music. One of the Villa supporters confronted Robert Hopkins and a fight broke out. Everybody chased everyone else. The scene was like a cross between the Keystone Cops and the Grand National: chasing across the dance floor and jumping over couches.

The result was me getting hit by a Toby jug pint glass, splitting my head open, and another trip to hospital for stitches. The fact that I was able to join the rest of the lads a couple of hours later in an Indian restaurant reflected the mood of the time.

We sat there for a few hours discussing how we were going to explain my scars to the gaffer. We had to get our stories straight. In the end, we concluded that it was probably best telling the truth. One of them threw a glass: end of story. The gaffer's relationship with Villa wasn't the best after the way he left the club. We figured he might take sympathy on us.

The next morning it was time for confession. 'We did them in though, gaffer,' someone reasoned. Ron smiled. 'You're fined a week's wages – don't go out in that place again.' Although he was strict, the gaffer's punishments were not arbitrary so long as we were just as committed during games.

He hated players who acted big off the pitch but were cowards on it. He appreciated too that the Birmingham press weren't all that keen on him for moving across the city. The press used our behaviour to get at him, often exaggerating the truth. That gave us a bit of leeway. Although we gave the press enough ammunition and we could have been shrewder, Ron appreciated it wasn't easy for us.

In one notorious incident an armed mob of Villa supporters decided to take me, Tony Coton, Robert Hopkins and Blakey on during a night out. We proceeded to give them such a beating that one of the original aggressors complained to the police through wired teeth after he sustained a broken jaw.

Hoppy was a winger who came to Birmingham – the club he supported as a boy – from Aston Villa. He was as hard-core as they come and the day he signed for Birmingham must have been the happiest day of his life. He was so mad about Birmingham, in fact, that during his last game for Villa it is said that he went to take a corner in front of their supporters and they noticed that he'd placed a Birmingham City badge over the Villa crest.

Understandably, I suppose, the Villa supporters went absolutely berserk and a few tried to jump over the fence in front of them to get at him. Hoppy responded to that by flicking a few V-signs at them before deliberately booting the ball out for a goal kick. A few weeks later, he joined Birmingham. After that sequence of events, the Villa supporters were always after him.

Relations between Birmingham and Villa, indeed, were not good at all and it ended up manifesting in full public view during derby games. In October 1983, we went to Villa Park and what followed was one of the most bad-tempered derbies in history. Six players were booked, Colin Gibson was sent off for fouling me and when the game was over Blakey head-butted Steve McMahon and was subsequently suspended for six games after the television cameras picked it up. Blakey also missed a penalty and had a goal disallowed. In the middle of all that, the referee ordered more than fifty free kicks.

On the terraces, there was chaos as well. One fan was stabbed and eighty others were arrested. The *Sunday Mercury* ran with the headline 'THE HORROR SHOW' on its front page while the Birmingham *Evening Mail* called it 'BRUM'S DAY OF SHAME'. It really was as bad as it sounds.

The game should never have been played in the first place. Torrential rain had left the pitch sodden and, as a consequence, it was a bit easier to fly into challenges. Modern football supporters would not believe just how brutal an encounter it was. Mick Harford was well known as the toughest centre-forward in the First Division and he was a better player than people remember. Outstanding in the air, he was very skilled with the ball at his feet and of all the centre-forwards I played with, I probably enjoyed playing with him the most because he was incredibly unselfish. Mick was an absolute monster of a man. I've encountered some scary people in my life but I can say for absolute certain that I'd never want to cross Mick. A great fella off the pitch, but once on it his blood ran cold. In the first couple of minutes, Mick caught Villa's captain Allan Evans and from there, it all went off. Hoppy then caught Mark Walters in an off-the-ball incident. You can imagine how Villa's supporters reacted to that.

Even the goal that won the match was scrappy. Pat van den Hauwe's back pass got caught in a puddle and it enabled Peter Withe to round Tony Coton and roll the ball into an empty net.

Blakey thought he'd equalised after his header hit the post and seemed to cross the line before Villa were reduced to ten men when I raced free on goal only for Gibson to pull me down. Hoppy then nailed Dennis Mortimer and Steve McMahon did likewise to our captain Kevan Broadhurst. There were so many flashpoints, I struggle to recall them all. At the end of the game, there was a punch-up in the Villa dressing room as well when we chased their players down the tunnel. Somehow, the press never picked up on it.

What I do know is, we did not react particularly well to the defeat. In the next thirteen matches, we won only once and drew twice: a run that saw us drop from eighth in the league to nineteenth by January. This Birmingham team was a bit mad in every sense because after that six wins, four draws and a defeat heaved us back up to a more respectable thirteenth in the league.

We were looking quite safe in the build-up to the second Birmingham derby of the season – a return at St Andrew's – and in the week before the fixture, the level of intensity in training was astonishing. Villa had become the grudge match that everyone wanted to play in and, as a result, our squad kicked ten types of shite out of each other in an attempt to prove how much we wanted it.

Fortunately, we won this one and I scored the winner. What a feeling. All I remember is racing on to a long clearance from Byron Stevenson and smashing a shot under the goalkeeper before he could steady himself. It made the scoreline 2–1 and there wasn't long to go. I reacted by running over to the Main Stand and jumping on the metal fence in order to celebrate with the supporters.

I had scored at Everton earlier in the season and that was the only moment that could match the Villa goal for pure thrill. With other clubs, I looked forward to games at Goodison Park the most, more than even Anfield. There was too much baggage attached to Anfield – it was too emotional a place for me to perform to my very best levels. I never scored a goal in my career against Liverpool and, although maybe I wasn't good enough, I think there's another reason behind that. Maybe I couldn't even contemplate it.

Everton, though, were a different proposition. My record against them for Liverpool's reserves was decent. Most footballers will claim to be motivated for all games but for me, there was an extra significance – an extra motivation – to beat Everton.

Everton supporters booed me because I was a former Liverpool player. A section of the crowd made monkey noises. It certainly wasn't a majority, but it was a considerable, audible minority. I was desperate to beat them: to send the Evertonians home for a miserable Saturday night.

When the ball broke to me in front of the Gwladys Street end, I scuffed the resulting shot but somehow it deceived Neville Southall to give Birmingham the lead, going in off the post.

Most players didn't celebrate goals extravagantly in the 1980s but I enjoyed this one. I ran towards the corner near the Bullens Road and waited for my team-mates to join me, watching the disappointment drain across the faces of the Everton supporters. I could feel their hatred towards me. I was a Scouser, a Liverpool fan and a black footballer. They knew who I was: where I came from.

AFTER BEATING ASTON VILLA AT ST ANDREW'S, EIGHT GAMES OF the season remained. The victory put us twelfth in the league and the spirit was as good as it had ever been during my time at Birmingham. In those final eight games, however, we didn't win once. Four draws and four defeats sent us down, even though our goal difference was way superior to Coventry City and Stoke, who managed to find some form from nowhere and stay up.

In this period, we desperately missed Mick Harford. We'd played Coventry at Highfield Road and Mick came up against Sam Allardyce, the man who's now in charge of England.

As a footballer, Allardyce was a clogger. There were a few of them around: Tommy Smith at Liverpool; Graham Roberts at Spurs; Mick McCarthy at Manchester City; Derek Fazackerley at Blackburn; and, to a lesser extent, Mick Lyons at Everton.

As a centre-forward, you had to be ready for a fight. Reputations went a long way in football. I remember having a discussion with Colin Gibson, the Villa left-back, when we bumped into each other on a night out in Birmingham. He let his guard down over a few drinks and told me that he dreaded playing against me because he knew he'd have his hands full. From then on, I knew I was in control of him during games. It didn't provoke me to go soft on him, but harder. I was going to bully him worse than I had before. I didn't want to disappoint him. I suspect he thought that by being my friend after a few drinks, I'd be nicer to him as a result. No chance. In First Division football, it was survival of the fittest.

I couldn't shake hands with an opponent before a game. For me, it betrayed what we were trying to do. After, yes; before, absolutely not. Everyone tries to find a way to stage-manage a game. Other players had different approaches. They'd try and talk to you: to butter you up and make you lose an edge. You can be friends with opponents afterwards, for sure, but in the meantime you've got a job to do: a game to win. If you fall for the trick of someone else being nice, you've been conned. It happened to me at the beginning of my career in the reserves at Liverpool. 'You're a great player, Howard,' someone told me. I lost my edge because I listened. I went home having played shit and the other player was awarded man of the match.

Allardyce versus Harford was one of those occasions where no words were needed. These were the type of players who were defined by their actions rather than anything they said. Allardyce was an aggressive player but he did not have the same level of technical ability as Mick. When the pair collided in the air, Mick came off worst, busting his lip really badly. Robert Hopkins and I chased after Allardyce for the rest of the afternoon seeking retribution but the damage was done, even though we won that particular game and I scored the winner. Mick was out for two months and it ended up costing us dearly because we lost our target man and leading scorer at a crucial stage of the season.

Mick's absence contributed towards us slipping down the league table. I stood on the pitch at St Andrew's after the final home game, a 0–0 draw with Southampton, and wanted to cry.

We were relegated.

THE SEASON HAD ENDED IN GLOOM FOR BIRMINGHAM CITY, YET IT had been a good one for me on a personal note. I'd established myself as a First Division player and proved I could score goals at the highest level in a struggling side. Nine in 46 games wasn't bad considering I'd played on the wing as much as I did up front. A few of those had come in the final months of the season too, when Birmingham were without Mick Harford, the team was losing and the pressure was on to replace him. I think I'd proven that I'd turn up for a fight and that I wouldn't back down when the going got tough.

I was thinking about my summer holidays when Ron Saunders called me into his office and told me that I'd been selected for England. 'You're in the under-21s for the European Championship finals, Howard. You haven't quite made it yet,' he said.

The news came as a major surprise. Not once in my life had I seriously considered the possibility of playing international football. I was eligible for England, Sierra Leone and Ghana through my father and my mother.

My dad had floated the idea of playing for Sierra Leone but I didn't consider it the wisest thing to do. I'd barely made an impact at club level. At Liverpool, the staff discouraged Bruce Grobbelaar and Craig Johnston from playing for Zimbabwe and Australia because of the travel distances involved. They were concerned players would return from international duty with fatigue and it would result in them either not being able to play or a series of bad performances. The last thing Liverpool wanted to do was change the side.

I had such a big job getting into the Liverpool team, I thought Sierra Leone was a risk too far.

Club football had always mattered more to me anyway. So many footballers – particularly from my era – have claimed that playing for their country represented a pinnacle. For me, it didn't.

If I pulled on a Liverpool shirt with the *liver bird* on my chest, it made me very proud. If I pulled on an England shirt, which bore the three lions, it meant nothing.

There is a banner on the Kop that reads, 'We're not English, We're Scouse'. Many people in Liverpool do not consider themselves to be English at all. Liverpool is a city that looks out to the sea for inspiration rather than inland at the hills and beyond.

I certainly feel Scouse rather than English. But I feel African rather than necessarily Sierra Leonean or Ghanaian as well. I suppose I feel Scouse West African more than anything.

I've been to Sierra Leone a few times to connect with my father's roots and as soon as I've landed in Freetown, I've felt a long way from home. Sierra Leoneans can tell by the colour of my skin, the shape of my face and the sound of my voice that I am not really one of them. Yet my allegiance to West Africa is strong. My view is this: West Africa is a beautiful region that struggles because of Western influence.

I did not relate to the overbearing sense of nationalism that came with representing England. It did not appeal to me. I do not speak for every black player, as I know others who feel differently.

In the press, there was a negative attitude towards the fortunes of the country's national football team and it felt as though, sometimes, a story of failure was already written. It felt like the press wanted England to fail because the probability of that happening was greater and failure and scandal sells newspapers. The entire mood around the English national team, indeed, was wrong and certainly not progressive.

I did not feel the national set-up with England was inclusive, not at the time anyway. My perception of the Football Association was the same as of the government: run by a group of grey old self-serving fuddy-duddies.

I could not relate to the environment. The dressing room culture was built around 'fight for your country' types – as if everything foreign was the enemy. It certainly wasn't an attitude I subscribed to, and had I done so I don't think it would have made me play any better. If anything, getting so wound up about the opposition was to the detriment of a performance. I liked to focus on myself.

The mood on the terraces was another problem for me. I found it harder motivating myself for a set of supporters who one week might be shouting racist abuse at me at club level and the next week were supporting England. The moment something went wrong for England, black players were castigated by the crowd. As soon as you made a mistake, they were on to you.

The fans that follow England tend to come from small patriotic towns and smaller cities which have football clubs outside of the top flight. On England duty you see flags on the terraces from places like Kidderminster, Rotherham, Yeovil or Cirencester.

Many black players – and, indeed, top footballers – come from the inner cities: London, Liverpool, Manchester, Leeds, Bristol and Birmingham. The people who live in these areas tend to be proud of the place they live in rather than the country they represent. I know I was. Liverpool meant everything to me. I didn't even consider myself English.

So why should I be really proud representing England?

61 MINUTES IN MUNICH

*

RON SAUNDERS EXPLAINED TO ME THAT EVEN THOUGH I WAS nearly 26 years old, I was permitted to play at under-21 level as one of two overage players.

Ron told me that he'd spoken to Bobby Robson, who was in charge of the senior side, and that Robson had seen my progression at Birmingham and viewed me as a potential wildcard for the World Cup in Mexico in two years' time.

England had not qualified for the senior European Championships in France and there was a clamour for change. Robson wanted to have a look at everyone on the summer tour of South America, so I was placed on the stand-by list at senior level. It proved to be the tour where John Barnes scored one of England's greatest goals against Brazil in the Maracana Stadium before he was abused by his own supporters on the flight home.

In the meantime, I would play for the under-21s. The format for the under-21 tournament was different then to what it is now, with a knockout competition all the way to the final. With Dave Sexton in charge, England were scheduled to play a two-legged semi-final and a final (subject to progression) in the month of May 1984.

Before my selection, England had won five of their six group games and then thrashed France 7–1 on aggregate in the quarter-finals. I was called up for the semi-final first leg against Italy and the tie was played at Maine Road. Roberto Mancini started for Italy and we won 3–1.

I thought I'd done reasonably well on the night but I wasn't involved for the second leg in Florence. There, England protected a two-goal advantage and losing 1–0 was enough to progress to the final, where Spain were the opponents. The Spanish team included Andoni Zubizarreta, Emilio Butragueño and Míchel. The first leg was played in Seville and there was a big attendance at the Ramon Sanchez Pizjuan Stadium, where Sevilla play their home games.

I wasn't the only black player in the England team. Mark Chamberlain – father of Alex – and Danny Thomas from Tottenham Hotspur played in defence and midfield respectively. Danny Wallace and Brian Stein were also involved in the set-up.

It had been a strange day: very hot in the morning and early afternoon before the monsoon started. There was a chance the game might have been postponed or abandoned because the rain was relentless. It did not mask the noise from the terraces, though, with Spanish supporters serenading Mark, Danny and me with monkey sounds whenever we touched the ball. Mel Sterland, the Sheffield Wednesday right-back, scored the match-winning goal. When you beat a racist crowd with football, it's particularly satisfying. *The Guardian* described our performance as 'marvellously composed', and claimed that we were 'perfect ambassadors for the country'. I wonder whether the reporter at the match considered the level of provocation towards black players like me, whether it even registered with him that it was wrong. For some reason, despite it being clearly audible, there was no mention of it happening in the paper.

A week later, we finished the job off with a 2–0 second-leg victory at Sheffield United's Bramall Lane. Mark Hateley scored a stunning volley just after half-time, his sixth goal in the knockout stages, and two minutes later one of my shots slithered under Zubizarreta (who would later go on to achieve greatness at Barcelona).

Because of Spain's emergence as one of the best football nations in the world in terms of style, it is easy to forget that in the 1980s they were just as physical and often basic as England. Spain had a slightly more cynical football philosophy in those days and they did not go quietly: an elbow from Patxi Salinas left Mark Hateley with loose teeth and three stitches in his lip.

Mark and I combined really well. Like Mick Harford, he was a target man and very physical. Like me, he'd enjoyed a good season, at Portsmouth where he scored lots of goals. He would complete a fairy-tale summer by travelling with the senior squad on a tour of South America before joining AC Milan.

Mark Chamberlain and Nick Pickering had already made their full debuts, and eleven of the seventeen players involved in the final would ultimately graduate to the senior team. This, however, was no golden generation. Only three players reached ten caps: Hateley, the Norwich defender and future Everton captain Dave Watson, and Nottingham Forest's Steve Hodge. Those players are well remembered; others, such as Peter Hucker, Kevin Brock, Mich D'Avray and myself, less so.

Thirty-two years later, Dave Sexton's side from 1984 stands as the last England team at senior or under-21 level to win a trophy.

Does that fill me with pride? Not particularly.

I'm not even sure where the medal is.

SUNDERLAND, 1984

MODERN FOOTBALL TRANSFERS BEGIN WITH RUMOUR AND speculation because of the number of interested parties involved. You have the player. You have the player's representatives, of which there can be more than one. Then you have each club, for whom lots of people work. In the 1980s, the clubs held all the cards. The players acted as pawns. One day you could be at Birmingham. The next you'd be signing for Sunderland. You'd have no time to think about the potential consequences of the move: on whether the move was really right for you and the impact it would have on your life.

In the summer of 1984, I returned to Birmingham for pre-season training, excited about the future in spite of relegation. A nucleus of good players remained. We were young enough and talented enough to make things better again. We believed in our manager, Ron Saunders.

There was a friendly against Walsall at the training ground. 'Gaffer wants to see you,' came the message after the full-time whistle. I thought I was in trouble for something.

'Howard, Sunderland have made an offer for you and we've accepted that offer,' Ron told me. 'We think you should consider it.'

I wasn't happy with the gaffer at all. What a cunt, I thought. I've tried my bollocks off for you and you're shoving me out the door.

'All right then, yeah. See you later,' I responded. I didn't know what else to stay.

I was disappointed. I did not want to leave Birmingham. For the first time in my life, I felt a sense of place. I liked the city; I liked the people; I liked my teammates. I liked Solihull, where I lived. I liked the fact that Liverpool was only an hour away as well.

Sunderland's offer of £75,000, though, was acceptable and Ron made it clear that I was his most sellable asset, bearing in mind I was a European Championship winner with England Under-21s. It was a good time for Birmingham to let me go; at least they would make back the money they had spent on me.

The board at Birmingham were a conservative bunch – as boards at most clubs tended to be in the 1980s. The season before, Ron had asked them for money to buy a player to help with our fight against relegation after Mick Harford got injured. 'Will that stop us going down?' they asked. 'Well, I can't make a statement of that value,' Ron told them. So he didn't get the money. The board weren't really prepared to take gambles.

The financial implications of relegation to the Second Division weren't as grave as they are now. Clubs relied on gate receipts rather than funding from television rights or shirt sponsorship. If you were a big club with a sizable following, you'd be OK providing finances were managed carefully. Birmingham was a big club with a reasonable following – a club that has never realised its potential because the natural instinct was to sell someone as soon as they were doing well and there was interest from other clubs. It had happened with Bob Latchford and Trevor Francis in the years before.

The day we went down, I remember the fans singing, 'We'll be back in eighty-five'. I was desperate to try and help move it back into the top flight. Relegation was embarrassing and I viewed it as a stain on my career that I wanted to help put right.

I did not get that chance

Len Ashurst was Sunderland's manager. I liked him; he was from Liverpool and we spoke the same language. I received a call from Ron asking me about developments. 'I'm sad you want me to go, gaffer,' I told him.

He explained that he'd gone to the board asking for money to help strengthen the team again. Their response had not been positive. The only way that was going to happen was if he offloaded a few of the players the club had. He explained that I was the first player any other club had showed a firm interest in.

Subsequently, Noel Blake got sold to Portsmouth, Robert Hopkins went to Manchester City, Mick Harford to Luton Town and Tony Coton to Watford. All of these players went on to enjoy good careers. There was a nucleus at Birmingham that was good enough to form a core of quality players over a number of years. Unfortunately, nobody seemed to realise it.

The lads at Birmingham have other theories about the break-up of a promising team. Some believe that Ron knew the writing was on the wall for him as soon as relegation was confirmed. They say he did not want to leave the club with a potentially good squad of players like he had at Aston Villa before they won the European Cup in 1982 in his absence. He was canny like that, Ron. But I guess it seems a bit far-fetched. He lasted in the job until 1986, when he crossed the Midlands again to take charge of West Bromwich Albion.

He was the manager I liked working under most.

*

I WASN'T OVERLY KEEN ON MOVING BACK TO THE NORTHEAST. There was no black community up there. There were hardly any minority groups, only a few black players. Since I had played for Newcastle on loan the reputation for racist chanting at St James' Park had got worse. It concerned me that it might be the same at Sunderland.

I'd played against Sunderland for Birmingham and Roker Park was an intimidating place to play. I was so used to racist abuse from the terraces by then – it was part of the routine – that I was usually able to block it out. I went to all stadiums expecting to be racially abused. I couldn't tell you which ones were racist and which ones were not. For the most part, it had become white noise – in more ways than one – to me: an undesirable feature of my working environment.

Sunderland as a place, like Liverpool, was in decline. Margaret Thatcher had destroyed the docks and the shipbuilding industries. She was in the process of taking the mines too. County Durham was really struggling. The fortune of the town's football team was paramount to the happiness of the people. I knew that already through my short experience at Newcastle.

Uncertainty seemed to be everywhere. The unemployment rates were sky-high. Even Len Ashurst was on a short-term contract. After a long playing career with Sunderland, he'd entered management with Hartlepool, moving to Gillingham, Sheffield Wednesday, Newport County and Cardiff City. He explained to me that Sunderland's board had appointed him as a short-term solution after the sacking of Alan Durban but if he did well, the job was his.

It was comforting to me that the same summer I moved there, Len signed another black player in Gary Bennett from Cardiff City. Benno was a Manchester lad who got released by Manchester City before moving to Wales, linking up with his brother Dave and proving himself as a top centre-half. I had played against him in my days with Liverpool's reserves and appreciated just how competitive he was.

At the beginning of our times at Sunderland, Benno and I were the only black players in the dressing room. I knew whom to head towards first. Benno became a great friend – one of my closest in football.

Although fundamentally we wanted the same things, Benno and I had opposite personalities and I think that helped. He was a tiger on the pitch but one of the most laid-back people I've ever met off it. Whereas I'd fight problems, he was a bit more considered and maybe cleverer with words, perhaps less abrasive.

There were occasions when we backed each other up. Over a number of years, Benno had an on-going feud with David Speedie, the Chelsea striker who later played for Liverpool. It started after a League Cup semi-final at Roker Park. Benno and I weren't even playing because of injury, but after the game we were having a drink in the players' lounge when Speedie's father came over and started mouthing off, saying what his son was going to do to us in the second leg. Benno told him where to go in no uncertain terms and then things got ugly. I wanted to chin both Speedie and his father but Benno held me back from doing some serious damage.

On another occasion earlier in the season, Chelsea were involved again when Benno prevented me from diving into the crowd to confront someone who threw a banana at me. I'd learned to ignore the chants by then but I could not brush this off. Benno held me back. He could see my blood was boiling.

The atmosphere at Stamford Bridge was consistently bad whenever I played there. The National Front had infiltrated the terraces. Paul Canoville was Chelsea's lone black player and the level of abuse towards him was horrific. 'Trigger, trigger, shoot that nigger,' they used to sing.

'How do you play here, la?' I asked him during a break in one game.

'I don't know, mate,' he said. 'I really don't know.'

When I saw Canoville fighting a lonely furrow against the racists, it made me appreciate Benno even more. We were kindred spirits. While black players had become increasingly common at clubs in the south, they were almost unheard of in the less racially diverse north.

Benno and I both saw ourselves as pioneers. We wanted to try and change attitudes at Sunderland. Neither of us were willing to accept racism, in any form. Some black players of our generation tried to ignore it, get their heads down and carry on. I wasn't like that. I challenged it, whether it came from a manager or a team-mate. If something racist was said, I picked up on it and would ask them to stop.

With Benno by my side at Sunderland, I had someone to back me up.

ONE OF THE MAIN REASONS I SIGNED FOR SUNDERLAND WAS because Len Ashurst promised I could play up front. At Birmingham I'd been on the wing a lot and, although I'd done quite well there, I felt that I was at my best when I played through the middle.

There was a tendency for black players to be used on the flanks where our pace and power could be an asset. Aside from Remi Moses at Manchester United and Clyde Best at West Ham a little earlier, hardly any played in the key positions: central midfield and centre-forward. I am sure managers would argue that skill sets dictated selection policies but was there a level of distrust? Did they not believe black players possessed the responsibility to perform in a key position, especially in midfield, where you have to be really disciplined? Only the managers and coaches can answer those questions.

At Sunderland, Len kept to his promise initially but as the season progressed and injuries contributed towards the form of the team dipping, I found myself shunted wide again.

Exciting progress had been made in the League Cup. We knocked out Crystal Palace over two legs, then, against Nottingham Forest, I scored arguably the best goal of my career, dribbling past three or four players, cutting in from the left and releasing a beautiful curling shot. I felt great that night. The Sunderland crowd sang my name.

Having beaten Tottenham in a replay, we all felt we had something to look forward to. The town was buzzing because of the cup run and a mid-table position in the league wasn't too bad.

It was at this moment Len's future began to unravel. I liked Len. He'd been good to me: very honest, very reasonable. But after beating Spurs at White Hart Lane, his personality changed completely. Towards everyone.

At the start of the season, his future was uncertain. He knew he needed to win games to earn a long-term deal. The progress made in the League Cup convinced the board that he was the man to lead Sunderland forward, so they gave him a secure contract the day after victory over Spurs.

We were playing Leicester the following weekend at Roker Park. Len, for a reason known only to him, walked into the changing rooms before the game and pinned the team sheet to the wall. 'There it is. Anyone has a problem, come and see me in my office on Monday morning.' Then he walked out.

Everyone present was gobsmacked. There was a silence. He had dropped Gordon Chisholm, and Gordon had scored the winner against Spurs on the Wednesday. It was a baffling decision. Gary Lineker was playing for Leicester and he was quick. Gordon wasn't the fastest and initially I thought it was a tactical move. Yet Gordon's partner in defence was Shaun Elliott and he compensated for Gordon's lack of pace. It just didn't make sense.

The mood among the players dropped. We felt like we'd all helped Len get the job in the first place. Now he had his security, he seemed to act as though he could do as he pleased. Before, he'd held team meetings where he encouraged open debate, but they stopped suddenly after signing his new contract.

The immediate consequence was a 4–0 defeat, with Lineker and Alan Smith scoring two each. It was a thumping of the worst kind. Had Leicester beaten us by eight, it wouldn't have been unfair.

The defeat left us thirteenth in the league table. Len never recovered from his mistake. A five-match losing streak saw us drop to eighteenth and in the first week of January we exited the FA Cup in the third round, losing to Lawrie McMenemy's Southampton (more about McMenemy shortly).

After knocking out Watford and then Chelsea over two legs in the League Cup semi, the final was reached. During that time, however, three league wins in five months saw us slip towards the relegation zone.

Len had seemed to be a good man. But as soon as he gained control – thanks in no small part to our efforts – he turned into the big bad wolf. In one swoop he lost the dressing room because players lost respect for him and the decisions he was making. Many felt betrayed and the confidence of the players slumped. If he could drop Gordon just like that, who was next? He'd been on to a winner at Sunderland before because he was approachable and open to debate – even criticism. The ink was barely dry on his new contract and, wham! He changed.

It was a miracle we found a way to get past Watford and then Chelsea to meet Norwich at Wembley in the League Cup final. Ironically, we were scheduled to face Norwich in the league the weekend before the final. I'd been injured and returned to the match-day squad. After being introduced for Ian Wallace, I set up David Hodgson to score our third goal in a 3–1 victory at Carrow Road.

Through the season, I'd delivered in big games. I was convinced Len would pick me for the final ahead of Ian Wallace, who was struggling for form.

Yet by then Len was drowning. Problem after problem. Strange decision after strange decision. Colin West had scored three goals against Chelsea over two legs in the semi-final but he decided to drop him altogether for the final after a blazing row had led to the pair of them squaring up in the changing room.

If anything, Westy should have been on the bench instead of me because of his efforts in the semi against Chelsea; but Len, seemingly, held a grudge against him. In the end, he decided to go with Wallace up front.

The attendance at Wembley was huge: of the 100,000 people, there must have been at least 60,000 from Sunderland. The fans turned up but unfortunately the team representing them did not.

Gordon Chisholm scored an own goal and Clive Walker missed a penalty. Len sent me on for David Corner but we played really badly against a side we'd beaten easily only a week before, a side that, like us, was battling relegation. Ultimately, we didn't do enough to win the cup and Norwich deserved their victory.

We weren't able to recover from the disappointment.

Relegation was soon confirmed: my second in as many seasons.

LEN ASHURST WAS SACKED AND WITH LAWRIE MCMENEMY'S appointment, Sunderland became national news.

McMenemy was considered a spectacular coup for the club. He had chosen to leave Southampton on 1 June 1985 after steering them to fifth position in the First Division. At the Dell he had won the FA Cup in 1976 and had built a reputation for himself as the next bright hope of British coaching, following icons like Brian Clough and Bobby Robson.

McMenemy had bought illustrious players like Alan Ball and Kevin Keegan to Southampton and they had become the second favourite side of many people because of their smooth style and, indeed, their improbable success.

Press reports told that McMenemy – who was from the Northeast and a former Coldstream guardsman – had become the highest-paid manager in English football by moving to Sunderland. There was speculation over his annual salary, with the figures suggested ranging between £175,000 a year and £300,000. His arrival at Roker Park was viewed as a tremendous accomplishment by the club considering it had just been relegated. Thousands of Sunderland supporters waited outside Roker Park to welcome him at the introductory press conference.

Accounting for what McMenemy had achieved at Southampton, it seemed to many that he was the man Sunderland had been waiting for – not only the man to take the club back into the First Division, but to even be competing with Liverpool within two or three years.

If he could get a smaller club like Southampton into Europe the possibilities with a bigger club like Sunderland appeared endless. The fans were happy and it was nice to see the town buzzing again.

It was tempting to join in and get carried away with it all. Yet I wasn't convinced by McMenemy. I'd encountered him before and my experiences had not been positive.

On my competitive debut for Sunderland, we beat Southampton 3–1 at Roker Park. It was the opening day of the 1984/85 season and it proved to be one of few high points in the campaign. The game had a lot of needle because of the characters involved. Southampton had Mark Dennis, or Damien as he was known from my Birmingham days, as well as Reuben Agboola and Joe Jordan. Sunderland had Gary Bennett, Gordon Chisholm and myself.

We blew Southampton away in the opening few minutes with goals from Benno and Barry Venison. All through the game, McMenemy was there on the touchline trying to gain little advantages by winding up our players with his comments. So when Mark Proctor scored our third to confirm the win, I celebrated by running past the dugouts and sliding on my knees. I really wanted to rub it in. McMenemy had been complaining to the referee all the way through the match and having a go at some of our lads, trying to wind them up. His reaction to my celebration was furious and I ended up telling him – dismissively, I guess – to pipe down: 'Shut your trap.'

The impressions we had of each other only got worse. I felt like McMenemy treated me badly from day one.

Before his arrival, I'd been carrying a knee injury following another late tackle by my old foe at Aston Villa, Steve McMahon. It ruled me out of Sunderland's last two games and an arthroscopy proved unsuccessful because it did not get to the root of the problem. I carried the injury with me over the summer, hoping it might go away naturally, and in the meantime McMenemy was appointed at Roker Park.

A few days before the start of pre-season training, I got out of bed at night and my leg locked. I couldn't move. I had the phone number for the specialist in Durham and he told me to see him straight away the following morning. He had a look at it and could see that the condition had deteriorated and my cartilage was torn. We decided there and then to operate and get rid of the problem. I realised it would rule me out for four to six weeks but it was necessary.

News reached McMenemy. I hadn't even met him. He called me and his first words were something like: 'Who do you think you are diagnosing an injury and making a decision about an operation without consulting me?'

I told him that the problem had lingered for a few months without being solved and that I didn't think it was sensible to delay the process, just so he could have a look at it. Besides, I didn't diagnose the injury – the specialist did.

I finished the conversation believing the only reason he wanted to have his say was because he wanted to sell me. Now that I'd had an operation, other clubs might know about it and look even more closely at it during a medical. Equally, he couldn't sell an injured player, could he? Especially over the summer months when he was attempting to reshape the team.

Upon my return to training, there was no recovery plan. It was like I didn't exist. Initially, McMenemy made me run, run and run some more. I told him that I thought it was dangerous considering the nature of the injury. For that, he made me train with the reserves. We were at loggerheads from then on.

During pre-season training, I can remember him doing his own running session around the perimeter of the training ground pitches. He looked like Steve Zodiac out of Fireball XL5, as if strings were pulling him along. He was really struggling. Me, David Hodgson, Eric Gates and Benno could see him from the raised viewing platform on the clubhouse and we were pissing ourselves. We started shouting stuff at him. It was only light stick.

He came charging off the pitch looking to find the identity of the culprits. 'Who was that?' he boomed. As soon as he said it, we knew he didn't have the answer, and nobody was going to grass. Everyone was trying to keep a straight face. He was fuming. It looked like his head was about to explode. Hodgey couldn't contain himself and started laughing. McMenemy completely lost it with him.

It said to me that McMenemy thought very highly of himself. He was top dog at Southampton. It was natural for him to think that he could do at Sunderland what he had at the Dell: to become an all-controlling power. Any manager has to earn that right, though. Any manager has to convince his players that he knows his onions.

Because of his appointment, Sunderland were made favourites by the bookmakers for an immediate promotion. Yet I knew he'd never played the game beyond non-league level. He was spoken about as a genius because of his achievements at Southampton but I thought back to Liverpool and the people in charge there: how brilliant they were compared to him; how humble, indeed, they were compared to him. I'd had problems with Bob Paisley but that didn't mean I couldn't recognise his brilliant football eye.

McMenemy thought he was the dog's bollocks and was very dismissive of the Sunderland players that had been there before his arrival. By signing so many new players for Sunderland during his first couple of months in charge, he clearly felt a revolution was needed to turn things around.

Six newcomers – Eric Gates, George Burley, Dave Swindlehurst, Frank Gray, Bob Bolder and Alan Kennedy – came in, all of them with a lot of experience behind them. It is always a gamble signing so many at once because if they don't all click pretty quickly, you find yourself struggling for results. Their presence fragmented the dressing room, driving a wedge right through it. Maybe his tactic was based around dividing and conquering. It certainly didn't work.

At Southampton, perhaps he'd surrounded himself with experience to mask his own inadequacies. These were players he did not have to coach. When he did the same thing at Sunderland, the approach failed.

I felt that McMenemy was contemptuous towards the players that had been there before. 'Look at these new lads,' was the message. 'They'll show you all what to do.' It was disrespectful to speak like that.

McMenemy gave his son a job and appointed Lew Chatterley as his assistant. Chatterley in my opinion was a yes man, who brought nothing to the atmosphere of the club. The lads worked McMenemy out quickly and eventually the players he brought in turned on him too.

What followed was beyond belief. First of all, we lost each of McMenemy's first five games in charge without scoring a single goal. There would have been a sixth defeat had it not been for two late Dave Swindlehurst goals at Grimsby to give us a point.

The team was absolutely abject and it never, ever got any better. Victories were lucky and scrappy; defeats were regular and deserved. Roker Park became a home for aged footballers, well past their best, and visiting clubs loved taking our scalp because we were title favourites in the old Second Division.

There are so many stories that reflect what I consider McMenemy's incompetence as well as the mood he created.

David Hodgson had been with Liverpool at the same time as me and had similar problems with McMenemy. After being dropped for one game, McMenemy called him into his office and said that the decision was made because he'd been spotted drinking after games. Hodgey denied this but McMenemy said it was pointless arguing because his car had been spotted in the car park of the Pear Tree in Felling every afternoon for weeks. 'Yeah, that's right,' Hodgey explained. 'It's because my parents are running the pub and I am living with them!'

Training sessions were repetitive and boring, stop-start, with McMenemy blowing his whistle every couple of minutes. We practised set-piece routines for hours; one week, McMenemy had Frank Gray taking free kicks on both sides of the pitch. When half-time came on the Saturday, and with Sunderland losing, McMenemy stormed into the dressing room, berating Frank for not taking a single set-piece. Alan Kennedy had been on them instead. Frank sat there calmly and, after the tirade was over, he said, 'Yeah, well you shouldn't have left me on the bench for the game, you stupid twat!'

McMenemy liked to practise kick-offs religiously. He wanted to get the opposition on the back foot immediately. The lads were lined up on the pitch like they would be at the start of a game. Eric Gates kicked off and the ball was laid back to Gary Bennett. Benno turned round to kick it back to our goalkeeper, Iain Hesford, but Iain was behind the goal still putting his gloves on and the ball rolled in the net.

So there we were, playing against no one, 1–0 down after ten seconds.

*

IN 1986, AT THE END OF LAWRIE MCMENEMY'S FIRST SEASON IN charge, Sunderland were on the verge of a second successive relegation. The air had shifted from the absolute high of appointing of someone who was considered the most sought-after manager in English football to the depths of despair when it became obvious that he simply wasn't up to the task of taking the club forward.

We'd been on a nine-game winless run and were staring into the abyss. McMenemy's solution in the middle of that was to play Scarborough in a friendly, to rack up a few goals and get some confidence back. Fair enough. The lads decided to use the trip as a bonding exercise so it ended up as a booze-fest by the sea with quite a bit of shagging. We struggled to a 2–1 win but at least we gained something in spirit by the night out afterwards.

Very few of us liked McMenemy but we certainly didn't want to be the group that consigned Sunderland to a second successive relegation. We were nineteenth in the Second Division. The atmosphere needed to be lifted for us to get out of danger but when he found out about the boozing and the shagging, he wasn't happy at all.

We were running out of games. It was April and we hadn't won in the league since January.

After beating Fulham 4–2 and gaining a valuable 0–0 draw at Norwich, we travelled to London and stayed in a hotel near Epping Forest. A rugby league team were there and Huddersfield Town came in for their breakfast too. Huddersfield's winger, Terry Curran, had played under McMenemy at Southampton and I remember him verbally abusing McMenemy from across the car park in front of everyone, calling him every bad name under the sun.

Yeah, that's the McMenemy I know too, I thought.

After the Scarborough trip, two decent results and with morale lifting among the players in the squad, there was surely no way McMenemy was going to change the team. But at Plough Lane – against Wimbledon – that's exactly what he did.

I'd taken my clothes off and was ready to get changed into my kit when

McMenemy came over to me. 'What do you think you're doing?' he asked.

'I'm putting my gear on,' I said.

'Not in that number you're not – you're sub.'

This was done in front of the team. Everyone could hear.

I was close to telling him to stuff it – that I wasn't playing for him any more. Instead, I simmered on the bench while we lost 3–0. Wimbledon smashed us all over the place. We were bullied. It was just the sort of game I would have enjoyed playing in as well.

I was fuming all the way home. It was a long bus journey.

*

IN THE LAST GAME OF THE 1985/86 SEASON SUNDERLAND NEEDED to beat Stoke to guarantee survival. It had been a dreadful campaign and I wasn't proud of some of my performances, nor the team's results. The players had to take some responsibility, of course, but it is the manager who sets the mood for the working environment.

McMenemy had tried to change things too quickly and had been too brazen with it. His character rubbed people up the wrong way. On a personal level, I only wanted to play well to prove him wrong and maybe do enough to impress another club to take me away. I loved playing for Sunderland and I related to the supporters. But McMenemy had made the experience joyless.

Fortunately, Stoke were beaten so we avoided relegation, although the game was not without its flashpoints. When McMenemy substituted me with twenty minutes to go, I was so frustrated that I threw my shirt at him, walked down the tunnel and sat alone in the changing room.

'It looks like Howard Gayle's time at Sunderland is over,' a radio commentator said.

He was right. My contract was up the following week and I'd figured this was McMenemy's way of having the final say, reminding me that he was the one in control.

My time at Sunderland was over. McMenemy requested that the squad meet on Monday morning for a debriefing. The contracts of a number of players, including me, were at an end and he was going to tell us whether we were getting kept on.

I didn't bother waiting around. I went into the kit room with a bin bag and lashed my boots in there. David Hodgson did the same. We both knew too much. Our education at Liverpool had taught us a lot about the game. Both of us had McMenemy sussed out. McMenemy's son Chris was on the staff and after seeing us do this, he went upstairs and told his dad.

The rest of the squad were sitting in the changing room. I passed McMenemy on my way out the door. The conversation went something a little like this:

'Where are you going?' he asked.

'Well, you're not going to give me a new deal are you?'

'What if I did?'

'Well, I won't be signing it.'

When I reached the exit he stopped me again. 'You're right,' he said. 'And you as well, Hodgson.'

SUNDERLAND SUPPORTERS VIEW THE MID-1980s AS ONE OF THE worst periods in the club's history. Not many have a good word to say about Lawrie McMenemy. They were difficult times for the town. They were difficult times for the football club. There wasn't much to be positive about.

A second relegation in as many years wasn't something I was proud of after the Birmingham experience. I was a part of the team that started the rut, which became deeper with McMenemy's appointment.

Yet when I go back to Sunderland, the reception I get is positive. People remember me for my goal against Nottingham Forest. They remember me too because I never hid during the tough times. I'd have a go and try to make it better. If we lost a game, I always took time to salute the supporters because I knew the sacrifices that came with following a team long distances. I'd been there on the terraces myself with Liverpool.

The year after my departure, it did not get any better at Sunderland. In fact, it got a whole lot worse. Relegation to the Third Division was a month away when McMenemy finally left the club.

DALLAS, 1984

SECONDS TURNED INTO MINUTES. MINUTES TURNED INTO HOURS. Hours turned into days. Days turned into weeks. Weeks turned into months. I waited for the telephone to ring. I'd returned to Liverpool for the summer knowing I would not be going back to Sunderland. I needed a new club for the 1986/87 season.

I began to write to managers, offering my services. In the summer of 1986, I must have written forty letters. Feedback was slow. So I made a list of the clubs across the top three divisions, looked in the Rothmans Football Yearbook for numbers that might help, and started cold-calling training grounds. I'd get up at eight in the morning and start dialling around half an hour later, just as managers were turning up to begin their working day, when all was quiet.

I'd introduce myself and tell them I was available. Some of them would tell you straight up that they were well stocked for players. Others would promise to get back to you only not to bother. In some instances, it was players who you'd played with that had become managers that let you down.

Ideally, I wanted to play at as high a level as possible with a club in the northwest of England and be closer to Liverpool than I had been at Birmingham or Sunderland. I was reluctant to contact some clubs, however, based on my experiences of racism at places like Burnley and Blackburn, even though the towns were close enough to Liverpool.

Silence.

Some footballers would have found this process humiliating. I know quite a few players who were in the same boat as me. They'd been released by clubs but didn't have the confidence to advertise themselves. I didn't take anything for granted. Experience had taught me that just because you've played for Liverpool, just because you're European Championship winner with England's Under-21s, just because you've scored goals at First Division level, it doesn't mean clubs are going to be battering down the door to sign you.

I had more money but it was like being seventeen again: uncertain of the future and feeling unwanted.

I had some investments in shares, pensions and bonds. A financial adviser had helped me save my money. During a conversation with him, he suggested trying to find a club in America. Feelers were put out and from there, Dallas Sidekicks got in touch. The idea didn't really appeal to me. I wanted to play in England. It worried me that once you've played for a smaller club outside the UK it is more difficult to get back in.

There didn't seem to be many opportunities in the UK though. I did an interview with the News of the World where I told the reporter about the problems I'd encountered at Sunderland under Lawrie McMenemy. This was back when the *News of the World* was still read on Merseyside, before its sister paper, *The Sun*, printed vile lies about the role of Liverpool supporters in the Hillsborough disaster.

I'd played for five clubs by the time I left Sunderland. At each I'd experienced problems. I realised that part of the challenge in finding a new club was convincing people I wasn't as difficult to work with as some claimed. I'd gained a reputation as a black militant; someone who wouldn't back down to bullies, even if they happened to be in authority positions. I realise too that football is a small world and everyone speaks, trading secrets and opinions. Stories travel fast and it was no secret among the community that McMenemy and I did not get on. Maybe it put other managers off signing me.

The offer in the States was good money: double the wages I was on in England. The whole package was £62,000 for a year, including accommodation. It wasn't to be sniffed at.

I couldn't turn it down. I wasn't in a position to be fussy.

*

FORGET NEW YORK CITY OR LOS ANGELES, IN THE 1980s DALLAS was the place in America everyone wanted to be.

I was a big fan of the *Dallas* television series, which revolved around the wealthy and feuding Texan family, the Ewings. I loved the start of the show: the camera swooping in on an eight-lane freeway. There was scorched earth and high-rise buildings in the distance surrounded by blue sky. Then the theme music kicked in.

I'll never forget the heat as I stepped off the plane. It was dry and enough to singe skin. I'd spent the previous two years playing football at Roker Park, a few blocks away from the North Sea. I knew straight away that Dallas was going to be a very different experience.

Dallas Sidekicks competed in the Major Indoor Soccer League (MISL). The league included clubs with other interesting names. There was Baltimore Blast, Chicago Sting, Cleveland Force, Kansas City Comets, Los Angeles Lazers, Minnesota Strikers, New York Express, San Diego Sockers, St Louis Steamers, Tacoma Stars and Wichita Wings.

We travelled all over the country. The North American Soccer League (NASL), which featured outdoor teams, had collapsed. Critics had claimed Americans did not like 45-minute halves and that shorter fifteen-minute quarters of four would hold a greater appeal. Each club had two teams – one on the court and another off it – so mass rotations took place.

I wasn't really prepared for just how different the football was. Games were played on hard indoor pitches. If you fell on the floor, you were in danger of serious injury; friction burns were commonplace. The game was physical and fast. You were allowed to shoulder-barge opponents into the walls of the pitch. There were lots of fights and regular sin-binning.

The indoor league had a strange format. Each club had two teams and games were played for an hour, consisting of four quarters. The court was split up into three thirds and each team had to keep a striker in the last third; if they came out of it, you'd concede a penalty. The rules were a cross between football (or soccer), ice hockey and basketball. During power plays, one of the teams would be reduced from six players to five. The team with the spare man would have an opportunity during these two-minute periods to try and score, taking an advantage. Each time the ball went out play, the clock would stop.

My position on the pitch was what the Americans called 'point', which in

English terms is centre-forward. Dallas's star player was a Brazilian called Tatu, who also played as 'point'. His style was a bit like Kenny Dalglish's: he was strong with his back to goal and quick at turning and shooting in one movement.

Having done well with Tampa Bay Rowdies in the NASL, Tatu moved into indoor football with Dallas before I joined and became a league legend for his goal celebrations. Each time, he'd throw his shirt into the crowd, home or away. It became a gimmick. There were some high scores and when I was there it was common for him to go through five or six shirts per match.

I could understand why the club liked his behaviour because it was promoting Dallas and promoting the league at the same time. Television stations would feature Tatu as a news story. His presence was good for the development of the game but it wasn't good for me because he was hogging the playing time. During hour-long games, sometimes I'd only get to play nine minutes. Tatu was usually preferred.

There were a few people I knew over there. Vic Moreland was a Northern Ireland international who was at Dallas with me. Keith Weller, a Leicester City legend, was the assistant manager. Arsenal's Chris Whyte was on loan at New York Express, while Stan Cummins, my former team-mate at Sunderland, played for Minnesota Strikers. All of us had the same idea, I think: a new experience in the sun and get paid a lot of money for it.

America was an eye-opener for me. In some ways, the football was ahead of its time. Pre-match warm-ups did not exist in England. Over in the States, it was compulsory. Routines were synchronised where you'd skip and clap above your head at the same time. It looked daft but it made sense in terms of injury prevention, ensuring you did not pull a muscle needlessly.

Texas is a wealthy state and Dallas stunk of money. Oil was all over the place. The clubs and bars were heaving, a world apart from Liverpool and elsewhere in England in terms of size, noise and intensity. I'd never experienced a superclub before. These were on a different scale.

I lived in an apartment in a suburb called Valley Ranch, which was a gated community close to the Dallas Cowboys training ground and near Fort Worth airport. The complex had a communal pool, which I used every day to escape the heat.

I wasn't used to being so far away from home. I'd look out of my apartment window in the quiet times and count the airplanes flying in and flying out. Fort Worth was a hub airport and relentless, one coming in every thirty seconds. I wondered where they were coming from and where they were heading. It made me feel homesick.

The schedule was ridiculous. Frequently, we played back-to-back games: one in Dallas on the Friday night, another in New York on the Saturday with a four-hour flight in between. It was all built around razzmatazz: being introduced to the crowd over a public address system accompanied by impressive statistics detailing your contribution towards the team. There was music and cheerleaders going on all the time.

The thing that made me miss home the most, though, was the fact I wasn't getting as much playing time as I'd have liked. Tatu was the main man. He'd been there a couple of years and everyone loved him. My position was the same as his. The travelling wouldn't have been so bad if I'd been playing the majority of games. But when you fly the width of an entire country – coast-to-coast – for six minutes of football, it becomes demoralising after a while. I felt like I wasn't contributing anything.

Keith Weller took a radio with him to away games and would tune in to the BBC World Service. The British lads would sit around the radio in the airport waiting to board a flight. The pangs for home became greater when I heard Watford beat Arsenal 3–1 in an FA Cup quarter-final at Highbury. It made me miss English football and it made me think about my own role in Dallas.

I went to see Gordon Jago, who was our coach. He was from London and had managed Queens Park Rangers and Millwall in the 1970s before returning to the US, where he'd previously taken charge of the national team.

I asked Gordon whether it would be possible to return home to the UK to see if I could find a club before the closure of the transfer window at the end of March, which was only a couple of weeks away.

I liked Gordon a lot. He was a lovely person: very intelligent, very caring, very sympathetic. 'I understand how it is, Howard,' he said. 'Do whatever you have to do.'

I flew to Heathrow, unsure again where my future would be.

61 MINUTES IN MUNICH

*

DURING MY TIME AT SUNDERLAND, LAWRIE MCMENEMY HAD TRIED to sell me to Stoke City. Mick Mills was the manager there and Mick had played under Lawrie previously at Southampton. I refused to move in spite of McMenemy. I wanted to leave on my own terms, not have him force me out.

Two years later, in the 1986/87 season Stoke had an outside chance of reaching the newly introduced promotion play-offs in the Second Division. I was desperate for a club and Mick was still keen on me. He wanted to improve his attacking options in the final month and a half of the season. I was available and willing to sign a short-term contract at a club that had shown some interest in the past, one that might be able to offer some long-term solutions.

Had I stuck it out in America, I would have won a league winners' medal. A few months later, Dallas Sidekicks beat Tacoma in the grand final series, after which Tatu was voted as the competition's most valuable player. By walking out on Dallas Sidekicks I was leaving a big contract behind as well.

What followed was two goals in six games and an eighth-place finish; we missed out on the play-offs by six points. I liked it at Stoke. Lee Dixon and Steve Bould, who later became fixtures in Arsenal's infamous back four, were there. I'd played with Mark Chamberlain in the England Under-21 side. Tony Kelly had been an apprentice at Liverpool and he'd cleaned my boots. When he later moved to Bolton Wanderers, supporters labelled him 'Zico' because of his ability on the ball. He was a really special player but struggled to keep his weight down, which maybe explained why he was not signed by one of the biggest clubs. Otherwise, he had the talent.

It was difficult for me at Stoke because the training at Dallas had been based on speed rather than stamina. Because players were brought on and off the pitch at regular intervals, fitness was based around achieving sharpness rather than endurance. Going back to the outdoor game on much heavier pitches, I struggled. I don't think Stoke appreciated where I had been and, as a result, they didn't see the real me.

There was a lack of medical knowledge at all the clubs I'd played for and Stoke was no different. I'm pretty certain Mick and the coaches at Stoke thought my legs had gone. I looked fit and healthy so they thought I should have been ready to play football matches.

Quite simply, my body just wasn't ready for the rigours of the English Second Division having played in the heat and on hard ground for the previous six months in the States. I was able to make an impact from the bench, but starting games was a different matter.

I left Stoke, returning to my position of a year earlier where I was ringing around clubs asking for trials. Again, demoralising for some, but it was something I couldn't afford to think about.

I spoke to Graeme Souness, my old team-mate and ally at Liverpool. No luck. Graeme had been appointed as player-manager of Glasgow Rangers. He told me he was looking to sign Mark Walters from Aston Villa, who played in my position. Soon, Walters became Rangers' first black player.

One morning, I was reading the *Daily Mirror* and there was a story about Blackburn Rovers offering a trial to a player, whose name I can't remember.

This is a club recruiting players, I thought.

But it was Blackburn, one of the clubs I'd been reluctant to sign for the summer before because of the problems with racism on the terraces and the presence of the National Front in the town.

What should I do?

I appreciated I wasn't in a position to be so picky. Beggars can't be choosers. There was nothing to be lost by ringing Don Mackay, Blackburn's manager. He'd probably tell there were no opportunities at the club anyway.

So I called him.

DON OFFERED ME A ONE-YEAR CONTRACT AT BLACKBURN AFTER A two-week trial where I'd got my head down and proved my fitness. Tony Parkes was one of the coaches and I got the impression he didn't really like me. I didn't particularly like him, but it wasn't time to start wars with people I barely knew.

I was fortunate that Don believed in me. He was born in Glasgow and had been a goalkeeper in his playing days. Like me, Don's career had taken him to Dallas in the 1960s, so straight away we had common ground.

Don brought in other players that maybe had lost their way. He didn't have lots of money, so he had to be creative in the transfer market. My contract was £300 a week: the lowest of my career. But it was an opportunity to try and earn promotion back into the First Division with a club that wanted me. So I was happy enough.

Scott Sellars had already joined Blackburn from Leeds by the time I arrived, while Simon Garner – who became my partner in crime up front – was already well on his way to becoming the club's all-time top scorer. I know Liverpool had looked at the possibility of taking both players to Anfield, where I have no doubt they would have proven a success. Scott was a really classy player, while Garns would have scored goals for any team because he had that knack of moving into the right position.

Don Mackay supplemented those talents by bringing in bigger personalities. Straight away, that impressed me, because although I wasn't a big player I had a forceful personality.

Ossie Ardiles came from Tottenham Hotspur, there was Frank Stapleton, Kevin Moran and Gordon Cowans: all top-class experienced performers. We had Colin Hendry in defence and Nicky Reid in the centre of the park. Don was able to spot players that were off the radar at other clubs but able to fit into the system and work ethic we had at Blackburn.

My first season at Ewood Park, though, was a struggle. I pulled my hamstring right at the start of the campaign and the club's medical team never got to the bottom of the problem. In the end – just as I had at Sunderland (much to the annoyance of Lawrie McMenemy) – I sought independent advice and an osteopath diagnosed it as a back problem, which was contributing towards pressure on lower parts of my body.

He clicked my spine into place and taught me a few exercises. It allowed me to finish the season reasonably strongly as Blackburn lost out in the promotion play-offs to Chelsea.

Thankfully, Don had seen enough to offer me another year's contract. The 1988/89 season would be my best as a professional footballer.

*

THERE WAS NO SIGN THAT BLACKBURN'S FUTURE ANY TIME SOON would take a dramatic upward trajectory. The ground was antiquated, attendances were low, the pitch was rutted and the training facilities were basic. There did not seem to be the potential to go much higher than their usual position halfway up the Second Division.

Things began to change when an industrialist with a personal fortune of more than £600m called Jack Walker became involved with the club at the invitation of the then chairman, Bill Fox. Jack donated funds to build the new Riverside Stand at the dilapidated Ewood Park. Over the next few years, he invested more money.

Walker was born and bred in the town and from a working-class family. He'd left school at fourteen and joined his father's small sheet-metal business; he worked variously as a sheet-metal worker, welder and a conscript craftsman in the Royal Electrical and Mechanical Engineers. In 1951, he took over the family firm with his brother, Fred.

Together they transformed Walkersteel from a back-street scrap metal business started by their father after the war into a steel-stockholding concern.

By 1990 they had built up the business so successfully that it had become the largest steel stockholder in Britain, employing 3,400 people at fifty sites. In 1956 the turnover was £46,000. In 1988 the business was making an annual profit of £48m. When the Walker brothers sold to British Steel for £360m in 1990 it was the highest price ever paid for a private company.

With that, Jack retired to St Helier in Jersey. Having stood on the terraces of Ewood Park in the 1950s, watching the team's local-born England internationals Ronnie Clayton and Bryan Douglas excel, he continued to commute regularly to Lancashire for Rovers games.

By 1991, he was ready to commit himself fully to the club. Effectively its owner, he remained officially no more than vice-president, although everybody knew who was in command and who signed all the cheques and paid all the bills.

In the early years, only some of Jack's money went towards the team. It enabled Don Mackay to sign some players that were previously out of reach in terms of finance. I didn't fall into that category, but Ossie Ardiles and Steve

Archibald certainly did. Although Don's name was a major pull, so was the money. Ossie was a World Cup winner. He'd never heard of Blackburn when growing up in Argentina.

Jack was a local guy who cared deeply about the club. Although he later invested heavily, it was his intention to make Blackburn successful – not to make more money out of the club. It wasn't a status symbol, either. He genuinely wanted Blackburn to do well. In 1995, all of his efforts resulted in Blackburn winning the Premier League, becoming league champions for the first time since 1914. It was a remarkable achievement – even with all the investment that followed after my departure.

In the late 1980s, his involvement contributed towards a better feeling than there had been at each of my previous clubs, Birmingham and Sunderland.

Don could work knowing that Blackburn's best players were not going to be sold against his wishes in order to keep the club afloat. Jack Walker wasn't throwing millions at it initially, but his backing acted a safety blanket.

The environment was happier. I was happier. I approached the 1988/89 season in a confident mood, having scored a number of goals in the pre-season campaign. I felt fitter than I'd ever been. Don had chosen Simon Garner and me up front in most of the warm-up games and that encouraged me a lot. Having been through successive relegations with Birmingham and Sunderland before two years of uncertainty and injury, I was really optimistic.

Six wins from the opening seven games increased the mood of positivity. Simon Garner and I were scoring goals and the local press labelled us the 'G-Men' because of our surnames. Scott Sellars was finding himself as a top player and, thanks to his service, Garns and I finished as the league's top strike-force. In forty-five games I scored nineteen goals. Garns scored a few more than me as well.

Don was the first manager to give me an entire campaign in my preferred position. I'd always seen myself as a centre-forward but often found myself on the wing, where managers and coaches thought my pace would be an asset. At Blackburn, I recognised that the club did not have great resources and that most players would need to be flexible – including myself.

Ally Dawson was a left-back who could play across the defence; David May

– who later had a good career at Manchester United – became a centre-half but played in the full-back positions during his early days at Blackburn. Nicky Reid, our captain, switched between centre-half and central midfield. Tony Finnigan was another versatile player. We all had to muck in.

Garns and I complemented each other, though, and I was at my happiest alongside him. A lot of his work was inside the penalty box where he was ruthless, while I was better in the channels and dropping deep and bringing others into play, stretching the game if necessary. At 29 I had a better understanding of what it took to perform on a consistent basis.

Garns and I were also different personalities. He was a hero on the terraces of Ewood Park not only for his ability but his loyalty as well. That's what fourteen years of unbroken service does. In 2007 Garner was voted the best player in Blackburn's history by the fans, ahead of Alan Shearer (Britain's greatest post-war striker in my opinion). That shows you just how good Garns was and how highly people thought of him.

Like the previous season, Blackburn reached the play-offs, a format only introduced by the FA for the 1986/87 campaign. In its first two years, it involved the third to fifth-placed teams in the Second Division and the third to bottom team in the First Division. In 1988 Chelsea were too good for us but a year later, we felt more prepared.

After Watford were knocked out in the semis on away goals, we faced Crystal Palace over two legs. Earlier in the season we'd beaten them 5–4 in a remarkable game at Ewood Park.

In those days the play-off finals were contested over two legs, and during the first leg at home I scored twice (and missed a penalty) in a 3–1 victory. I also set up the team's third goal. I have to admit I thought promotion was almost a certainty because we travelled to London for the return game absolutely buzzing.

I wish things had turned out differently because it would have crowned a perfect season on a personal level. Unfortunately some of the Blackburn players froze on the big occasion and decisions by the referee George Courtney went against us.

Palace had Ian Wright and Mark Bright up front and our defenders could not deal with them. It resulted in a 3–0 defeat.

Our promotion dreams were shattered.

I was convinced, though, that I would play with Simon Garner the following season, develop our relationship further and go up automatically this time. That's why I accepted a new three-year contract and a pay rise to £500 a week. A few clubs contacted me but I wanted to be loyal to Blackburn and Don, who had given me a chance when nobody else would touch me.

Don's other option in attack was Andy Kennedy from Birmingham City, who was a person I liked but also a player I thought I was better than. Andy brought some good attributes to the club. He was a character everybody liked because of his enthusiasm around the changing room. He was a Scot with the nickname 'Mad Dog'.

When the new season started, Andy was up front and I was back out on the wing. I had just enjoyed my best goal-scoring campaign and Blackburn had gone close to promotion. Objectively I asked myself – and indeed Don – whether I was better than him.

Don reasoned that he believed I could offer a better goal threat than the wingers he had. To me, though, it felt like a vote of no-confidence.

It was OK playing on the wing if you were at a club like Liverpool who passed the ball, because you had more freedom and would get plenty of touches. Blackburn were not like that. I remember one game on a Saturday afternoon and looking at the stadium clock. It was 3:12 and I hadn't touched the ball once. Do you lose discipline and go looking for it so the team is out of shape? The pattern ended up frustrating me. Our players in the middle of midfield were Nicky Reid and Ronnie Hildersley, but they were both ball-winners. There was a limited supply line to the wide areas.

Don seemed to lose his confidence in me. And that made me lose confidence in him.

*

IN 1991, I WENT BACK TO ANFIELD AS A BLACKBURN PLAYER FOR AN FA Cup third-round replay where the attendance was less than 35,000. It was one of those occasions where Anfield became an echoey place because the capacity was down. There were open spaces on the terraces and that meant you could hear people shouting at you.

It did not concern me what sort of a reception I got whenever I returned to the stadium I considered to be home. I'd been back with Birmingham and Sunderland. It only concerned me what the supporters of Birmingham and Sunderland thought of my performance. Those clubs were my paymasters, not Liverpool.

This was the ninth time I'd played against Liverpool. Previously, I'd been on the losing side four times. I'd never beaten them. By then, Liverpool were 'them' rather than 'us'. It had to be that way for me. It would be unprofessional to think otherwise.

The original tie at Ewood Park was drawn in controversial circumstances. Blackburn were leading 1–0 thanks to Simon Garner's goal. We were on the verge of a cup shock until Mark Atkins' own-goal in injury time. Jimmy Hill, the famous football pundit, was working for the BBC and he blamed the ballgirl for throwing the ball back into play too quickly, contributing towards Liverpool's equaliser. Hill gave the impression in his commentary that he resented Liverpool's success. He always appeared to be trying to knock the club down. This attempt was really unfair because it prompted the media to focus on the young girl and she was devastated.

It contributed towards the tension ahead of the replay. It had not been a good time for Liverpool and Kenny Dalglish was a month away from resigning because of stress. By beating Blackburn, Liverpool would draw Everton in the fifth round a month or so later and, after a famous 4–4 draw at Goodison Park, Kenny decided to walk away from Liverpool. Ultimately – soon enough – he'd be Blackburn's manager after Jack Walker moved heaven and earth to bring him to Ewood Park following a short period away from the game.

I'd had many run-ins with Steve McMahon over the years. They went back to our days in the reserve games between Liverpool and Everton. In the replay Ray Houghton and Ian Rush made it 2–0 to Liverpool. McMahon should have already been sent off by the time he was ordered off for a tackle on me, raking his studs right down my calf. I didn't know he'd even been given a red card until the end of the game. I was down for so long and in so much pain, I didn't know what was going on around me.

The crowd responded by booing every time I touched the ball. The media made quite a big deal of it because it does not happen very often to former players. I'd left Liverpool eight years before. I've got a sense of pride about myself, and if you can get one over on people who chant what they chant or say what they say, it's satisfying. I used the hostility towards me as a motivation. It's the only way to be in my opinion. You either do that or you go under; make mistakes or take the wrong decisions. I had to focus on the positives: on the Blackburn fans in that ground singing my name. Ultimately, I know Liverpool supporters because I am one. They'll always try and protect their own players. Ultimately, I wasn't one of them for ninety minutes.

My brothers were fuming, but I was thick-skinned by then.

We lost 3–0, Steve Staunton scoring Liverpool's third and final goal.

I PLAYED IN OTHER GAMES FOR BLACKBURN, BUT LIVERPOOL AWAY was the last big one.

The 1990/91 season was really disappointing for the club. After finishing in the play-off positions three seasons in a row – we had lost in the semi-finals to Swindon in 1990 – only to end up failing in the quest to earn promotion, we finished this campaign just four points off the relegation zone in nineeenth place.

Having operated in the background for three years, Jack Walker bought the club in his own right in January 1991. He promptly invested £20million in reconstructing Ewood Park before securing new training facilities.

Pressure fell upon Don Mackay to justify the investment by Mr Walker, who declared early on his ambition that Blackburn would return to the top flight, establish themselves as a top side in England and eventually go on to compete with the very best clubs in Europe.

His response was to replace Don with Kenny Dalglish. Kenny was refreshed after nearly eight months' rest and I remember travelling back from a game with Ipswich Town as the pressure was mounting on Don. The players were discussing what might happen on the bus and I suggested that Kenny would take the job. Within a week, the club made their move and it became public that he was Jack Walker's primary target.

I appreciated that I was 33 years old and at the end of my career but I hoped that Kenny might give me one last chance to prove myself. It had gone a bit sour between Don and me. I'd suffered from injuries. Negotiations between Kenny and Blackburn ran on for a few weeks and, in that time, I decided it was a good idea to put my injury problems behind me by booking myself in for a hernia operation. I did not want to miss the opportunity to get back into his plans. It was against club policy to have operations without consent but I felt like I was left with no choice. The club didn't have a manager and I couldn't afford time to pass by: valuable time that might be the difference between me earning a new contract or not.

Kenny isn't the type of person to let past acquaintance get in the way of progression, though. He doesn't do favours just because he knows you when professionalism is involved. I went to meet him in his office and he told me straight up: 'We're not keeping you on, Howard.'

JIMMY CASE WAS MY OLD TEAM-MATE AT LIVERPOOL. HE WAS 38 years old and still playing in the Football League. Jimmy loved football and, like me, had emerged from the parks to Liverpool's first team in a short space of time. Like me, he was from the south end of the city. He was an aggressive midfielder and technically outstanding. A bit like me, I guess, he fell foul of Bob Paisley's system and was sold to Brighton and Hove Albion in 1981 for getting into trouble on nights out once too often.

I liked Jimmy. After five good years at Blackburn, he was the first person to pick up the phone and ask how I was. In the summer of 1992 he moved from Bournemouth to Halifax Town and their manager John McGrath was looking to add further experience to his team.

I was living in Blackburn and Halifax was an hour away. Jimmy put a good word in for me and, after a month-long trial, I was offered a month-to-month contract. There were no other offers on the table so I had to accept it.

I played only five games for Halifax. My debut was at Cardiff City's old Ninian Park ground and the first half did not go to plan. At half-time we were 2–0 down and I'd sustained two dead legs. McGrath wasn't happy at all. I was the first person he had a go at. I said to him, 'My legs are fucked here and they have been since the twentieth minute. But I didn't want to come off because it would leave you in the lurch.'

I ended up coming off ten minutes into the second half. The following game, I was dropped out of the squad. It felt like a punishment for having a go back at him in the dressing room.

'Why am I dropped?' I asked him.

'You're not fit enough,' he said, knowing I didn't have the benefit of a full pre-season campaign behind me. I needed games to get fit. I stayed at Halifax for a month or so until McGrath told me he wasn't going to extend the deal any longer.

The next morning I was on the phone again, ringing around. I knew Dave McCreery from my short time on loan at Newcastle ten years earlier. He was Carlisle United's manager. So I called him. 'Any chance, Dave?' He gave me a trial and I did reasonably well.

In negotiations, Carlisle's chairman Michael Knighton, who'd come close to buying Manchester United, offered me £150 a week until the end of the season. The deal didn't even cover the cost of petrol, never mind living, considering all the driving potentially involved.

There was no way I could justify accepting it.

At the age of 33, my professional football career was over.

RETIREMENT, 1993

JOE FAGAN HAD A QUOTE THAT HE WOULD ALWAYS MUTTER around the players at Liverpool. "The grass isn't always greener on the other side," he'd say.

Liverpool had adopted a philosophy of not fixing what wasn't broken even when things weren't quite working.

Liverpool developed a culture that insisted on a format of continuity. The team virtually picked itself week after week, which was a major factor in the early success and the domination of English and European football.

Consistency and routine were core values and it contributed majorly towards Liverpool becoming an unstoppable juggernaut. If Liverpool were winning and everyone was happy, the process would stay the same.

Of course, players who were trying to break into this phenomenon would be frustrated by the lack of opportunity in the first team. Some players who had come through the youth system had spent many years playing reserve team football without being able to get anywhere near selection.

It reached the point where many of the young players would moan amongst themselves and to Roy Evans about the lack of opportunities to play for Liverpool. Realistically, though, we all knew that while the first team were winning and senior players kept themselves fit, those opportunities were few and far between.

Some players were able to make the step up to first team level but even then would find that a return to reserve team football in most cases would be the outcome soon after.

Football is no different to any other industry in that you have players who will climb the greasy pole to get ahead of the rest.

There are a lot of players who come into the world of football who have wonderful skills only to fail because of a lack of mental toughness to cope with adversity and what could be termed as a lack of progression.

My childhood did not let me be that way. If I saw something I didn't like, I'd try to do something about it straight away.

Outside football, I'm a straightforward person. If someone upsets or disappoints me, I'll either forgive and forget or tell that person what my thoughts are.

Just because I am honest with other people doesn't mean I always make the right judgement calls. There are some things I regret like the way I have treated the girlfriends and partners I've had throughout my life. When I look back at some of these things maybe I could have done things in a different way.

Being promiscuous tended to be a part of football culture. I found it hard to have a total commitment within relationships. A lot of the mistakes I have made have been mistakes that I am solely responsible for. I blame myself for the breakdown of failed relationships with some wonderful women who have played a meaningful role in my life. I have been fortunate throughout my life, indeed, to meet some intelligent and loving partners.

Growing up in Norris Green, the main focus of life was playing football. As a teen, I started to become attracted to the opposite sex. I never really had the confidence to ask a girl to become my girlfriend because I always had an underlying feeling that a girl might have a complex about being seen with me. I was always wary of rejection too. Her thoughts about me may have been compromised by her family's views on race.

The racism and negativity towards me in the early years meant I formed an opinion that may have been skewed but in the back of my mind I was always conscious of the experience of going to a friend's house where the father would put his hand across my chest to stop me walking through the door while others were allowed in.

There was one girl, Cathy Bullen, who I went to school with from nursery to senior school. Cathy had a bubbly personality and a lovely family. We used to walk to school together nearly every day and when knocking for her I would always feel the warmth of a family who I felt really comfortable with.

Our mothers would often stand talking at the gate of our house and this alone was something that indicated to me our friendship was noticed by our parents. Cathy is one of my oldest friends and although she now lives in Australia we still keep in touch with each other.

Cathy was a girl that I felt really comfortable around and someone I was attracted to but because we had such a close relationship and because I didn't want to risk spoiling that relationship, coupled with my fear of rejection, our relationship never developed beyond anything else than a close friendship.

After leaving school my first meaningful relationship with a girl from Norris Green was Pat Fletcher. Pat lived in the Broadway area of Norris Green and we met at a disco that was held on a Thursday night. I plucked up the courage to ask her if I could walk her home. For me, this was really hard to do.

Pat didn't go to my school. She was a lovely person who had a kind way about her. For the first few weeks our courtship involved walking around the streets in the evening and me taking her home before stopping a few doors away where we would kiss. The term in Norris Green for this was 'necking.'

Pat lived at home with her mum, her dad and her grandparents. She was an only child and was well loved by her family. We used to sit in the kitchen in her home and sneak little kisses on each other's lips. Her parents, like all parents, would concern themselves with the welfare of their daughter and would come in and out of the kitchen to check on us to make sure we weren't up to anything that we shouldn't have been doing. There were times when our emotions got the better of us and we came very close to overstepping the mark.

Eventually, our relationship petered out not long after I left Norris Green and moved back to the south end of Liverpool, Liverpool 8. Moving back to Liverpool 8, indeed, was a new adventure. This was a period in time where I felt really comfortable with the environment I was living in. Although I kept in contact with some of my friends in Norris Green, this new area introduced me to a culture which I could identify with.

Liverpool, in my opinion, has some of the most beautiful women on the planet. For the first time in my life I was around lots of black women my age. In the mid-70s many black women wore Afro style haircuts and they had a confidence which was new to me.

I had a group of friends which included both girls and boys. There was Donna, Lorraine, Tracey, Rose and Gayle. Then there was Joe Biggs, Touchy, Johnny Cat, Eric, Block Up, Bull, Tommy Bean, Melvin, Mogsy, Valie, Browny, Smeady and David and George Osu, just to name a few.

There was also an older generation in Liverpool 8 who acted as social mentors as we entered the nightspots of the city: Manor Brown, the Bass, the older Osus, the Morris's, the Cokers, the Dohertys and then Paul Wright and John Baker.

This was a tight knit group which wasn't a gang out for trouble but a gathering of people linked by different generations of family linked by brothers, sisters and cousins which formed the basis of a social community.

One of my closest friends became Stephen Skeete. Together, we made the decision to not even think about marriage until I was 35 years old. That was the golden number: 35. By then, I hoped that I'd have sorted myself out financially. I'd been cheated on by a girl when I was young, which left me not wanting to commit myself: not wanting to give my heart to someone else, only to find it broken. Life experience had taught me to put a shield up to protect me from being hurt.

I'd witnessed my dad's treatment of my mum. I did not want to become that person either. Perhaps it explains why I wasn't ready to accept the responsibility of being a father. All those years earlier my first son Chris was affected by my actions and the toxic relationship I had with his mother at the time.

My second son, Howard, was born in 1989. His mother was Doreen. We'd met in Sunderland after my relationship with Lorraine broke down. Doreen, from the North-east, was a lovely person and we fell in love very quickly.

Doreen had two other sons from a previous relationship, Saul and Lee. Doreen was an excellent mother who raised her children by herself, producing, with Howard, three wonderful, well-mannered young men.

Unfortunately, my relationship with Doreen became difficult after leaving Sunderland. There was only one real option on the table and that was to move to America to play indoor football for Dallas Sidekicks. This didn't help our relationship. Although we spoke over the phone our long distance relationship was strained and I felt lonely and knew there was something missing in my life.

Although Doreen was able to pay a visit to me in America, as soon as she returned home I felt there was a big gap in my life that needed filling. This had an impact in me becoming homesick and wanting to return to England.

I signed for Stoke on a two-month contract hoping they would sign me on a full-time basis. Because Stoke did not achieve promotion there was no further offer to keep me there.

My next club became Blackburn Rovers and I remained there for the five years. From Blackburn, Doreen and I continued a long-distance relationship but unfortunately I felt that our relationship wasn't how it was before and at Blackburn, I met Samantha, falling in love with her.

If there is one lesson that I have learned from our separation it is that I did not realise how much I hurt Doreen by not telling her my feelings and how they had changed. I still loved her but I wasn't in love with her and she did not deserve not to know that. I should have had the decency to sit down and explain to her my feelings.

Unfortunately for me, what goes around comes around and in the future it was going to come around for me.

It would be easy for me to reason that sleeping around was embedded into the culture of football. It went on at all of the clubs I played for. It certainly wasn't expected of you in any changing room I entered, but it was the done thing because the opportunities would always be there. You'd walk into a bar or a nightclub and, almost immediately, you'd be surrounded by attractive women. Some were gold-diggers and others were determined to be around sporting personalities. This was before footballers were really considered as celebrities and, indeed, before certain newspapers started running kiss-and-tell stories. There were no cameraphones so it was easier to keep your private life private.

It was hard resisting temptation. I couldn't help myself. I enjoyed the positive attention. It wasn't something I'd grown up around and it made a nice change. The environment was intoxicating. It isn't an excuse for my behaviour; it's an explanation.

At Blackburn, I met Samantha. I'd told her that my relationship with Doreen was coming to an end but that wasn't the case, certainly not to Doreen's knowledge. It took a phone call from someone at Blackburn – possibly one of the other players' wives – to tell Doreen what was going on. Samantha's phone number was supplied and from there my relationship with Doreen unravelled.

Samantha fell pregnant. Before going on a pre-season tour to Sweden with Blackburn, she hadn't been too well. I travelled to Sweden before a message arrived at the team hotel telling me about complications with the pregnancy and that I was to return home immediately.

Samantha's parents were from the Isle of Man and I'd left her with them before leaving for Sweden. So I called her mother first. 'Samantha's lost the baby,' she said. I flew home immediately and Samantha's dad picked me up at Manchester airport and took me straight to the hospital. As soon as I saw her, we both broke down in tears.

The baby was stillborn. Because of the struggle, Samantha was told that she couldn't have children in the future. We were devastated. Her mum's suggestion was for us to get engaged so that marriage would act as something for both of us to look forward to. So that's what we did.

Inwardly, I couldn't escape that saying, 'What goes around, comes around'. I'd slept with a lot of women causing them to fall pregnant: women I didn't really know, and certainly not ones I was in a relationship with. In the aftermath, I suggested the idea of abortion and they went through with it. It happened three or four times. I'm not religious at all and I don't necessarily believe in karma or anything like that. But if you keep living on the edge, life tends to bite you back eventually. I saw this as payback.

I loved Samantha but I realise now we married for the wrong reasons. We wrongly believed it would smooth over the pain. We lasted fifteen months.

Again, I was to blame for the way it ended. Samantha went on holiday for a week and while she was away I drove to Sunderland for Gary Bennett's testimonial. After the game, everyone went out to a club known by all the players called Finos. Friends of mine, Mike Emerson and Bob McKenzie, ran the place. He took care of the Sunderland players by cornering off an area of the club so we'd never get pestered.

I got chatting to a girl that night and, though nothing happened between us, a story that told otherwise made its way back to Blackburn and Samantha that I was up to no good.

It proved to be a tipping point. I tried as hard as I could to convince Samantha that the story wasn't true and that I still loved her. But the strain of her losing the baby and the fact that I was now unemployed ended up in separation and Sam applying for a divorce.

I remember driving back from Blackburn to Liverpool. I was that angry that I took my wedding ring off, wound down the window and threw it on the M6 motorway.

What goes around comes around.

*

YOU RETIRE FROM FOOTBALL. YOU HAVE HAD A MODEST CAREER.
You know the money you have earned will run out quickly. You have not really
got a long-term plan. What do you do next?

As a footballer, I'd been used to everything being done for me from dental
appointments, to doctors' appointments to finding houses and financial advice.
Now, I was back to a world where I was on my own; going through a divorce and
hanging on to the belief that I still had something to offer the game of football.

It became apparent in the first few weeks after moving back to Liverpool and
moving in to live with my dad in Liverpool 8 that there was no role or place for
me in front line professional football. I spent countless hours ringing and writing
to football clubs to see if they would take on an experienced player who I felt still
had something to offer to the game as a coach. This world is a lonely one.

A lot of ex-footballers speak about the difficulties they face in retirement.
They reveal stories of depression: not being able to replace the adrenalin of a
match, filling all the empty hours, trying to find something to do. I can understand
why this happens because at one point I felt so low. Everything had gone.
My career was over. My marriage was over. I'd ended up back in the place where
it had all started.

I was lucky that I had a strong family who helped me through this period.
Some other footballers aren't that fortunate and it's only in recent years that
football has recognized the serious issues around mental illness and depression
amongst players who have become victims of a world that is unforgiving once
you have kicked your last ball.

THROUGHOUT MY LIFE, I'D ALWAYS LOOKED AT WHAT WAS GOING
on around me, surveying and judging the landscape. That's why I signed for
Birmingham City. I went there because there was a core of black players in
the squad. I understand that professionally there should always be a challenge to
prove yourself. But as a black player, I had to go to places where I felt comfortable
in order to flourish. If you're making decisions based on reasons of race, you're

one step behind everyone else and at a disadvantage from day one. That makes it incredibly hard to prove yourself professionally.

At the start of the 1990s, I wasn't aware of any black coaches. There certainly weren't any black managers. Then again, there were fewer black players than there are now.

Of the 230 clubs that made up the seven tiers of English football at the start of the 2014/15 season only fourteen employed black managers. In the Women's Super League, there were two black managers among the eighteen clubs. In the top four divisions of Scottish and Northern Irish football, there were no black managers at all. In Wales, there was one. In coaching, the situation was even grimmer. In 2015 a study revealed that of 552 key coaching jobs in English football only nineteen were occupied by people from black and minority backgrounds.

If you think this is a depressing statistic in 2015, imagine what it was like two decades before in 1993 when I retired and was looking for my first job as a coach. It concerned me that there would be the same mistrust about black coaches and black managers as there was about black players.

I applied for several jobs. The longer time passed, the lower I looked. Although based in North Wales, Colwyn Bay were in the English pyramid, competing in the Northern Premier League. I read about their manager being sacked in the *Daily Post* and decided to give it a go.

I met Colwyn Bay's chairman in Ruthin near Wrexham and explained to him that although I was nearly thirty-six years old, I could still play part-time. He would get a manager and a player in one deal, in turn saving some money.

Colwyn Bay was an hour or so's drive from Liverpool and I knew the club could attract a lot of players from the city of Liverpool. Welsh clubs had always contained lots of players from Liverpool. With my contacts, I was confident of building an aggressive, streetwise side capable of competing at the top end of the table. Historically, non-league clubs containing Merseysiders had been successful. I wanted to incorporate young local players capable of playing at a higher level. Hopefully, they'd be good enough for us to sell them on and keep reproducing. That way, the club could run as a successful business. We didn't have to rely on cup runs.

Maybe my ideas were too progressive for them. Maybe I was viewed as too militant. Football is a small world. Everyone knows everyone else's business and reputations endure. I'd been outspoken on racism. Maybe Colwyn Bay viewed me as a hot potato. Maybe they thought I'd bring the wrong sort of attention to their club. I don't really know.

Because the rejection letter I received was short. They did not even grant me a phone call. It was demoralising. They'd chosen a seasoned non-league manager with an abundance of experience.

*

I GOT A BREAK AT TRANMERE ROVERS.

Twelve months before I left Blackburn I started doing my coaching badges. That was my idea: to carry on with football, passing my experience on to others. But no opportunities were forthcoming until I became a youth coach at Tranmere several years later.

I spent five years at the club's centre of excellence and had a great relationship with Warwick Rimmer and Glyn Salmon.

One of the age groups that I coached was an under-12s team. We had a really good side, going two years unbeaten. There were some really good players who I thought had a chance of eventually progressing to the first team.

I had a discussion with Glyn and expressed my wishes for the team to develop a system of playing football out from the defence. Aaron Creswell, who now plays for West Ham United, along with Terry Gornell, who became a professional were players in my team.

Cresser was a talented player who had an educated left foot and playing this way suited his game because he was of a diminutive stature. Playing with the ball at his feet enhanced his ability and you could see that if pushed in the right direction, he was going to go far.

Terry, meanwhile, was a striker who lacked pace but was very good with the ball at his feet. He went through a period where he lost his confidence because he was frustrated that his pace was inhibiting his development.

I took Terry to one side and told him that rather than being an Ian Rush going in behind defences, which he didn't have the pace to do, I asked him to adapt his game and become more of a Dennis Bergkamp type of player, who would drop deeper for the ball. To be fair to Terry he took this on board and it transformed his game. Terry's had a good career, playing for Tranmere, Accrington Stanley, Shrewsbury Town, Rochdale and Cheltenham Town.

I really enjoyed my time working at Tranmere. Yet lifespans at football clubs are short. Attitudes change. Warren Joyce ended up replacing Glyn as the centre of excellence director and he had his own ideas about the way he wanted the set up to be run. Warren is now involved at Manchester United. After leaving Tranmere I had a spell as a scout at one of my former clubs, Stoke City.

*

I HAVE FIVE KIDS. AIYANA IS THE YOUNGEST AND SHE LIVES WITH me in Liverpool's south end. Aiyana's mum is Gill and she died in 2007 from cancer. We'd separated long before her passing but I still think about her every day. I wonder whether we'd have got back together.

Aiyana's brothers are Faisal and Malik. They are grown men and although I am strictly their stepfather through my relationship with Gill, they are sons to me.

Chris is my oldest son. I am so proud of Chris and how he has turned his life around after a difficult start. Chris has a son called Brandon who he has a close relationship with and who he is a good father to. Brandon lives on the outskirts of Liverpool in Huyton with his mother and Chris takes every opportunity he can to visit from Scotland where he lives with his fiancée to whom he is looking forward to marrying in 2017. Chris's mother Atonia has done a fine job in raising him.

Malik, the second eldest is also doing well for himself. At present he is studying to be an electrician and he also has an interest in music, creating beats for artists. He lives with his girlfriend and has produced a wonderful grandson in Malik junior.

Next comes Howard. Howard still lives in the north east in Whitburn near Sunderland. He's a qualified health and safety officer. Again, Doreen has done brilliantly raising him to become the man he is now.

Our Faisal now lives and works in London and has a degree in law.

This leaves Aiyana, who is my world. She's studying at sixth form and is hoping to go into politics. I am sure that she will achieve this because she never stops arguing with me at home.

Malik, Faisal and Aiyana have come through some tough times and they have had to grow up quicker than most children when losing their mother at the age of 40.

I am so proud of them.

*

IN THE 1990s, THE WAIT FOR WORK WAS AGONISING AND THERE were some difficult years after retirement from football. It prompted me to sign on at the dole office.

I was in a relationship with Gill at the time and obviously my unemployment put pressure on both of us. I was close to taking a job stacking shelves at the Asda supermarket, but I couldn't bring myself to do it. I don't mean any disrespect to anyone who stacks shelves at Asda. I wanted a more meaningful job that would challenge me and allow me to use my experience.

I've always had the attitude that something will come along if you hang in there and persist. My solution was to go right back to the beginning and start a coaching programme in Toxteth Sports Centre on a Friday night. There was an indoor hall and Astroturf pitches. So I rented one out with the idea of providing coaching and making a relatively small amount of money out of it.

Quickly, the coaching sessions became popular. The kids wanted to test their skills in competition. We evolved into a team and eventually we became Stanley House – one the first multicultural football clubs to my knowledge in Britain. Anyone could play for us: whether you were black, brown, Asian or white, it didn't matter. The badge was a black hand and a white hand.

We won leagues and we went on tours. We tried to mirror everything that happened inside the academies at professional cubs. We wanted the kids to understand the levels of discipline and dedication required in case they got picked up. I have known of many young players who go straight from the street to professionalism and they don't know how to deal with discipline and complex issues around football clubs.

The aim, though, wasn't primarily to raise professional footballers but, more importantly, good human beings. We wanted to raise professional individuals that could walk into any sphere of life and have the confidence to succeed.

More than one hundred young boys and girls played football at Stanley House from season to season. Kids came from as far afield as Southport to play. Soon, we were able to work in conjunction with local schools. If a child wasn't behaving or not attending school, they wouldn't be playing football with us. That offered them an incentive.

Most adults look at young people when they misbehave as a mark of resentment against discipline or an organised structure. What they seem to forget is that many adults have also been through the same processes themselves growing up. I think the experiences I had growing up form a large part of the template that I use in developing young people, helping them maximise their own potential and future well-being.

A lot of the skills and experiences that I carry with me are based on my own life and others close to me, whereas back then, when I was young, there was no complaint system or a particular body or figure you could go to with a complaint. You had to work it out yourself and, if you got it wrong, face the consequences. If you got it right, in most cases you certainly wouldn't get any praise for it. Today, young people have to understand the values and culture of other human beings and embrace those cultures rather than segregate themselves from it.

I really believe discipline and respect is missed in modern society. There is a big difference between discipline and overzealousness. You can be firm and get your point across without coming across like an unswerving fundamentalist. In my childhood, it was dished out ruthlessly. But it didn't work because I was disobedient on the street. Maybe if I'd felt able to speak to an adult about my problems, my behaviour outside of the home would have been better and consequently things would have been different for me.

If you reach out to a young person before it's too late, I'm convinced that you can teach them that there is always a way forward. Unfortunately, kids are as much part of a structure as adults: a structure that says if you're a black person, you're not as good as a white person; if you're a poor person, you're not as good as a wealthy person; if you've been brought up in care, you're not as good as someone who's been brought up by parents; if you've just been brought up by your mother, you're not as good as someone who's been brought up by both parents.

There is a pecking order and kids pick up on it. Constantly, it makes them feel like they're missing out on something. The process is damaging. Kids are told they are disadvantaged from the outset. The more you tell someone they are something, the quicker they become it.

We made great strides with Stanley House. One of our players, Les Afful, ended up playing professionally for Exeter City. Ralph Welch signed for Liverpool before becoming a professional at Blackburn Rovers, though he never made a first-team appearance. Gary Roberts, a white winger, broke into the professional game with Accrington Stanley before spells at Ipswich Town, Huddersfield Towns, Chesterfield and Portsmouth.

Bala O'Rourke went to Liverpool and I thought it was the wrong decision by him and his family. Bala and Ralph were two of our best prospects at Stanley House and I felt both of them could have developed into good professional footballers. I was hoping they would be the next generation to graduate out of Liverpool 8 and make it into Liverpool's first team. Both players, in my opinion, should have achieved more with their football careers. Instead, Bala became disillusioned with football after being released by Liverpool and Ralph, while he went to Blackburn, ended up playing in non-league. Ralph is now a football coach within Liverpool 8.

There were other boys who were just as talented but did not get the breaks. Scouts were watching Mark Wong (or Ace as he was known) – a half-Chinese kid, someone who was supremely talented. Martin Crowder was another: a goalscorer who could have signed for Exeter City with Les Afful but chose Everton instead, where they played him at left-back before his release.

I always asked myself why after breaking through at Liverpool as the first black player, there hasn't been a steady stream of other black players being recruited from within Merseyside. People call me a groundbreaker but I'm not so sure about that. If I was a groundbreaker, why there hasn't been more black players in the team after me: boys who emerged from the streets of Liverpool? The next was Tony Warner, a goalkeeper who holds the record still as the player with the most appearances on the substitutes' bench without ever getting on the pitch. Then there was Jon Otsemobor and Lee Peltier. I find it strange because I know there are some really good players.

In Liverpool Football Club's history, only three players from the local black community have represented the club, making a total of sixteen appearances between them. Don't you find that astonishing, considering Liverpool's black community is well established and has been here so long?

I know I do.

*

TOXTETH HAS CHANGED. I SEE A DIFFERENT PLACE NOW. THE change is audible and sensory. In the 1950s, it was dominated by African immigrants and Caribbeans who took on work or set up businesses.

Now there are more Arabs and Somalians. There are more refugees. You meet people from Iran and Iraq. The Chinese community is growing bigger. You can smell the cooking as you walk down the streets. You can hear their voices.

The main shopping thoroughfare used to be Granby Street. It had bars and clubs: numerous places to meet for the West African community particularly.

Now, Granby Street struggles. There has been a regeneration project inspired by local leaders in recent years but there is still some way to go to get it back to the way it was in the 1950s and 60s.

Today, Lodge Lane is the area where Liverpool's migrant community bases itself, a few roads inland. There are restaurants and small shopping markets but fewer social venues.

I realise things do not stay the same forever wherever you go. Places evolve, taking on different identities. What saddens me is, what remains in Liverpool 8 is overwhelming unemployment. Social problems from the 1980s are still there.

If you walk through the main business district in Liverpool, across the other side of the city centre near Exchange Flags, you don't see many black faces. This was the place where Liverpool grew from, where the cotton traders who made their money off the back of slavery in the Americas grew wealthier. It is called Exchange Flags because it is a place of trade. The destinations of the cargo on the ships would be identified by the raising of a flag in this square.

A lot of people believe racism is born out of ignorance and fear. At a secondary stage, that's certainly true. Originally, though, it came because of greed: the level of greed shown by European slave traders. The British Empire was created by rampant capitalists who searched for new ways to make money. Black people in the Americas and West Africa were vulnerable and therefore exploitable. Seeing black people as lesser beings justified terrible deeds. Once you repeat the action, the status becomes defined. This explains why, for so long, attitudes within Liverpool were depressingly hostile towards black people.

Liverpool, indeed, has the oldest black communities in Europe but these are barely represented in the city's most prosperous and supposedly enterprising district. So clearly, we have some way to go if integration and acceptance is to be completed.

Liverpool has become a more welcoming place, nevertheless. The 1980s changed the view of many living there. It is a myth that Liverpool has always been a left-thinking city that welcomes all. I think my story reflects that and my story is certainly not unique.

When troops returned after the First World War, Liverpool's black population grew to about five thousand. Black and white ex-servicemen competed for work and politicians suggested sending people who had fought for Britain during the war back to their countries of birth.

In this tense atmosphere an argument in a pub turned into a riot and police raided the homes of only the black people, who in turn retaliated. Charles Wootton, a 24-year-old black seaman who had not been involved in the fighting, ran out of one building and was pursued by a mob along with around 300 residents before being battered to death with bricks and thrown into the Queen's Dock, though the official version of events suggested he jumped.

In the 1950s, 60s and 70s Liverpool – where black people accounted for roughly 8 per cent of the population – remained a difficult place to live, particularly if you moved outside of Liverpool 8. Attitudes were nowhere near as relaxed as they are in some areas now.

Thatcher's government then tried to break the morale of Liverpool but she failed thanks to the will and resistance of working-class people. It brought a wider community together – regardless of colour or creed. My hope is it would be easier for a black family to move into a white community like Norris Green in 2016.

In football, the outlook has changed for the better too. There is a tendency for society to blame many of its ills on football when the reality is football has done more than most to eradicate racism from its sport.

2016 is the twentieth birthday of Show Racism the Red Card, for whom I am a campaigner and an ambassador. My work takes me into schools where we do workshops with young people to educate them and make them aware of their role in accepting different cultures and genders which will hopefully help them form a better understanding of the differences in cultures that they may face in the future.

In England anti-racism campaigns such as Show Racism the Red Card and Kick It Out have helped drive racism away from stadiums. They are safer places for black people to watch and play now.

Racism is society's problem, not football's. If racism exists in football it's a symptom of the society we live in, not the cause. I don't think any government has done enough to rid society of the problem. Punishments are not reflective of the damage it does and the legacy it leaves behind.

I cannot see the fight for equality ending. Racism has existed since time began. Human beings have always put fences up to segregate themselves from one another. All we can try to do is try and stem the tide.

It worries me that we live in a society now where lots of people only deal in black and white conclusions. They want definite answers: definite endings. With racism, these people will be waiting a long time.

The struggle goes on. Maybe the victory is in the struggle.

*

ON 8 AUGUST 8 2016 I RECEIVED A PHONE CALL FROM GED GREBBY from Show Racism the Red Card. He informed me that along with two other campaigners, I had been nominated for an MBE honour.

Immediately, I refused the nomination. Ged's reply was, 'I knew you would.' The conversation stopped there. I did not ask him any further questions about it and he did not ask me.

I knew that the nominations would be disclosed in the press. In order to make people understand the reasoning behind my decision I posted a short explanation on social media of the reason behind my decision.

I explained that accepting an MBE would be a betrayal to all of the Africans who were killed or who suffered from slavery. This was the main reason.

I would have liked to have disclosed the sexual abuse that was acted out upon me as another reason. For that as well, I could not accept an MBE. The fact that Jimmy Savile had been awarded an OBE and had been honoured with a knighthood before his death weighed heavily on my mind.

I also thought about the families affected by the Hillsborough disaster, who had also suffered from 27 years of lies, deceit and corruption which was projected on them by the establishment.

I had supported the Hillsborough Justice Campaign and I felt that it would have been a kick in the teeth to those families if I accepted the honour as they had been victims of this system.

I had previously posted on social media my support for Kenny Dalglish to be knighted and the reasoning behind this was the unequivocal and passionate support that Kenny and his family had shown in their support in the quest for justice for the Hillsborough families.

I fielded many questions since in relation to how I could nominate someone else for an award but refuse one myself from the same establishment.

My answer was simple: the decision not to accept an MBE is based on my own principles and views of a historical event which has impacted my life, the lives of my family and billions of other people. It does not mean that I am anti-British. My conscience would not forgive me.

There has been a lot of debate on this subject since and I am grateful and humbled by all of those who have supported my decision from around the globe.

*

ACKNOWLEDGEMENTS

THERE ARE MANY PEOPLE I WOULD LIKE TO THANK. FORGIVE ME IF
I have forgotten someone.

The extended Gayle family: Atonia, Christopher, Antonia, Brandon,
Gill - RIP, Malik, Simira, Faisal, Aiyana, Malik Jnr, Howard, Doreen, Saul and
Lee Stafstrom; Alan Gayle, Ann Lopez, Janice Gayle Jnr, Khalid, Farees,
Khalisah, Junade Gayle, Djuane, Garrett, Lee, Demi, Lea, Dre, O'
Shea, Demmere, Denzil, Denica, Donnell, Lee, Lashone Garrett, Shaquille,
Tyanna, Shyhiem - RIP, Chavey, Panero, Celeste; Abdul Saleem Gayle (Paul),
Helen, Joyce, Claire, Anthony, Lynne Spindler, Wayne, Nisha.

From the community I am from, there are many families. Starting with the
Thompsons: Aunty Francis, Norman Snr - RIP, Kevin Thompson Snr - RIP,
Jackie, Kathleen, Kevin Jnr, Spencer Duncan, Hayley, Rachel Duncan, Wayne,
Norman Jnr, Ben, Natalie, Neika, Gloria, Robbie − RIP, Courtney McAuley,
Josh McAuley, Elis McAuley, Lorraine Thomson, Courtney, Jordan; the
Armstrongs. The Fontenots: Albert, Lyn Beers, Denis, Carol, Jade, Ryam, Rael,
Aaron, Esmee, Danielle, Elliot, Jessie, Amanda, Leah. The Bartels: Les, Jackie,
James, Joanne, Gary, Willard, Marilyn, Teresa, Audrey, Willard, William, Mikala,
Barry, Lou and Leanne Philburn. The Hampsons: Nicky, Hadam, Les, Ike, Phil,
Neal, Rob. The Skeetes: Bull, Leo, Jeff, John, Carl, Sandra, The Tagoes: Jeff,
Norma, Jeff Jnr, Sharon Jnr, Sharon Snr, Chantelle, Rikaya. The Walkers:
Bernard − RIP, Joey, Larry, Eddie, Jo Jo, Yvonne, Betty, Dave Goodall, Sam;
and the Chins: Pat, Lorraine, Deli, Sandra, Susie and Christine Sheba.

We also have: Maria, Steve Mo Chris & amp; Sue Brown, Dave Clay, Sugar Dean and the family, the Contehs, Dave Scanteberry, The Real Thing, the Amoo family, the Jacobs family, Mibbs, Michelle Charters, Anna Rothery, Lyn Pie, the Jones girls, Paul Wright Snr, John Baker, the Dohertys, Dylan Williams, Gill Williams, Robbie Savage, Pam Savage, Brian Omar, Lee Omar, Jade Omar, Jane Potts, Ste Griff, Paddy Rooney, Geoff Thomson, Eddie Johnno, Nicky Alt, Dave Kirby, Peter Diboe, Ruth Diboe, Val Reed, Tall Boy, Austin, Yellow, Hutchy, Rocker O'Rourke, Bala the Weavers, Val, Smiler, Speedy, the Lunts, Donna Marie Kassim, Mandy and Brenda Gray, Donna Alleyne, Kelvin Alleyne, Curtis Warren, Ste Nse, James Nse, Phil Nse, Michael and Delroy Showers, Giselle Ouerd, the Jones girls, John Baker, Paul and Michael Desson, Alan and Christine Johnson.

I would also like to thank the Jacksons, Julie, Nyenessnah Jacobs, Elaine – RIP, Aida, Andrew, Martin, Keith Palmer, the Grahams, Eric, Nada, Sonsha, Nelson Asu, Joe Biggs, Barber, Clare, Paula, Peter Lynsey, Joey and Dot Marshall, Joseph, Jordan, the Morris family: Michael, Tony, Teresa, Susanne; the Singh family: Gary, Betty, Gareth, Andy, Cush, Ash; Mr North at St Teresa's, Mr Jonranau, Mike Small Jimmy O'Hanlon, Jimmy Wilson, Mike Small, Ste Shelly, Paul Williams, Ste Maitland, the Westheads, the Ashtons, Steve Lawley, Farah Sadiki, Debbie Mendy, Kate Kassim, Zara Law, Pauline Payne, Ashley and Danny Molynuex, Paddy Payne, Rose Byrne, Gareth from the garage, the Boreses, the Littles, the Robinsons the Whitakers, the Cannons, the Todds, the Howards, Alison Cooke, Dan and Racheal, Pippa McC, the Patersons, Natalie and Sam Moore.

From Norris Green: Tony Kinnear, Perry Walker, Pop Freeman, Jimmy Wilson, Phil Burns, the Lodge family, Babs and Bev Keenan, the Blighs, the Nelsons, the Bullens, Joyce Smith, the Kavagnahs, the Littles, Tony Pillians, Anthony Hanna, Dot Riley, Mike Pines, Paul Williams, Ann-Marie Butchard and Lenny the green grocer.

From Stanley House: Mark Wong (Ace), Rab O'Shea, Tony Dunn, Gary Roberts, Timothy Ojapah, Leroy Paris, Adrian Weaver (Speedy), Kyle Samson, Robbie Punch Wayne Tagoe, Daly Corrie, Martin Aggalomani, Toby Ottabor, Julian Tagoe, Ali Magazachi, Kareem Desmond, Les Afful, Lee Powell, Jama Estridge, Nathan Mebie

From Show Racism the Red Card: Ged Grebby, Paul Kearns, James, Gavin. From Kingsley School: Don Ford, Jenny, Sophie, Pat, Alicia, Aunty (Mrs Coker), Nathan, Flora, Mandy, Maureen. From Redbank Community Home: Mick, Alex, Everton, Neville, Mary M, Phil, Pete, Glen, Russell, Ste Gagan and Colin.

And finally, football people. From the early days: Eric Dunlop, Mala, George, Joe Garcia, Joe Orr, Billy Mercer and Pat. From Fulham: Bobby Campbell, Les Strong, Teddy Maybank, Tony Gale, Richard Money, Hilton Philips and John Beck. From Newcastle United: Arthur Cox, Kevin Keegan, Terry McDermott, Chris Waddle and David McCreery.

From Birmingham City: Ron Saunders, Lenny, Keith, Doigy, Noel Blake, Robert Hopkins, Tony Coton, Mick Harford, Mike Halsall, Pat Van, Ian Handysides – RIP, Martin Kuhl, Kevin Broadhurst, Mark McCarrick, Jim Hagen, Byron Stevenson, Gary Coles, Rupert, Jnr B, Cuddles.

From Liverpool FC: John Bennison, Bob Paisley, Joe Fagan, Reuben Bennett, Tom Saunders, Geoff Twentyman, Terry Littlewood, Tom Parry, Phil Lynch, Tony Morton, Tony Iron, Willie Miller, Mark Walters, Michael Thomas, Sammy Lee, John Barnes and Mike Marsh. From the reserves, where I helped win four Central League titles: Roy Evans, Oggy, Jeff Ainsworth, Colin Irwin, Brian Kettle, Max Thompson, Trevor Birch, Dave Bamber, Colin Russell, Alan Harper, Avi Cohen, Kevin Sheedy, Ronnie Whelan, Stigger Foley, Alex Cribley, Ian Rush, Sammy Lee, Robbie Ditchburn, Mark Hodder, Jimmy Williams, Mick Halsall, Phil Thompson, Emlyn Hughes, Ian Callaghan, Dave Fairclough, Jimmy Case, Dave Johnson, John Toshack, Stevie Heighway, Ann and the dinner ladies.

Sunderland AFC: Len Ashurst, Gary Bennett, Clive Walker, Chris Turner, Davy Corner, David Hodgson, Stan Cummins, Barry Venison, Sean Elliott, Mark Proctor Gordon Armstrong, Gordon Chisholm, Nicky Pickering, Pete Daniels, Eric Gates, John Corrnforth, Reuben Agboola, Lid, Frank Gray, Rodger Wylde, Brian Murphy, Bob McKenzie, Mike Emerson and Norman Massey. From Dallas Sidekicks: Gordon Jago, Keith Weller, Victor Stride, The Doc, Pedro, Wes, Haiden. Then Stoke City: Mick Mills, Tony Kelly, Mark Chamberlain, Lee Dixon and Steve Bould. At Blackburn Rovers: Don Mackay, Jim Furnell, Ken Beamish, Ally Dawson, Scott Sellars, Simon Garner, Andy Kennedy, Terry Gennoe, Tony Diamond, Sean Curry, Lenny Johnrose Chris Sully, Ian Miller, Nicky Reid, Keith Hill, David May, Ossie Ardiles, Kevin Moran Frank Stapleton, Steve Archibald, Gordon Cowans, Gareth Ainsworth, Mark Atkins, Jason Wilcox and Tony Dobson. Halifax Town: Jimmy Case and John McGrath. Tranmere Rovers: Warwick Rimmer, Glyn Salmon, Dave Bleasdale.

BIBLIOGRAPHY

Recommended reading

Fletcher, Mike, *'Making of Liverpool'*, (Wharncliffe 2004)

Frost, Diane & Phillips, Richard *'Liverpool '81: Remembering the Riots'*
(Liverpool University Press, 2011)

Onoura, Emy *'Pitch Back: the Story of British Black Footballers'*
(Biteback, 2015)

Phillips, Mike & Trevor *'Windrush'* (Element, 2009)

Turner, Alwyn *'Crisis? What Crisis: Britain in the 1970s'* (Aurum, 2013)

Recommended viewing

Olusoga, David *'Britain's Forgotten Slave Owners'* (BBC, 2015)

Places to see

International Slavery Museum, Liverpool

Museum of Liverpool, Liverpool

ABOUT
THE AUTHORS

HOWARD GAYLE WAS BORN IN TOXTETH, LIVERPOOL IN 1958. When his family were moved out of L8 by the council in the early part of the 1960s, a childhood spent in Norris Green had a profound influence on the rest of his life. A Liverpool supporter, he followed the team home and away as a self-confessed football hooligan before he emerged from the terraces as a first team player. Howard later joined Birmingham City, taking in spells at Sunderland and Blackburn Rovers also. He now lives back in Liverpool's south end, on the streets where he spent his earliest years.

SIMON HUGHES WHO HAS COLLABORATED WITH HOWARD ON this book, is a writer, journalist and editor who focuses on Merseyside football in the *Independent* and elsewhere for The *Sunday Telegraph*. Simon is the author of four books: *Secret Diary of a Liverpool Scout* (2009), *Red Machine* (2013) - winner of the Antonio Ghirelli prize as Italian soccer foreign book of the year, *Men in White Suits* (2015) and *Ring of Fire* (2016).

Touching Distance
Martin Hardy

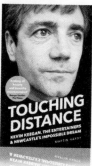

Make Us Dream
Neil Atkinson & John Gibbons

Up There
Michael Walker

The Unbelievables
David Bevan

Love Affairs & Marriage
Howard Kendall

When Friday Comes
James Montague

Hasta La Muerte Scunthorpe
Iñigo Gurruchaga

The Acid Test
Clyde Best

The Binman Chronicles
Neville Southall

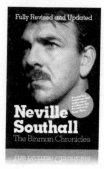

decoubertin.co.uk